Lou H Alwood

WHY?

♦ ♦ *The Journey 1965* ♦ ♦

Produced by:

FriesenPress
Suite 300 – 852 Fort Street
Victoria, BC, Canada V8W 1H8

www.friesenpress.com

Distributed to the trade by The Ingram Book Company

Table of Contents

DEDICATION

This book is dedicated to

JOYCE MARIE MYHON
(J.C.)

Aug. 15, 1931 – Jan. 23, 2008

A True Companion

This journey took everything we had. I had never met anyone before, who had the courage and the stamina to pursue and carry on to the end. This woman was remarkable. She came into my life, with a short phone call, (I will go with you). Shortly after the Journey, Joyce left for another adventure. Never to have seen her again. These journeys never end, my friend. You were a true companion. Never to be forgotten. You can bet there were many campfires, with her guitar, and tales to tell. I was blessed to have known you J.C. May you rest in peace.

May those campfires keep you warm, with Belva-Dear by your side.
May we meet on one of those trails again.

ACKNOWLEDGEMENTS

Thank you to my Mother Helen Marie Massey, who kept track of the journey in its entirety- newspaper clippings, photos, and covered expenses when we got a little low.

Thank you to my daughter Dana for sticking by me, and helping me through the process of proof reading and editing, as I come with little patience. Thank you to my family for caring for my little girl, while I was away, Eileen and Bruce Taylor, and my sisters, Katie Dol (Ormiston), Deanna and Albert Ollech, and her grandma Helen Massey.

Thank you to my cousin George L. DeFrane, for all the camp-outs and fishing trips over the past years, where we learned most of our survival skills, on Vancouver Island. I had his encouragement and found out later that he would have gone with me. Thanks "Pepe."

Thank you to all those great people we met along the trail, all the bales of hay, and oats, friendship, and encouragement. Also all the Vets, for the care of our horses.

A Special Thank-You, to the families we were so fortunate to of been able to spend an overnight with, and those who helped pick us up off the road and mend our wounds. A special thanks to the Avery family and the Young family for our twenty-seven day stay at the (Bar X) at Sault Saint Marie. Not to be, forgotten. Also thank you for the loan of Sailor Boy and Duke. You truly made the ride possible.

P.S. We forgave you boys, for the attack on our camp, near the Saskatchewan border. Looking back, we made a mistake in not reporting you!

Note: In this manuscript, I use miles instead of kilometers, as that is what it was in 1965. In addition, the First Nations People in 1965 were referred to as Indians.

This Journey was written from a daily log of all events from April 20, to October 22, 1965, and the events that followed.

PREFACE

Fall 1964 – January 9, 1965

I had no idea that my journey would ever take place. Something I just had to do was ride horseback across Canada. It was never that far in the back of my mind since I was a small child. I talked about it to anyone who would listen, and I set it on the back burner many times. In 1963 two women thought, that would be fun. We talked about it many times, after ball games and get togethers.

As time passed, the friends I had planned on going with, cancelled re: their jobs, and life circumstances. I had quit my job at the plywood plant, and was up in Chase B.C, working at Mom's grocery store, preparing for the journey. A few days later, I received a phone call in the late evening. The caller stuttered somewhat, but I made out, "Horseback trip. I would like to go with you, and I will meet you, and call back later."

I got off the phone, and my Mother said, Oh, who was that, I said, I don't know, but they want to go on the horseback trip with me." The look on my mom's face was, well (I call it the Massey Stare). She replied, you are not going are you? You said when you were nine years old; that you were going to ride horseback across Canada, but that was kids stuff." I never replied, but heard, WELL ARE YOU? Yes Mom, if someone will go with me."

I went to Vancouver in the fall of 64, and met Joyce Myhon. We purchased the saddles, and all the gear necessary. I knew now, my dream would come true. YES! We checked around and found two people we could purchase horses from. One in Langley, and the other outside of Millard Ville area. We agreed to come in the month of April to purchase them.

I left Vancouver with my five-year-old daughter Dana, who later on, was going to stay during my journey with her Aunt Eileen, Uncle Bruce Taylor, and their six kids, and occasional week-enders with my other sisters Katie and Deanna in Port Alberni B.C. until I returned, from Apr 13th 65 to end of journey. It, was all arranged.

On the 08 January 1965, Dana and I left Burnaby for Hope around 11 p.m. We slept in the car a couple hours at Hope, woke up and had a snack. We weren't tired so we decided to drive on to Chase via the Hope-Princeton. While driving up through there, it was raining and a real miserable night. I was going to find a place to pull off the road until it cleared up a bit. Driving along, looking for a spot, we passed a vehicle. Then I spotted a light up ahead, thought at first it was another car, but turned out to be a small café. We pulled in for coffee, hot chocolate, and a piece of pie.

As we, were being served the pie, a Vehicle pulled in. The driver came running in, and was yelling "My God the whole #### mountain just came down!" He was beside himself. "You have to get help, you have to get help. There was a horrible slide." I told the waitress that we had passed a car. There was nothing we could do. We finally left, heading for Chase.

We travelled over an hour and never passed a single vehicle. Help must have come from the other end. We drove through the night to Chase.

We heard it on the news the next day, that the highway was going to be closed indefinitely. It was a terrible tragedy.

Later I thought about the journey east, and called Joyce. We made decisions and planned on leaving from Merritt or Ashcroft. We were blessed to have missed the slide, and so sorry to have heard about the victims. Joyce, had heard the news and was glad to hear from us.

April 13th – April 21st, 1965

Left Port Alberni on April 13th, 1965 in a 1946 Chevy. I stopped and picked Joyce up in Burnaby with her gear. We headed out up thru the canyon to Boston Bar, then on into Ashcroft, enquiring about horses for sale. Then we went to Clinton to stay the week, to prepare for this ride. We stayed with my father during that time. We had plans of being on the trail by April 21st to make it to the East Coast, prior to winter.

We had calls from several people enquiring as to what kind of horses we were looking for. Well, I never thought about what kind of horse to purchase. I asked Joyce and she said "Let's go see them.". Neither one of us had much experience riding prior to this journey.

Met a woman named Moira Ziola, who had a mare for sale for $150. She said she was very tame, and the horse looked good. That was in my price range, so I purchased her. She was a seven-year-old mare, brand T4. She said I could pick her up on the 20th of the month. She also knew where we could probably get another one.

She directed us to Kenneth Graff's place. He had two horses for sale. Two geldings: one five year old, brand T.S, and one nine year old, brand Rafter M lazy H. We agreed to come on the 20th and purchase them for $150 each.

We came on the 20th with our saddles to his place, picked the two up, and rode them back to Dads place that evening, as he had a fenced grassy area out back. We also brought a halter and a rope to pick up the mare.

It was eight miles back to dads, and took us four and a half hours. We were excited, as we were all prepared to venture out the next morning.

That afternoon, on the 20th, a Clinton man trimmed and put shoes on all three of the horses for us, for Five dollars each horse. It was very interesting to watch. Another Clinton resident, Ralph Moon, gave us a packsaddle for the journey. Dennis Taggert, a local man, showed us the 'Diamond Hitch' several times.

Our gear consisted of:

3 days Food	2 Jeans & Shirts each
Jean jackets	1 Hatchet
2 Pocket Knives	2 Sleeping Bags
Fishing equipment	1 Two-Man Tent
First Aid supplies	1 Ground Sheet
1 Rifle (.22) and Scabbard	Needle and Thread
2 Canteens	Horse Shoeing Equipment
1 Bucket	Horse Liniment and Suave
Pots, pans, utensils, plates, mugs	6 Horse Blankets
2 Rain Slickers (coats)	Pack Saddle
2 Saddles	3 Halters
3 - 50 ft. ¾ inch rope	30 lbs. of oats
Waterproof container and matches	1 Small Radio
My mare I named. Frankie, 7-year-old, brand T4.	
Joyce called her gelding. Belva-Dear, 5- year old, brand TS	
The packhorse we called. Scout, 9 year-old, brand Rafter M Lazy H.	
Mary Aikin witnessed Sale.	

Lou H Alwood

WHY?

♦ ♦ *The Journey 1965* ♦ ♦

BRITISH COLUMBIA

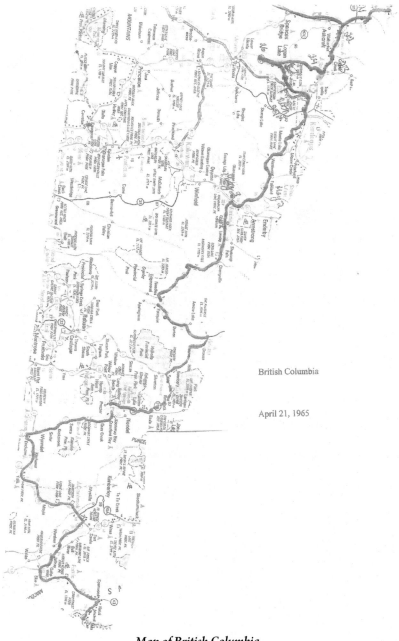

British Columbia

April 21, 1965

Map of British Columbia

I

April 21, 1965
The Beginning

They say that this is a typical spring day in Clinton. It is a cool one, but sunny. Clinton is a small western town, that lies in a hollow approximately 190 miles N.E. of the Vancouver area. Our horses have cleaned up their hay from last night, and we have given them their oats. We are ready to start out for Cache Creek, then east. It is 7:30 a.m. and the horses are fit and ready to go. A few Clinton residence gathered around to wish us all the best.

We talked of our plans, and some just smiled. The majority of them wished us the best. As we were about to leave, a woman from the local newspaper arrived, She took down notes and took pictures. (To put in the local paper next week).

Leaving Clinton

April 29, 1965
Serving Clinton, Cache Creek,
70 Mile and Ashcroft Areas

We finally got on the road at 9:00 a.m. heading West for Cache Creek. Then, East towards Halifax Nova Scotia. The air was fresh and cool, and a slight breeze had picked up. We were in the best of spirits.

We were about to start out to do something that I've ALWAYS wanted to do, with a new found friend, who was willing and ready. Out of the past, we were in western gear, a packhorse with a 'diamond hitch', spurs and a rifle, and of course a map of British Columbia. I was 28 years old and Joyce was 33.

We started out three abreast and only ten minutes from our starting point, two of the horses were not co-operating. (As I saw it then). The packhorse was tied to the rider's saddle horn, when they decided to take different routes around one lone tree. The packhorse got quite excited. He reared up, and stepped on the slack rope pulling it ever so tight across my leg. Oh, boy that hurt! The first lesson learned! (No slack rope!)

Clinton was still in sight. After a few grimaces, and a few choice words, on we went. All was going to be fine, but 'phew' that hurt. My mare would do nothing but trot (smooth mind you). Both of us were quite stiff from riding yesterday for the first time.

We rode up past David Stoddard High School, looking back at the little town of Clinton. We travelled along the countryside, and a couple miles out, we stopped to check the gear at the rodeo grounds. After you leave that area, there are several alkaline lakes throughout the countryside. Seeing only a few older farmhouses made it quite interesting.

We pulled in at six mile lake to water the horses. Then we headed west. Beautiful scenery, rolling hills, sand and sage, and saw several deer along the way. We arrived at Maiden Creek, approximately 18 miles west of Clinton, and decided to stop for noon grazing.

We unpacked everything, and tethered the horses out. We fell asleep on the hillside. At 3:15 p.m., we started to pack up. We already had forgotten the 'diamond hitch'. We put on what the farmers call a 'Mexican diamond'. It sort of crosses here, and twists there, but managed to stay on remarkably well.

Behind the store at 16 mile, we turned off the highway and onto a back country road along the hillside. We made another ten miles then camped in a rancher's field. There didn't seem to be any stock on the land. In and over a little bridge, which crossed a beautiful little stream (Bonaparte), the horses were not sure they wanted to cross. With a little swat on the rump away they went. Staked our horses out, made camp, and gathered firewood for a nice fire. Soon we were hungry as wolves, and could smell the stew cooking. We walked down to the creek to wash up. (A thought passed through my mind, I bet there's fish in here. I will have to come back one day.)

The warm fire made us realize how chilly the night air was. Standing back, relaxing around the fire, we noticed way out in the field there were at least ten head of horses. They were heading our way on the dead run. Something we were not going to do was panic. Somehow, I guess we forgot, and our horses started to get excited. We headed for the brush, grabbing pots and pans. We started clanging them and swing branches. They turned and charged over the little bridge and out of sight. It was a real tense moment.

We untangled our horses, and went back to our now slightly burned biscuits and stew. Mind you, it sure tasted good. We sat around the fire, and talked of our first day on the trail. As the fire died down, we roped off our sleeping area, and took the horses down to water. We noticed we were tucked into a wooded area, and had no knowledge as to why the horses were running, and it kind of put us on edge. We could see nothing in the field, and wondered if bears were out. We kept an eye out, and listened for anything. Then we crawled into our sleeping bags and still had a good night sleep. This was the end of our first day.

April 22, 1965
Bonaparte

6:30 a.m. came early. Getting out of our warm sleeping bags was harder than we had expected. "OH", we were some stiff! We got a nice fire going. Within minutes the remainder of stew and biscuits with coffee took what chill there may be away. We washed in cool water at the little creek. It felt so good, as both our faces were wind burned. My leg was swollen quite badly from the rope burn.

We tended to our horses as the sun was coming up. It looked like this was going to be another great day. We threw away our pack boxes and rolled the supplies in our sleeping bags, making a much neater pack. The horses had grazed well and were quite frisky. We gave them their oats, and little did they know this was going to be the longest journey of their lives. There was no sign of our guests from the previous night.

We decided to name our horses: the bay gelding we will keep his name 'Scout'; the other gelding, will be called 'Belva-Dear'; and my mare, I'm calling her 'Frankie'. The narrow road along the old highway is quite peaceful. Rolling hills, open range, dotted for miles with the beautiful sagebrush, and cactus, and the odd farmhouse. The hillside looks painted with gold, reds, and browns. They say it is slag from mining back in the hills.

A groundhog poked his nose up over a pile of stones and watched as we rode through his territory.

Crossing the highway to Lillooet, staying on the old country road through to Cache Creek, we ran into an old Barkerville Stage coach stop. We travelled down onto the old historic wagon trail road and past some buildings that were built between 1860 and 1905. There were freight wagons with passengers that went through here back then. It was so quiet passing through. We met a local resident who said, it 'was known' as the 'Bar X'. Some of the buildings were the Hat Creek House and the BX Barn.

There was no one in the area, and it looked abandoned. We followed through for about another mile, still along the Bonaparte, and came upon what looked to be an old burial ground. We tied up the horses and went for a closer look. There were at least twenty head of dead cattle, and alongside them lay their young. It was quite a strange thing to see. We heard later that they died giving birth, apparently from the lack of vitamin D (hmm). We stopped to take pictures and the packhorse decided to take a nap. Down he went, pack and all.

The pack looked good; so on we went, travelled thru a small reservation, and back out onto the highway. Two miles this side of Cache Creek, the pack slid under Belva-Dear. Being a wee bit lazy, he never seemed to get as excited as his two companions did. A loose rope was stepped on, and the entire gear was all over the side of the highway. A car swerved, and a Clinton resident stopped and showed us the 'diamond hitch.'(Once more.) (Dennis Taggart). He got a good laugh out of that, as we were sure we knew it the first half dozen times he showed us, prior to leaving Clinton. We thanked him, and headed into Cache Creek crossing the Bonaparte.

We stopped to water the horses, turned left after the bridge, to the hillside, and unpacked for noon grazing. This fresh air all at once, sure does wonders for the appetite. We were more wind burned than we thought we would be, but the cool air is helping a lot. It's the breeze that's causing the wind burn.

4:30 p.m. saw us back on the road toting a 'Mexican diamond'. We decided to take a short cut across country over the hill to the Kamloops highway, as there was no fences. It proved to be very exciting. As we reached the top of the hill, we met a short stalky man. He was very angry, (I mean VERY angry!). He said we were cutting through his property. He got flustered, red in the face, used some very choice language, and was holding a rifle. (Phew!) Being somewhat nervous, we turned our horses and rode away. He kept yelling, "What did you see? What did you see?" Waiving his gun and yelling, "What did you see?" It was a little scary for a few minutes. We could still hear him going at it when he was off in the distance. We had seen no signs anywhere.

Once we were across the other side, we wondered what it could have been that he was so mad about. We laughed and wondered, did he find the 'Lost Miners' gold, or was it a crime scene? We were sure glad to be out of there.

We were wondering where we could camp tonight when a 'Perry" ranch hand pulled up and invited us to stop over for the night, as they had heard we were coming. We rode on to the ranch, and they were waiting for us. They gave us a bunkhouse, cared for our animals, and gave us the run of the ranch. We hauled water from the horse troughs and washed our badly sun burned faces. We were still wondering why the old man was so cranky, and mad, and why did he have a rifle. We cooked a hot meal, and decided to have an early night. We did approximately 28 miles today. We are ready to bed down. We checked the horses, and they were eating hay that was tossed out to them.

April 23, 1965
Perry Ranch

The sun started to come through the window of the little bunkhouse. All that could be heard was a tractor off in the distance. Already there was life all around us. The two riders in the bunkhouse were feeling the effects of the two-day ride. I got up and lit the fire, putting on the bacon and coffee. That woke Joyce up.

Looking up at me from her bunk, she started to laugh hysterically. "What's wrong with you?" was the reply. She sat on the floor and laughed holding her sides. I just ignored her. However, even a good hardy laugh, can only be ignored for so long. I started to laugh with her, and there was something terribly wrong. The tears that began to run down my face started to burn. My lips were cracked and bleeding. "Look in the mirror" Joyce replied when she caught her breath. My God, it took her ten minutes to tell me, from laughing hysterically, "You look like a basketball with two oranges attached". From being, so wind burned my face was swollen, my eyes were two slits, and my ears were blistered.

No more could we laugh. We sat across from each other at the table and tried not to make eye contact. If we did, there were a few more snickers. We were exhausted and wanted to crawl back in our bunks and sleep for a week. We have never been so stiff. Joyce was sunburned but not swollen. My leg was still puffy and sore. I said, "What a pair we are, and we've only travelled a couple days."

We went for the horses, and they were fighting. They had rolled in the mud and were a fine mess. They were loose in the corral and were not going to be caught. Believe me, this is not a time to be cranky. A lariat soon fixed this. I may not ride well, but I'm not bad with a rope.

By 9:30 a.m., we were packed and ready to leave. The Perry Ranch riders asked us to come and stay with them again and drop a line. We thanked them before we pulled out. Scout and Belva-Dear were following the mare as we headed out across country. They started to act up. So Belva-Dear was led by the mare this morning. That put a stop to the fighting. Belva-Dear and Frankie were the two that had roamed free together for so long, but there wasn't a mare involved. She seemed to care less.

Along a country road, there was several ranches. These rolling hills are a wonderful place to ride on horseback. They are quite beautiful. The smell of the sage is something in itself. We understand the value of our Stetsons, and will wear them today. We look like bandits, with bandanas over our ears. There wasn't much of a breeze today at all, which will be in our favor.

We cut across the main highway and down over the other side onto the old highway. So silent and peaceful, and such a big country. Off in the distance you could hear bawling cattle. It was branding season, and the young were being separated. It was something neither of us had seen before. The fire was hot, and the cowboys knew what they were doing. They were putting brands on all these young calves to show ownership as western cattle sometimes are set free to graze. You could hear the bawling for miles.

We could see the Thompson River and valley below. Everything was starting to look greener. We passed a couple old log cabins looking about 100 years old. About seven miles from the Perry ranch it got quite windy. The area had more rolling hills and the wind started to pick up. After several hours, we stopped for noon grazing. We looked around the area and stretched our stiff legs. The very first thing the animals do when unsaddled, is roll and snort.

We came to a little stream. We got water for the horse, filled our canteens and wet our bandanas to use on our faces. Phew, sure felt good. 4:30 p.m. the wind has really started to pick up. Down over the road we went and came to a fence that had a sign on it saying 'Government Property'. There wasn't any 'No Trespassing' signs, so in we went, closing the gate behind us.A small piece of tumbleweed blew across the trail in front of us. The wind was coming up even stronger now. A few black clouds were rolling in, in the distance. We decided to make camp when, up over the hill, came a picture that could not be painted. Standing in the wind, across the sand blown ground, stood a Palomino Stallion. His tail and mane were snow white, and blowing in the wind. This young fellow pawed the ground, snorted, and looked like he meant business. It appeared he had six mares down in the hollow, and we were trespassing. It was a frantic dash for the gate. Scout decided to protect Frankie. Hell, what a time to be a hero.

Through the gate we went. The sand was blowing up into our faces, and a piece of tumbleweed hit Belva-Dear, and caused him to be very un-co-operative. We headed for a hollow to wait it out. Forty minutes later, we were back on the road heading for Dead Man's Creek. This was to be our night's camp.

There was no grazing until we hit this spot. It was sandy country with a lot of sage and tumbleweed, and of course, cactus. Night began to fall fast. We were on the highway after dark. Finally, here we were. This spot had been seen from the road many times. It was green most of the year round, with a lovely little flowing stream.

Off the road we went, pulled our gear off, and started to make camp. I took the horses to tether them and apiece of cactus flew up and stuck in between my knees. When I walked, it dug in. I thought an arrow had hit me. I fell to the ground into more cactus. Damn, that was it! Away went the horses, all three of them.

They stopped when a young filly came down the mountain and ran down to greet them. The loveliest little bay mare we had ever seen, bearing no brand. We managed to round up our horses. This little filly put on quite a show for us. How she could prance around and not get stabbed to death, was a mystery to us.

We finally tethered the horses outside the fence. Somehow, that seemed to be the only place we could feel no cactus. My God, we had to choose each step very carefully. Back into the camp area we went. We had to get our pocketknives out to cut a space to put our bedrolls down. While preparing a meal, Joyce sat on a cactus. The words that came out of her can't be mentioned. Oh Lord, that had to be painful.

After our meal, it took no time at all getting into the bedrolls. Throughout the night you could hear the horses snorting. What a day this has turned out to be. The wind has come up a lot more now, and looks like quite a storm. Soon all was silent, and darker than the inside of a cat.

April 24, 1965
Dead Man's Creek

Horses are doing well. There appears to be no more rub spots that we have noticed while combing the horses down this morning. We took extra time to make sure there were no cactus nettles in the horse blankets or gear. It's an extremely bad area to camp, with or without horses. Oh boy did we sleep. Never did know whether it rained during the night or not.

5:30 a.m. found us both awake and quite cramped. We never dared move during the night for fear we'd roll into more cactus. Not having much experience with them, we discovered that where the thorn enters your hide, it soon would swell. If you didn't take them out right then, it would be quite painful for some time to come. We managed to get thorns in places such as posterior, inside the knees, and 'groan' the fingertip, which bothered us the most.

We definitely decided that this day would not be rushed. A better thought, pack up and go home. After the third night we were: sunburned, wind burned, rope burned, stiff, full of cactus, scared by running horses, ,cracked lips, threatened by miner, wind chill, cranky, cold, and lost gear on the highway. We haven't had the chance to get to know each other yet, but we both agree we won't quit. We thought we would sit by the creek and drop a few lines to the folks. Joyce said she can't sit, (Oh I forgot that!) and the writing finger has a thorn in it. That takes care of the pen in hand. It's cloudy and windy this morning, but looks like it may clear. We definitely have to make some plans, as we cannot stay here. The way Joyce walks, I can tell she's in pain.

The young filly disappeared during the night. She was as wild as the wind. Guess she knew it was no place in 'cactus land', to spend the night. We moved the horses, gathered our gear carefully, and moved it out to the roadside. We checked the gear again. While coiling our ropes we managed quite nicely to pick up several more thorns. After camp was cleared, we went over to the creek bed, took out our pocketknives, and tried to cut some of them out before they swelled. This was a very painful job, and we now have the most tender hands in the province. Thought came through our minds, third night out, and we are totally exhausted. We really need to talk about it. First, we have to get out of here.

"Hello Girls" came from the highway. Walking down the bank, towards us was what appeared to be a family. A man, woman, and son. They were dressed in western gear. They were very cheerful people, and introduced themselves as the Howard Allen family. They saw us leave Clinton and were wanting us to stay with them, last night. They were only four miles or so away. We could have cried. We sat and chatted for a while. They thought this was a wonderful thing to do, to ride horseback across Canada, and how proud we must feel to take on such an adventure. They said they admired us. I said "Gee how long does it take to learn to ride?" with no idea where that thought came from. They replied, "You've never rode before?" We chatted awhile, they left wishing us all the best.

After they left there was no discussion. We just stared at each other for a moment. I asked Joyce, How are you going to ride? I just got a look, then, she started to gather up all the gear very carefully, neither one speaking, and rode out. Leaving Dead Man's Creek, looking back, you would never expect such a beautiful looking location to be such a nightmare.

We travelled on a ways and ran into the Allen's. The Father and the son, on horseback. We rode along five or six miles with them, and they told us all about the country. They were extremely helpful and very nice folks. They then turned into where they had a spread on the river, wished us the best, and we left heading east.

As we got near Savanah, we had to cross an old steel bridge. You could see the river below. WELL, one-step forward, three steps back. I had to blind fold the mare and lead her across. The other two followed. It was quite a chore stopping traffic, but everyone was great about it. As we reached Savanah, who should come along with a bale of hay, some oats and a picnic lunch, the Allen family. It was good to see them again. We decided to stop for noon grazing.

It had warmed up, and we were in much better spirits. We truly enjoyed their company. They were our very first visitors on the trail. We asked them what kind of horses were theirs. They owned probably the only half Morgan/half Arabian with a full mustache in the country. We told them that someone in Clinton said ours were Mustangs, and that Belva-Dear was a wild horse once. They asked about our plans from Savanah. "We've decided to go south over the mountains, then directly east." When they left, they asked us to stay with them anytime we were in the area.

We washed our sunburned faces and packed up camp. A cowboy came along and left us fifty pounds of oats. He never said who he was. He just wished us the best and then left. (Thank you) We've decided to go south over the mountains, then directly east, (YES) against our better judgment. So, south we headed down past Lake Tunkwa and Lac La Juene.

Spring is in the air and the horses are ready. We travelled about ten miles off the highway and camped in a fenced-in area. The grazing isn't half-bad. We won't be turning them loose though, as they are too close to home. Probably like us, wish they were. Being from open range and doing as they pleased, who can blame them? They are still very high spirited. The slightest sound or a sudden noise, and you are away on the wildest, damnedest, nightmare of a ride you can possibly imagine. If you are lucky you fall off. Frankie (the mare) spooks at her own shadow, falling leaves, honking horns, and anything out of the ordinary. Even mailboxes. She is spooked so easy that when she takes off she nearly goes down every time. It can be very scary at times.

Its 6:30 p.m. and we got a great fire going. A stew with homemade biscuits is about the nicest thing you can have on a chilly night around a camp fire. Now getting up is another thing. Why it hits the knees is something else? Believe me, stiff is, putting it mildly. Joyce said, rigor mortis has set in. Wind burned a bit more, we are so nice and brown, we look like typical natives, we have been asked if we are Indians, and where we are from.

The horses are lying down. It looks like it's going to be foggy and cold tonight. We are much higher in the hills now than we have been on the whole trip. The country in this area appears to be all farms. A few beautiful older homes. We are just up from Durand Creek. We've cared for our horses and combed them good tonight. We are hitting the sack about 8:00 p.m., and we both believe we could sleep a week.

We watched the fire die, and talked for about half an hour after we were bunked down. We decided we'd take one day at a time, and see what tomorrow brings. We both talked about how much beauty there is in living out doors, and totally tried to forget yesterday by thinking about how beautiful the fresh air, cooking out and the scenery could be. B.C. is certainly a beautiful province. The chill of a light breeze made us pull our heads into our sleeping bags. Soon, almost sound asleep until I said "Shouldn't the bears be coming out soon?" I heard "Jesus!"

We both feel that spending time with the Allen family gave us the strength to carry on, as we were pretty down.

April 25, 1965
Durand Creek

Have you ever woke up with your heart in your mouth and terrified. There was a very loud bang and an echo. The horses were very excited and Frankie was on the run. We both sat straight up in our sleeping bags. We could see a pick up backing up. A man got out of his truck,, and was walking slowly over to the fence. He looked at us sitting there and looked around at the horses. For a minute neither one of us spoke. He questioned us as to why we were there, and where were we going. I yelled out "Halifax". He raised his eyebrows, put his head back and said "NO, NO, Halifax Nova Scotia? I think he didn't believe us but was very polite in not saying so. He said he owned the land, and it was all right that we stayed there. He said he was really, sorry he scared the horses, but he thought they were moose. He chuckled then left.

I took the rifle out just in case someone came along and thought they were moose again. About an hour and a half later, the man came back with half a bale of hay, tossed it over the fence and left. We never got a chance to thank him. Spread the hay out between the horses and went back to bed.

Awake at 5:30 a.m. and up at 7:00. We were too groggy and stiff to crawl out before that. All the gear was frozen. The tent, ends of the blankets, even the canteens were frozen. So this is spring morning in the mountains is it? Well another day was in the making when our horses whinnied out to us. We had to light a fair size fire to dry our gear before we started. We took care of the horses and Joyce remembered to put her watch ahead an hour.

We started the day at 10:30 a.m. still heading south, and made real good time this morning. We came to a dead end road, and kept going across a field hoping the road would come out the other end. It appeared to be going nowhere. There were signs of snow. It was about 1:00 p.m. when we decided to turn back, and ended up where we had started out this morning. We stopped and watered the horses. We took out the map and tried to figure out where we were and why the road had stopped. We had to really move, it was going to be dark within a couple of hours.

We kept back tracking. I led the packhorse who was tied to the horn of my saddle. He stepped on the slack rope. My God! How could I forget? The pain that went up my side almost caused me to black out. It was something that cannot be described. Within half an hour it was badly swollen. Joyce helped me down from the saddle and we stopped for twenty minutes. I could walk so I knew my leg wasn't broken. Joyce said, "I'll bet you will never do that again". It was not a good time to discuss it.

Managed to get back in the saddle, and to the nearest farm for hay. They had no cattle, let alone hay. They were very friendly and told us about a vacant farm down the road. There was no new grass, but it would do for the evening with a good portion of oats. We saw more dead cattle. They say the lack of vitamin D killed the heifers and their new born calves (which we had heard near cache creek).

The country up through here is absolutely beautiful. The remains of old abandoned cabins were probably homes with families at one time. They were not new to Joyce, as coming from Wells area she had seen a lot of these types of cabins. For myself, I was in awe, and wondered what it was like living back in those days, and who the families were?

We pulled in and camped at Witches Brook again. We combed the horses down and found out the packhorse has another small rub spot that we will watch closely. Nothing serious at this time. We tethered them out and gave them their oats. The grazing isn't too bad. It looks like a good spot for fishing in warmer weather. The little creek glowed as it twisted across the valley. It was so beautiful. We were so tired that we just gathered firewood for the morning. There was snow all around and the temperature is dropping.

We were up 63,000 ft. and in April, boy it is cold. I used a bread bag and filled it with snow. I wrapped it around my swollen leg with an old t-shirt. We threw tarps over our sleeping bags and huddled together to keep warm. We laughed for an hour. Neither one of us could find a thing funny to laugh about. We were just damned good and tired, and cold. We talked about the daily events, which got us laughing again. One thing for sure I will never have slack rope again when leading the packhorse. We won't give up now. After all, we just started five days ago. We will take one day at a time.

For some unknown reason when you ask your friend why they are laughing, they say they don't know.

With tears rolling down our faces we respond "why are you?" So you both laugh until you could nearly pass out. What's the answer? Stress! The next day it came up again. What were we laughing about? Away we went.

Log cabin

Joyce cooking

LOU H ALWOOD

April 26, 1965
Nicola Lake Turn Off - Witches Brook

You could hear the creek running during the night. It was quite comforting. The crooked little brook we followed for so many miles seemed to twist across the meadow like a spring wanting to unwind. It was 5:30 a.m. and there was two inches of frost. We are staying in bed until the sun comes up. Jack Frost can certainly paint a beautiful picture even though you could hardly bare the cold at this altitude.

9:30 a.m. and a new day is in the making. Got the fire crackling, the horses are answering, and all coming towards us at once. They were trying to beat one another in getting their oats first. Oh the nice warm fire, the smell of hot cakes, bacon and coffee sure can start the day off right! We hate to leave this lonely little deserted farm. It also makes you wish the remains of the buildings could speak, tell the tale of the past, and who lived here. What was their life like? I could go off in my own world thinking about it. A good campfire sure can put a spark in you. We could just stay here another day by the fire, but we know we need to move on for better grazing.

Tonight with a good days ride should find us several hundred feet lower, and hopefully warmer weather. We have decided today to pack Scout instead of Belva-Dear. Joyce will ride Frankie, and I will ride Belva-Dear today. The horses are faring well. We rode to the Lower Nicola Lake turn off where we met forestry workers who said we could not get through the trail because there was fifteen feet of snow. This certainly has altered our plans considerably. We had planned to get new supplies at Nicola lake camp. This leaves us with half a day's supply of groceries, and two and a half days still to go. Both of us have the feeling that this has not been very well planned.

We will now have to rely on our ability as hunters for our food supply. We are not too worried as there are many ducks in the area. We then spotted a 'fool' hen and went for the gun. No shells, they were packed away. Another lesson learned. Joyce leaped from her horse and began hurling everything in sight at it. Probably weighed no more than a quarter of a pound. It sat there and dodged everything that came at her. We were laughing like darn fools as she took off for an upper limb of a tree off in the distance. Grouse was not to be our noon meal. She perched about ten feet up on a limb looking at us from way back in the bush. Between us was a small swamp.

Off we rode towards Lac la Juene as we had to make up time. The horses were full of life. Once again the country is remarkably beautiful. Belva-Dear certainly is rough riding after being used to the mare, yet Joyce likes him best. Scout seems to be a much better packhorse. He leads easy while Belva-Dear had to be convinced. The mare, impossible to pack as she's too nervous.

It has warmed up and our arms are sunburned. Our faces are peeling. We look weather beaten. We travelled eight to ten more miles and made camp this side of Lac la Juene. We have not eaten since this morning, and are starving. Joyce has taken the gun and gone to the other side of the lake to see what's to be had for dinner. There are fresh moose tracks everywhere. We are four miles off the forestry road.

I began unpacking and putting the camp back together. A shot, was heard quite a distance from camp. It was now getting dark and I'd be glad to see my partner back. The fire was blazing and I got the makings for supper ready. All that was left in our saddlebags were, one small frozen onion, half a cup of flour, one potato with a horseshoe nail in it, and of course there would be the duck that Joyce was bringing for supper.

The minutes passed and night was falling fast. It is quite eerie miles in the bush from nowhere. I heard a noise off in the bush, and was expecting to see Joyce. I turned instead to see a young cow moose heading towards the far end of the lake and back into the bush. This was the first large animal I had seen so far. Minutes later Joyce came back with one male squirrel, which she skinned, boiled, fried in flour, and roasted over the bonfire. Then we tried to consume it all within half an hour. Joyce claimed it tasted like rabbit. As I went to take a bite, she asked if squirrels belong to the rat family? Instantly I lost my appetite for squirrel stew.

I headed for the back of the tent. Within minutes the day was gone. I've never been sick on an empty stomach before, as normally things like that don't bother me. I told her she might have said that 'after' we ate. Besides, it was too tough to eat, (boiled rat). I see she managed to enjoy it anyways as there were ribs in the fire pit the next morning.

Note: We didn't bother pitching the tent tonight. Belva-Dear got tangled several times this week on the road. He's clumsy, lazy, and the fastest walker of the three when he wants to move. He gets along with the mare, but backs off when Scout is around. Scout has a mind all of his own. He is moody and very cranky at times. He cannot be pushed when his mind is made up. He appears to have been pouting for a week. Then, there is Frankie and she does not much care what the other two do. Everything frightens her still. From falling leaves to white lines on the highway, and anything else that is in her vision.

We slept out under the trees, and never saw the moose again, then watched the fire burn down. We talked about the past five days on the road. I told her about the moose I'd seen. We laughed about all the mishaps and how things could only get better. I packed snow on my leg again. We bedded down around 9:40.

April 27, 1965
Knutsford

Fresh moose tracks were found in the camp this morning. The horses couldn't have been too alarmed, as we never heard a sound. Saw three sputniks during the night, all within half an hour. We were up at 6:15 a.m., got a fair size fire going and Joyce is heating up the rest of the "Squirrel Stew" as she calls it. I put the coffee on, and I told her that two burnt legs is not stew. I told her I saw the ribs in the fire pit and had hoped she had eaten it all. When you are as hungry as we are, squirrel stew with coffee isn't that bad. This is the end of our supplies. We will try to make it thru to Knutsford, just outside of Kamloops. All the forestry trails to Merritt are closed.

Heading back to Kamloops and into the area, which we passed just four days ago. It was against our better judgment in the first place to take the mountain route. However, the experience in the past four days and seeing new countryside has been well worth it. (Leave out the rope burn). Leaving another camp behind we travelled for two hours and took the road into Lac La Juene Park, to see if we can get supplies. The road to Kamloops was only forty miles.

At the park, we met a man painting boats in preparation for the spring opening. He introduced himself as John Whittaker. He said he was sorry he had no supplies whatsoever, and was just there for the day. We talked a while and thanked him.

We left the park and pushed through until nearly 1:00 p.m. Came upon several bales of hay, which appeared to have been lost off a truck. We pulled up for a couple hours, split a bale and fed the horses. We washed clothes in the creek and let the horses rest and have their feed, before we headed eastward.

The country road looks like one I'd seen in Europe. Little farm houses set off in the distance with many tiny bridges, over a rippling creek. It looked like a storm was coming up behind us. The sky was black and you could hear the thunder rolling in. It spooked the horses making for better time. We finally began to see cattle and other horses. The horses seeing other animals seemed to pick up their spirits considerably. I noticed that the mare was limping a little. I stopped and checked her out and found a small stone in her hoof.

The narrow country road running between fenced in pastures, wasn't exactly an ideal spot for a lost bawling calf to be. She ran ahead of us for a long ways. We backed off, and she was able to find a break in the fence and head back toward her mother. We finally came out at Knutsford about 6:00 p.m. The storm was heading north, and the sky appeared to be clearing.

We picked up a few groceries and camped just south of Kamloops under two pine trees. The horses are travelling well, and the grazing appears to be much better. We tied up to a farmer's fence, and a young man came over and asked us why we were there. I just shook my head and ignored him, then walked over to the fence to get the horses out from under the tree. I was slapped in the face by a branch bringing tears to my eyes.

After untying the horses from the fence, I tied them to the tree. He was still standing there and complaining. We told him very nicely that the horses were no longer on his property but on the road allowance. I then told him that he should 'BUGGER OFF' as we were far too damned tired to listen to him complain. I assumed he never expected that response, as he left right away.

Note: We pulled in off the road near a power line and camped for the night. We made forty miles today. So far, this has been our biggest day. Their shoes are holding out remarkably well, considering the country we've crossed. There were many leaves around making for a nice soft bed. All is well, but very cold. We bunked down early.

April 28, 1965
Kamloops Area

Slept well last night. Leaves made a good soft bed. The sun was coming up at 6:00 a.m., but not the riders. Cold old man winter sure can be cruel. We realized we needed more winter clothing, as we didn't prepare properly. It's crisp and clear. The air smells so fresh.

Up at 6:30 a.m. A truck stopped and a cocky young punk slinked over and said "Where you from? What are you doing here?" We replied "From Vancouver, why?" He replied "I'll see you're moved. This isn't your land." So I asked him if it was his and he said no. So I told him not to worry as we are leaving soon, but go ahead and do whatever you feel you have to do. He left. (Two cranks in 24 hours, there must be something in the water.)

We had the rest of the macaroni and water for breakfast. The wind is starting to howl and we will be glad to get moving this morning. Hope the horses travel well today. It looks like we will be riding into the wind. While packing Belva-Dear, he bit Joyce on the left leg. She cringed in pain and her leg bruised instantly. My God! Between the cold and the bite, the day for her wasn't starting out well. It left a perfect set of teeth marks on her leg. She said, she's o.k.

About 15 minutes later we were leaving camp and heading down into Kamloops through the outskirts, which is the highway east. It's quite a beautiful little city from the top of the hill. You can see north Kamloops and the center of town, the river, and the Shuswap Lake. Things were starting to move in the city as we passed through. The horses were a little jittery and nervous, as the traffic buzzed by with horns honking. Some kids on their way to school came over to see the horses.

We rode off of the highway as there was too much commotion. Their steel plated shoes made quite a clatter on the pavement. You could see people peeking through their still drawn drapes, probably wondering who we were, riding down their streets so early in the morning. We felt a little uncomfortable, as we knew, no one knew where we were going or why. In addition they didn't seem to believe it when we told them. Sometimes we feel the same way.

Joyce's bite seems to be bothering her a lot. Phew, I'm so sorry. We were glad to get to the other side of town and off the pavement, for all our sakes. It was warming up a little but the wind still bit at you. The air was so clean and fresh we decided to stop and rest the horses for an hour. There was a beautiful grazing area behind a gas station, where we also could clean up. Joyce showed me where she got bit. I tried not to laugh, but it was, the most perfect set of dentures I had ever seen. Her leg was swollen and purple. Never seen anything like that before. I'm so sorry. God how painful that must have been.

We had only been on the road a week and we were craving apple pie. We went and sat in a booth for an hour. Joyce got an icepack from the waitress.

We started out and then half an hour later stopped again east of Kamloops at the valley view market. We tied the horses to a picket fence. Recess for the school kids proved to be quite exciting. All the kids came running over to see the horses at once. This made the horses very nervous. When I went to put the groceries on the pack horse from the wrong side, he kicked, snorted, and kicked the fence. Pickets flew everywhere. I got one on the shin-bone which was very painful for a few minutes. Damn, it was on the same leg. The SILLY ASS!

We got pails of water from the owner of the store and watered the horses. I put the fence back together and we started out again. Both of us bruised and battered. We turned off at the Par 3 Golf course. The country is hilly with little farms all round. Its real beautiful country. Travelled on to Campbell Creek and watered the horses again before we made camp on the other side of Barnhartville. We will pick up more oats tomorrow at Duck Meadows.

We took turns riding Belva-Dear as he is quite stubborn and can really wear you out. We are experimenting with the horses. We rode through Barnhartville. It looks like a little old frontier town. We found the folks to be very friendly. We camped three miles the other side of town at 4:00 p.m. and went up thru the field and back up off the road to the trees, where you could see a creek down in the gully below. The grazing was not that good. It appears that spring hasn't arrived. We have a bale of hay that was dropped off by a kind hearted rancher as we were making camp.

After the animals were unsaddled, and while grooming them, camp was in the making, Joyce yelled "The horses have bugs". I went over to take a look and sure enough they had ticks. We checked all three of them and found eight more on their bellies. We picked them off and burned them. Oooooo, it makes you feel crawly all night.

We were in bed writing in the diary at 7:45 p.m. It is too darn cold to stay up and Joyce's bite is extremely painful and colorful. I didn't mean to laugh when I saw those perfect teeth marks again. I was promptly told, that it was not funny. Believe me, it really isn't. You have to see something like this bite, to believe it. I'm sure it's going to be sore for some time to come. Both our knees are quite sore and a few more spots are a wee bit tender, but mostly cold.

The wind is very strong and cold tonight. We are sleeping under the stars and listening to the weather forecast. We were going to write home but Joyce said she would rather commute with nature instead. We're sleeping on a hillside with our feet pointing down the gully. There is a hill on the other side of the creek and the sun is hitting the top of it. It is quite spectacular. It is so silent, not a sound at all. You can see the creek down below but cannot hear it running. It was total silence.

We lay there talking of the trip. We laughed at our many errors and the experiences we have had. Oh how little we knew about horses, what is out there, and what tomorrow will bring.

We watched another sputnik before there was twenty stars in the sky, then watched it follow the curvature of the earth. There is nothing more beautiful than nature. We never expected so many injuries in the first week. Rope burn twice. Oh yes those horrid cactus. That was the very worse night on the entire trip, until Joyce was bit. She said it couldn't get any worse than that. We had a few chuckles and the thorn in the finger still hurt after a week. Then, the flying fence rails. No more slack ropes, and pack-horses do not lead.

We are ready to call it a night. We are very tired and wind burned from fighting the wind all day. We had hoped to find a creek around noon to wash our clothes and to stop for the day. Really is amazing how tiring it can be to ride into such a strong wind for six to eight hours a day, even though we had stopped for an hour. The horses appear to be in good shape. Belva-Dears feeding habits are starting to improve a little. We dozed off around 9:00 p.m.

April 29, 1965
Robins Creek – Duck Meadows

We woke up stiff and everything was damp. We were restless all night as the ground was so hard. It seemed to be a lot harder to get a nice fire going as we found out we had lost our hatchet. It looks like it's going to be a nice day. No clouds and the sun is already up.

We are having rolled oats with toast and coffee. We tried rubbing horse linament on our legs to see if it would improve the circulation, as we sure are stiff this morning.

We packed up camp and left the area at 9:30 a.m. All is well. We were sure glad that the wind had died down last night. Joyce's hands were blistered. We travelled on for several miles to Robins Creek. It's a great day to do our laundry. The grass is green and the horses are feeding even before we unpacked. It's a really good spot for all of us. We lit a fair sized campfire and boiled all our clothes in a bucket. Everything came out grey as a black sock got in with the whites.

We strung up a clothes line to dry out our underwear, (panties, bras, and long johns), all was well as we were way back off the road, back in the country. We heated up another bucket of water to have sponge baths from. We each took turns going back into the trees to strip down and bathe. Then, out of nowhere came a loaded logging truck. Phew! Thought he was going to lose his load. We didn't think he saw us and hoped it must have been the garments hanging on the line. Oh well. Who would believe his story back at camp?

It is just another day. It was the fastest bath we have ever had, as it was very cold. We were so thankful he never decided to stop, and come and see what was up, as then no one would believe him. We decided to have an early dinner and let the horses roll. We will haul water for them before we start out.

Laundry

While packing Scout he reared up. Something had spooked him. I went to grab the rope and stepped on it in the tall grass. It jerked me off my feet. I managed to grab it and was dragged several feet over a pile of rocks. Oh Brother! My hands were rope burned. I had a hard time breathing for a few seconds. I thought I'd broken my elbow. Oh Boy! I just stayed down a minute still hanging onto the rope. I looked at my partner and she just shook her head. I slowly got up. Not a word was spoken.

My nose started to bleed. We looked at each other and started to laugh hysterically. We both laid out on the grass for twenty minutes. (The pain!). Joyce said her bite still hurts. Then I thought to myself, who cares? We started to laugh again! (What are we doing here?)

We packed up the best we could and I bet we were both sharing the same prayer, that the horses would walk gently to our next camp. We are heading for Robins Creek. We heard that Duck Meadows is a good grazing spot. So, we decided to stop and graze in a farmer's field for a while. There are so many different bird sounds, the only two we recognize, were the Robin and the Owl.

The mare still spooks at everything. When she drops, she drops on all fours and nearly throws me each time. I've never seen or heard anything like this before. We found out she's also afraid of parked cars, wrecked cars, pieces of paper flying in the wind, cement barriers and barking dogs. I actually am starting to worry about her. If it keeps up I may have to trade her along the way, as I feel it's quite dangerous this close to the highway. It would be quite sad to have to swap her though, as she's proven to be the best horse so far. Easy riding, she's a leader and the other two always stay with her. When they broke loose, Frankie started to come back and the other two followed her.

After grazing a couple hours we started out again. We went through a farm yard with sheep in it. They had just butchered a few head of cattle and we really had our hands full controlling all the horses, who just were not going to go past this farm. But, they have to, as it's the only road through. Its a narrow road and its fenced on both sides. Somehow the mare found a small path along the fence. She snorted and carefully selected all her steps. Two forward, three back, three forward, two back. Then she took off on the run past the farm. Boy, we really made time. The others followed. They were not having anything to do with sheep or dead cattle. It was quite hilarious.

We travelled a few more miles then made camp for the night. We took a few more ticks out of the horses, and gave them a good grooming. There was a block of salt lying out in the field, which they all seemed to enjoy. Another day was over, we were glad to see this one end. Tomorrow has to be an easier one.

We took care of the horses and went to bed without supper. We were just too tired and battered. We snuggled in to our sleeping bags, and listened to the weather forecast. It says it's going to be another cold night. I am losing weight and Joyce is eating the best she has ever eaten in her life, she says.

Why? Sitting on ground with saddles

Note: We were starting to look a little weather beaten and feel like we've aged a few years. Not only in looks, as it feels this way clean to the marrow. We've also learned a great deal of knowledge about the old way of travelling. If some of their tales had been told, or understood, (would be a better way of saying it), it may be easier to understand, if you've lived it. The painful bruises and injuries you soon forget when you can see the sparkle of the running winding creeks for several miles. We really have to be more alert as our injuries are taking their toll with us. (Our experiences have taught us more than that).We honestly feel that what keeps us going are the beautiful warm campfires in the mornings and evenings, the animals, the birds, and the sound of rippling creeks and reflection of the moonlight. The cold evenings were beautiful due to the abundance of stars. I could lie there for hours, waiting for the next shooting star.

April 30, 1965
Monte Creek

Started stirring about 7:30 a.m. It's really damp outside and everything ached. We lay there damp but warm and wondered why we were still here. A bus full of school kids went by as we laid there. They all turned their heads with their mouths open at the same time. This managed to get a smile out of both of us, and just enough energy to get up.

From a horizontal point of view the horses looked just fine. We will try to make it to the other side of Falkland today. The country through here is beautiful. I hope to make it back through here by car some time. There is no place to light a campfire as we are travelling along the highway, so we decided not to have breakfast this morning. We will pick something up as we got a late start.

We stopped at Monte Lake and got some groceries. We got hot dogs buns, wieners, mustard, canned soup, carrots, stewing meat, bread, beans, onions, can of chili, and coffee. We saw cars that were in a race from Montreal to Vancouver, as they came thru Paxton Valley, the noise spooked the horses. We didn't manage to calm them until three cars had passed.

We had travelled three miles past the Monte lake store when I discovered my wallet was missing. I panicked right away, as that's all the cash we had. Joyce backtracked to the store, and I unpacked the horses for a rest. She returned with no wallet. I decided to back track again just in case she had missed it, as we had just left the store. There had been very little traffic. I figured it might have bounced off to the side.

Half a mile up the road, a highway patrol car came driving right at me. He stopped and asked, "Are you Miss Alwood?" I yelled Yahoo! he laughed and said he had found it on the road, and after travelling ten miles he saw the bill of sale for the horses while looking for ownership. He remembered passing us and decided to turn around and bring it to me. He was very pleasant and had gone out of his way to return it. I'm so sorry I never got his name. I was very thankful for such a thoughtful person. (Thank You).

We stopped outside Westwold and had lunch, hotdogs and cocoa. We went up to the WM Ranch. Peg and George Young said to follow them and they were going to give us some free oats. While Joyce was in at the farm I was trying to hang onto the three horses. Scout decided he wanted to fight with one of their young geldings. He broke free with pack and all. I had to let go of the other two as there was no time to tie them to the fence. Scout was kicking and snorting. He was starting to lose the pack, and was fighting mad. As I grabbed the rope. He hauled me off my feet. I hit the ground with a hell of a thud. This was it. I could not take another one of these.

When Joyce returned I yelled and hollered at her. I gave her all the devil anyone could give another at that moment. She took it well and never said a word. Well I felt like a big heel for getting angry and apologized. We laughed it off and rode on into Falkland.

Just this side, we camped in the rodeo grounds. We made a bunk in the hotdog stand as there was no one around. It looked like a great place as it was about to rain. We looked around and found a couple bales of hay over by the corrals. We unpacked and turned the horses loose. They rolled and snorted, then dug into the hay, cleaning most of it up by nightfall. They still have most of their winter coats. After rolling in the mud it's going to be quite a job combing them in the morning.

It has been cold and windy all day, shivering cold. Night is on us. Joyce went a few blocks and picked up a couple of hamburgers while I set up camp. We ate and tried to make the best of it. Sitting on a wooden floor, eating hamburgers, out of the rain, wasn't all that bad. The mosquitos though did not help.

We managed to keep ahead of a wicked storm all day. We put our rain slickers on twice today. We got lucky and managed to stay dry. The odd splash with the wind sure did not help much. As it got darker, it was a little scary in this six by eight hot dog stand, but we are dry. We talked about the journey and decided we can take the knocks, we just have to be more present.

May 1, 1965
Falkland

Cold and damp, so we are taking the privilege of sleeping in this morning. No use getting up any sooner as we are a ways from town and the stores don't open until nine. We laughed when I said, "I feel like I'm 90". Joyce replied, "Is that all?"

Even though the floor was quite hard last night we slept well. If we had a choice, it would be the ground, any day. The horses seem to be enjoying their freedom. Now comes the combing and they do not want to be saddled. Oh boy! Here we go again. They had it all last night, hay, oats and water.

We are in good spirits this morning. The newsman says thunder and lightning showers today. We don't even care. The horses look well (Well!) They are covered in mud. There's an hour combing to do anyway. We left the rodeo grounds at 8:30 a.m. with no breakfast, and will pick up a bite to eat in town.

Here we are in Falkland, a small western town and most of the folks here seem really friendly. We went into the general store, which sold everything from oats to soup. It had an old wooden floor. There were several people in boots and Stetsons, and we felt right at home. The clerk took a hundred pounds of oats out back for us to put on Scout. Wow, that's a heavy sack. We split it in half with the bag we had in the first sack. We unpacked the horses and decided to browse around in town for a bit before we rode out. I felt like this would be a swell place to settle down one day. We had breakfast and talked to a few of the local residents. Yahoo! Looking at our map over breakfast, we realize we only have 4,000 miles left to go to complete this journey. We purchased some fancy neckerchiefs, which we really didn't need. They were so nice looking we just couldn't resist them. Joyce said she bought hers to wrap around her sun burned hands.

Over to the post office we went to send cards home to the folks and friends, who were probably wondering how we were doing. We left out most of the details but told them all we are doing fine. The Post Mistress was very kind. She told us all about the town and asked us if there was anything else, she could help us with. We talked a while and truly enjoyed a couple hours in Falkland. The people were so friendly. Near noon we saddled up and headed out.

Starting out, the riding proved to be little rough as Joyce's arm is still quite swollen, and me being dragged the other day, and the other day, and the other day. Still can't get those denture marks out of my mind. Joyce says I'm still not funny. Like I said, you have to see it to believe it.

While grazing our horses this afternoon, a woman came along. She stopped us and said, "she was tired of doing her house cleaning" and remembered seeing us. So, she decided to come out and talk about it all, and, SHE DID. We enjoyed her company.

We had to go on soon as the black thunder clouds that we had expected all day, were all around us. We decided to make a shelter and fast. We headed down in a hollow area, covered all the gear and under we went. The horses were also down in the hollow in back of us. Being near an animal they say, is not the thing to do in a storm.

The lightning flashed and boy was there a lot of thunder. It was a heck of a commotion for half an hour. We were quite nervous but it all seemed to be over when we came out of our hiding place. We were surprised the horses were so calm. Frankie did one dance, but that's all.

This we will never understand, but where we were was not wet at all. The storm was all around us but the rain never hit the area we were in. The sky soon cleared so we saddled up and headed out for better grazing grounds, and our nights camp. The clouds were as black as I've ever seen. Off in the distance was the most beautiful rainbow either of us have seen, for ages.

We camped to the left in a hollow, down off the main highway. We could see water for the horses. It turned out to be a beaver pond. It was full of downed trees. There were a couple of beaver gracefully gliding through the smooth water. A loud splash was heard when we were discovered, and they both disappeared. We watered the horses, gave them their oats, and tethered them out.

8:30 p.m. the fire was blazing and the stew was on. We pitched our tent, with Stetsons on the pole, and the saddles and boots were nearby. We sat around the fire for a while and laughed about how we must look with neckerchiefs wrapped around our ears. Took pictures of the camp and watched the horses grazing. This is really a great moment. (Good meal, nice fire, clear sky.)

It was windy and cool all day but nice and fresh. It's supposed to go down to 32 degrees Fahrenheit tonight. It will be good to see July arrive with warmer weather. It would make sense that once we are out of the mountains the temperature at night would be better.

The horses seem to be adjusting to their daily changes in their grazing habits. We are only sixteen miles outside of Falkland. We both are still very stiff but slowly adjusting. We figure that when the saddles are no longer too heavy to toss up on the horses, then, we've got it made. Hitting the sack at 9:00 p.m.

Starting of the Day

Camping Out

May 2, 1965
Out of Falkland – Moffat Creek

Slept well last night at Moffat Creek. Cloudy but warmer. We camped about a hundred feet from the railway tracks on a turn in the road. We were just hoping that no train would come in the middle of the night and scare dear old Frankie. The horses seemed to be standing up just great and they don't appear to be as weary as the riders. It must be the long hours, the wind, and the dampness. It looks like its going to be a beautiful day. We are into some gorgeous country. There is not a lot of green grass yet, as we had hoped to see.

We got on the road at 8:30 a.m. The roads are a little narrow and some of these highway cowboys do like to take up a lot of it. It took us almost until 1:30 p.m. to reach the Okanagan Lake. We put the horses out to graze, and climbed a hill to the right, just across from what appeared to be an old racetrack. We walked up over the other side of the hill. Joyce saw her first wild canary.

We took a sandwich with us and sat on the hillside overlooking what appeared to be a valley. We found a couple pieces of old cardboard and slid back down the hill nearly three hundred feet. Had a great time (acting like two kids) Then we laid down in the tall grass for a nap.

Hit the road again about 4:30 p.m. It must have been the rest as we are extremely tired. When I think about the way the mare jumps around and acts up, and think what I was told when I purchased her, (about how quiet and smooth riding she was), nasty thoughts came to my mind. Nice calm horse hey?

Well she's done it again. Off just a running. Joyce phoned some friends in Vernon to enquire about the ferry schedule at Needles, and to see if horses are allowed aboard 'on the hoof'. They said they couldn't find out until Monday morning, but to please come in for the night, and a doctor friend of his would put the horses up for the evening. So, we proceeded into Vernon on highway 97. Frankie really had to act up. It just wasn't one of her days. (Oh Frankie!) I was not aware that Joyce knew anyone in the area, until the call was made. I asked if they were related. She only replied "No".

It was awful nice of so many people to have had the patience they did while they waited approximately twenty minutes while crossing the street. That darn mare could kill someone. The time to trade her is in the near future. Anyways we made it to the John Gracie residence on Okanagan Lake. What a beautiful place and real swell folks. While waiting for his friend to take the horses for the night, we grazed them up the hill on a 45-degree angle. We sat on our britches and slid down another hill, like two kids.(It was fun)

That evening we had the best steak dinner I have ever eaten, and Joyce agrees. We were so exhausted and spending the night with the Gracie family was a wonderful treat. We had hot baths and found it such a relief to lay down stretch out and let it all go. The pain. I told Joyce, that I think my hair hurts, (and I do not think I was joking). Got a good laugh. Next thing we knew, we were gone for the night.

May 3, 1965
Second night in Vernon

These folks let us sleep right on until nearly 10:00 a.m. I doubt if we'd even be up yet if they hadn't called us. They phoned about the ferries, and no one seemed to think there would be any problems boarding the horses. We looked outside, and it was pouring rain. We both are still extremely tired. It has to be the wonderful sleeping indoors that does it. Not waking up with frost covering us is a real treat.

When we were asked to stay another night, you could hardly wipe the smiles off our faces. The thought was, 'Oh thank you Lord'. We went to tend to our three horses down in the draw in case a storm came up in the night, and found out they'd already been tended too. These folks are so thoughtful.

The clouds were black, and the horses looked great. All we did for most of the day was visit, eat, sleep, and eat. This was one day we couldn't have been paid enough to mount and ride. It was even a horrible thought. The fact is, the idea of trading the horses in on a one way, ticket home, has entered our minds. Believe it! Two weeks sleeping out in the spring was quite an experience. This is truly a great break.

Joyce is not feeling well, and hasn't been for couple of days. We talked about it that night, and decided to get an early start. Tomorrow we will ride.

May 4, 1965
Vernon - Lumby

We got up at 6:30 a.m. and the Gracie family made us a breakfast that could have lasted us on into the prairies. We thanked them for the wonderful stop over. We packed Scout today. What a miserable old cuss he is, ears pinned down all day and snorting.

Leaving Vernon behind us and heading for Lumby. The horses started to pick up and were sure feeling their oats. Holding them back was quite a chore. We have little choice as we need to make up time. Looking at our map, we have some real rough country to go through yet.

We are taking a back road to Lumby and cutting through a few farms. The first stop was alongside the Coldstream Ranch. We chatted with the owners and they told us where we could find water up ahead. It's turning bitterly cold. Rain is all around us, but not in the immediate area. We are really thankful for that.

We wanted to make time while the sun shone. We were only half an hour on the road when I got the surprise of my life. I was sitting on the ground with the most surprise look of disbelief that Joyce had ever seen. A dog had jumped up on this old half buried car out in the tall grass, and barked. It was only a few feet behind me. Belva-Dear took off with such a sudden jolt that she left me straight behind. I was literally sucked out of the saddle. Joyce laughed so hard, that for a moment I forgot that I was hurt. I just sat there with tears running down my face. I thought I was fine. I managed to mount, and didn't want to discuss it for a while. (OH PAIN).

Half a mile down the road I looked around to see where Joyce was. She was about fifty feet back, bent over, and still howling. I thought my brains would fly out of the top of my head. We rode to within half a mile to Lumby, and started to unsaddle the horses in a mill yard. I had to lay down for ten minutes. Ive never had a headache like this one.

Along came six motorcyclists. We had quite a chat. They could not believe we were going to Halifax. In fact, neither did I. Then came people from the town, with a gal from the newspaper office who had heard of our story. I got up, and we unpacked and tethered the horses out.

A young fellow said he'd watch them while the rest of us went to town. In town we met more folks. I had to excuse myself to go to the washroom and get a cold towel for my head and eyes. My eyes were quite bloodshot. Now I realized that the fall really affected me.

While in town we had our dinner bought by two loggers. The waitress gave me two aspirin and two to go. Then they returned us to our horses to find out that a whole group was taking care of them. Thank you Lumby. It's a nice town and a heck of a lot of nice people. If you reverse the story that's written in the local newspaper you'll have it right.

Boy is it ever hard bedding down tonight in this tall wet grass. So many deer in the area, and they never seem to be alarmed or run from us. My headache halfway thru the night was unbearable, from landing on my butt. Just yesterday we were saying... No more. We are about two miles from town, and I felt I needed a doctor. Totally relaxing I fell asleep.

Setting up camp

Lumby logger

May 5, 1965
Heading over the Monashee

Woke up this morning quite damp but warm for a change. Belva-Dear managed to get his leg cut on barbwire during the night. It had to be tended to, but he's fine. The owner of the newspaper in Lumby came out again. He took pictures of us for the story his daughter wrote up the night previously.

Joyce is quite sick this morning but as usual, in good spirits. I'm not mentioning my headache but my eyes are swollen, red, and I am nauseated. We have no idea what time it is, or even care. It was hard to start this morning. We've decided to travel a mile at a time.

It's much warmer but snowing lightly.

As we were going through Creighton Valley this afternoon, a dog came up the bank (now let me explain). It was straight up one side and straight down the other. I was toting Scout, on fifty feet of rope coiled up on my saddle horn, and there was ten feet between us. Joyce was on Belva-Dear behind us. Well, they took off, passing us on the full gallop around a corner. Scout ran out heading for the other side of the road. We saw a sports car coming. He was heading between Scout and I. I grabbed the fifty feet of rope and tossed it up over Scout. It cleared the roof of the sports car, how I will never know.

Joyce went partially down the bank and it took at least two hundred feet before she stopped. It's like out of a horror movie. I said, "What the hell is next?" In a low toned voice, she replied, "I don't know".

Joyce lost her Stetson in all the excitement, and was on her way back for it.

On the corner, she met a young fellow who had just come up the same bank. They were surveying over the bank, and were just as surprised to see us. He had Joyce's Stetson in his hand. She snatched it, and then we left. We couldn't believe we were still alive.

It's the second encounter we've had with a dog in the last couple of days. Believe me, it has become very nerve wracking. We had a hard time laughing this one off. How many times can close calls happen? How lucky have we been? It's almost hard to believe. It's as if we're on a path of destruction. (Is there some lesson we have to learn?)

We stopped for half an hour near a creek. I had to put a cold wet towel on my head to try to relieve the headache. I fell asleep and woke up somewhat better, as long as I didn't move too fast. We gathered up and headed to Echo Lake. I had to get Joyce to toss my saddle up, as my headache was still there.

Rode on to the lake resort and met a game warden in the area. Got talking to him, and he said he'd seen us earlier in the week and wanted to know if we knew that the Monashee Pass had lots of snow on it. Its bitter cold and he suggests that we camp this side of the pass and get a long day in tomorrow in the crossing. We were glad to have heard of this. He also told us of this vacant log cabin this side of the pass in which we could stay. We thanked him. What a blessing.

By the time we stopped at the cabin, we'd been in the saddle eight and a half hours steady, except for one stop at the creek. We were glad to dismount and make camp for the night. Once the sun started to go down it soon became bitter cold. We made a shelter for the horses, gave them their oats and a bucket of water.

It was snowing off and on all day. We were so glad when that cabin came into site. We got a small fire going and had a hot meal with lots of coffee. We put our bedroll inside the door, straight ahead under the stairwell. All night we heard thumping and banging. We never ever had seen a night so absolutely pitch black as this one. We got some snow in our bucket, for my headache and wrapped in a towel.

We were in bed only about half an hour when above us we heard a scary thumping noise.. I quietly said to Joyce "What the hell's that?" she whispered back "I don't know?" Oh pain. If it only weren't so damn dark. The rifle, boots, and saddles were outside. We were using our saddlebags for pillows. We managed to find a candle and some matches.

Thump, thump, thump. This damn noise came down the stairs, over our head. We knew the stairs came down into a room, and around through a doorway at our feet. Then it turned left out the screen door. We stopped breathing for a few seconds. There was nothing, nothing at all. The silence was worse than the noise. I could just picture something crawling over us. Then we heard the sound of chomping coming from outside the door on the porch.

I knew our saddles were out there. They were our pride and joy. I threw my boot out through the doorway and quickly dove back into my sleeping bag. Seconds later, chomp. So, we braved lighting the candle and for damn sakes if this animal didn't jump back through the frame in the screen door, coming straight at us. Oh Pain! We both dove into our sleeping bags, and waited to die.

We waited and waited. Still don't know what happened to the lit candle. We figured whatever it was came in, made a right hand turn, and then went back up the stairs. Anyway, all night long we never moved, just slept until it was light enough to see all around us.

Joyce went outside to get a snow pack for me to put over my swollen eyes. I stayed down for about twenty minutes and it seemed to help some.

Cabin

Cabin

May 6, 1965
Heckman Creek

We found out later, that the animal was just a big pack rat. It really was scary, because we were lying on the floor, and as he jumped over the door frame, it made him look so huge. Being so dark, he was just a shadow moving.

Eventually we got up and on the road. We rode into the wind and headed up over the pass. We were having a heck of a time riding into the blowing snow. The visibility was very poor, and the horses were having nothing to do with this. There is about three or four inches of snow on the side of the road. We walked them up over the top of the hill, and going down the other side the wind had died down some. We travelled on down a long winding hill and we're hoping to hit better weather soon. We were very thankful we were, warned prior, not to continue on last night.

Joyce thought I had lost my mind when I filled my Stetson with snow and put it back on. She said "It's really that bad is it?" Believe me, it saved the day as my eyes were still swollen, but better than yesterday.

We camped twenty miles outside of Needles to have lunch and tend to the horses. Just before we pulled in, a doe crossed the road in front of us. She raised her head to get a scent. Obviously she never did, as she walked down in front of us for several minutes. Frankie danced and acted up like a crazy fool. It's nice to see a wild animal not panic and run off for a change.

It sure will be nice to see warmer weather soon. We are so thankful for the long johns, and the bandanas we have wrapped around our faces. Our eyes are just slits between our Stetsons and bandanas. Once again we look like 'Bandits', but we don't find it funny anymore. The horses look great. We will be glad when we hit greener pastures, in both ways.

We travelled on to a half mile this side of Needles, hoping to get the ferry in the morning.We are exhausted, had a trying day, and are calling it an early night. We opened a can of smoked oysters, threw the tarp over us, and were down for the night.

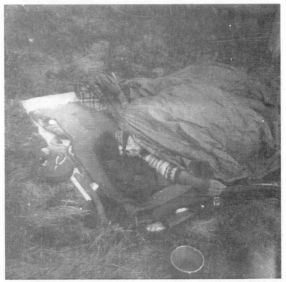

We are used to the ground now, and can stand the cold a lot better than we ever could. We were only in bed half an hour, when I had to get up and untangle Belva-Dear. I noticed after being out in the wind that short time, just how burned my ears were. They were actually cracked and bleeding. A lot of Vaseline and a wrapped bandana sure felt good. The night has cleared up. You can sure feel the temperature dropping. We will get the ferry in the morning. We both remarked at how beautiful it is to lay out and look up at a clear sky with such an abundance of sparkling stars. We soon drifted off to sleep.

little narrow dirt roads like you would see in pictures of an English countryside. We found out we still had ten miles to go before we hit the ferry at Needles.

The animals were in high spirits and stepped out real well this morning. Everything is starting to look a lot greener. We arrived at the Arrow Lakes. British Columbia sure is beautiful. We went to a store and then a café and had breakfast before we went down to the ferry. A lot of people wondered about the horses tied up outside. Some asked us, and we told them. They just grinned and said "Yeah Sure, Halifax Hey?" We smiled, but if they only knew how factual that statement was.

We boarded the ferry. One operator, us and the horses, were the only passengers. We chatted to the captain who ran the ferry. He was interested in our journey and wished us the best of luck. The animals were perfect on board, which was surprising. We got off the ferry at Fauquier and went up a wooden ramp and onto a dirt road up the hill, to the grocery store.

Needles ferry

We picked up supplies for the next few days: corn, cabbage, hamburger, potatoes, cheese, buns, chili, wieners, can fruit, beans, salt, porridge, bacon, and pancake mix. A woman at the store was very friendly and told us of a vacant house, which was about seven miles north.

The country spread out on both sides of the road. What a beautiful place for anyone to have to leave behind. We heard from people, that they were going to flood this area to put in a dam. So, we also knew, that we would never be over this ground again. What a waste of such beauty.

We arrived at a vacant house. Over to the left of the road (lake side) was a rabbit pen, old corral, barn, and an old car with spoke wheels. Up to the right side of the road, where the house was, was a chicken coop, another corral, and a rabbit pen. It had two creeks running through the property. We then noticed a sign on the door of the house that read 'Please pay for your hospitality by not breaking our windows, as they cost hard earned dollars." Therefore, we felt we were welcome to stay a day. Thank you Mr. Don Venard and family. This home turned out to be half way to Burton.

We took the horses, stripped them down, and turned them loose on the lakeside to roll and do their thing. Which is exactly what they did. We never entered the vacant home. We decided to camp right in front of the house near the creek. Here we could keep an eye on the animals.

We made camp about two p.m., had a bite to eat, and walked down across the road to the sandy beach. We just walked along the beach looking for driftwood, and laid around in the warm sun. We actually got a little more sunburned today, which we hadn't planned.

Both of us love the outdoors. It was almost too perfect. This is exactly what we needed. We talked about how rough it's been but decided that's behind us now. Joyce said that my eyes were still bloodshot. It's got to be better up ahead. It's wonderful how this beauty can put you in such good spirits. Our ears are still in bad shape, but coming along.

Between the tics, the wind burn and the cold nights, it sure can all play hell on you. I told Joyce our bucket has a hole in it. Our gear is showing some wear and has to do us for another five and a half months. Our tent is still good as a tarp, as it's now riddled and full of holes. We are at 14,000 ft. and the difference of this and coming over the Monashee, is like spring to dead winter. Neither of us would advise anyone to make this journey this early.

We went down to get the horses to bring them up to camp for the evening. Their tail and mane were totally full of burrs. It took two and a half hours to comb their tails alone, as we only had one comb. So, we decided to finally trim their manes.

After taking care of the horses for the evening, we walked down to the beach and had a wiener roast for dinner. The blazing fire and reflection off the lake was absolutely spectacular. Stayed until the fire died down talking about the different experiences and the people we have met. Decided to turn in for the night. Watched a million stars, and it was so silent that soon we were fast asleep.

May 8, 1965

Up in the morning and decided to stay another day. This time we grazed the horses down near the creek. Spent most of the day just walking on the beach, and had a bonfire. It was good to take one more day to rest, and we have learned to be more aware of our surroundings. We made a pact, we are going to complete this trail ride come hell or high water. No complaining, no looking back, just one day at a time. Together we will ride on into Halifax.

We woke up this morning about 7:30 a.m. and the horses were walking towards us, wanting their oats. Belva-Dear nearly walked on us looking for the sack, and Scout was snorting.

We gave them their oats and decided to lay back down and fell asleep. Woke up 9:30 a.m. and peeled out right away. It looks like it's going to be a beautiful day. Sure hope to make the best of it. We sauntered on down to the lake, stretched out our blankets, and fell back asleep.

We walked the beach, slept a little, and did a little fishing, in which we had no luck what so ever. I had found the hook at Deadman's Creek. We washed all our clothing. I hung everything over the fence to dry, while Joyce scrubbed out all the pots, pans and kettle.

While cleaning our gear, something green and purple squished in our saddlebags and had to be cleaned up. No idea what it was? We repaired our map until it was half-fit to read and figure out. So far, we have averaged nineteen miles per day. We figure this is approximately three hundred and forty five miles in seventeen days. Mind you, we got lost a day or two and had to turn back. We figure, if we keep up the good time, we will reach Halifax in the spring of '66. So, we stretched out our blankets on the beach and had another sleep. (Too much to think about.)

We hope to do better in the next couple weeks, as we are starting to be organized somewhat. I just came from the little house out back and had to run and get Joyce. There was four of the most beautiful mule deer, I've seen in ages, just grazing across the creek and up the draw. They were all doe's. They sure are bigger than the Vancouver Island deer.

I tried fishing again this evening but think it's too shallow to toss out the line. We try every day not to get a little more wind burned, but there's not much shade around. Wrote home today and tried to explain about this 'living out doors' and the beauty of the area up here. I told Joyce, if you leave out all the bad stuff, it sure would be a short note. How do you put that in words? We really hate to leave all this behind. I can't imagine the impact on those that had to.

We were going to leave this morning but decided to bed down early and try to make a big day tomorrow. There's no way to write home and tell about the complete journey, just we love you, and all is well.

P.S. I believe I love every moment. Not always right then, but… the journey.

Note: I'll always remember this place: The freedom and the smell of fresh air, stars, moon shining across the water, silent moments, and all those birds first thing in the morning. Joyce never comments about much. I haven,t gotten to really know her yet. I do know she is a real trooper. And so thank full she came on this journey with me. By the time we set up camp, take care of the horses, make dinner, and prep for the evening, there is not much conversation beyond that.

Joyce says that all her friends call her 'J.C.', and I laughed and said 'well all my friends call me 'Muggsie' a name I got in the Air Force as a rookie. So, in reference to Joyce, I will refer to her as J.C. And yes, she calls me Muggsie. My family call me Lou.

Joyce cleaning out our gear (J.C.)

May 9, 1965
Burton – Nakusp

Mother's Day today, and miss home for several reasons. Another hot day, but nice country to travel through. We started out this morning with some rolled outs under our belts.

(P.S. I am writing this journal nearly 50 years after the trail ride, and my daughter Dana is helping me put it together. She looked up at me and said, "Mom, why did you put the oats under your belt instead of eating them?" Just had to add that bit of humor! Kids)

Travelled on into Burton. We got ten dollars' worth of groceries and decided to stop at a café for dinner. The owners wouldn't let us pay for it. Thank you to the Schmitt family. These folks own race horses, and have to move from this area in Burton soon, as they are being bought out, within a week. They said the Columbia Dam is going in within two years, and plan on moving to Cranbrook. They sure are not pleased with it all. We talked to them for nearly an hour and thoroughly enjoyed their company.

We moved on towards Nakusp and the East Arrow Park. We stopped and rested the hay burners for two hours, tethered them out, and once again walked down to the water. I walked out knee deep and dunked my head in the lake. J.C. asked "Why do you do that?" I told her… "I can't complain." She just scrunched her face. It was a pact we had made at the cabin in the Monashees…no complaining.

We pulled out around 4:30 p.m. and a young man stopped us along the road. He gave us a half sack of oats for the horses. We thanked him and talked a bit. He just said his name was 'Jake'. Then, we ran into a bit of construction. It looks like rain, as it's clouding up fast. When we hit Nakusp, we will buy ourselves a couple of rain slickers, again. The other two are hanging on a tree limb where our clothes line was back near Duck Meadows.

We made thirty odd miles today and camped on the beach a few miles this side of Nakusp. Took care of the horses, and lit a big bonfire. It was a cold night on the water. We made a beautiful big pot of stew with hot biscuits and lots of black coffee. It was so quiet and peaceful. After dinner we curled up in our sleeping bags and watched the fire die down from them.

There didn't seem to be much conversation between either of us on the road today. It's extremely tiring, beautiful, and lonesome for moments at a time. This type of travel certainly gives a person a lot of time to think of who you are, why you are here, and where you are going.

J.C. has never talked about her family, and getting to know each other is difficult, as most conversations we have, are about what will happen and has happened. Travelling we are usually about twenty feet from each other, and toting the pack horse. Then when we stop we have the camp and the horses to deal with, and we are usually too exhausted and bed down early.

May 10, 1965
Nakusp

Up at 7:00 a.m. Lit a nice bonfire, heated up the left over stew, made coffee, and moved the horses for a couple of hours. Just sat around the fire, stayed warm, and enjoyed the water. We arrived in Nakusp at 9:00 a.m. I found it reminded me of the Alberni Valley. Beautiful swimming areas.

There doesn't seem to be many farms around. Looks to be mostly logging and mills. We see deer everywhere in this country, and we saw several coming into town this morning. We grazed the horses in behind a garage for a couple of hours, while we walked the streets of Nakusp looking to buy rain slickers and a bite to eat.

We ran into the Schmitt's again from Burton. They are the proud owners of a new black 'filly' during the night, and were quite excited about it. They hope to see us in Halifax in the fall. We finally found rain slickers and we were very glad as it had just started to come down in buckets.

We stayed in town and had dinner. We ordered fish n chips and a drink. $2.10 for two orders. We headed out again after dinner. It was around 4:00 p.m. when we were riding on into a place called Hills.

We noticed that four Holsteins were following us. They must have broken through a fence somewhere. Well, why not we thought. They were still following us, when a logging truck came up from the rear and scared the four old dolls right out in front of us.

As we were coming into Hills, a farmer stopped us and said "You ought not to chase them cows like that, as they are due to calf any time." We also got a nasty look from his wife. We had to chuckle, as they never seen them run past us when the logging truck came.

We rode another five miles or so to a Girl Guide camp on Slocan Lake. We decided to stop early and hoped to get a long day in tomorrow, as we've decided to cross the mountains from Hills to Kaslo. We would like to make it all the way in one day.

There's only an old overgrown road to Kaslo. A logger told us that there was a lot of bear through the mountains there. He advised us that if we insist on going that way, to go right straight thru, as he lost a string of horses while he was packing up there a few years previous. We kind of hesitated on whether we would go via Slocan to Nelson, but then we took the map, looked at it and decided to brave it.

We bedded down at 7:00 p.m. All is well.

May 11, 1965
Hills – Kaslo

Up at 6:00 a.m. and starving. It was cold and damp this morning. Got a fire going and made a half dozen hotcakes and a half a pound of bacon. The thought of meeting any bears is a little unsettling. If we keep going, we won't have to stop for noon grazing as long as we find water for the horses. We made the decision to take the chance, to take the short cut over the mountain.

It looks like an overgrown forestry or skidder trail that we're following. Heading East saw some real nice country and followed a creek most of the way. It turned out to be the Kaslo River. We passed a place where a mountain came down, and when the snow melted in the spring, it was a lake we heard later. We haven't run into any bears yet or seen any sign of them. It reminds me of the Fraser Canyon area.

We came across three old deserted camps, (mining or logging?). The first one we were told, was or used to be Florin Logging. The second was an old mining camp called Whitewater's Mining, which apparently was still in operation somewhere back in the hills called 'Blue star'.

At one of these places, sitting on a drum over by the mine entrance was an elderly gentleman all by himself, He just sat and looked at us. He looked like an old prospector. We waved and yelled hello, but there was no response. He just looked at us. We thought maybe he's just bushed and deaf. We yelled HELLO louder and waved. Still we got no response, so we decided not to approach him. It appeared he'd been there a long time. Not many people have been in the area as the road is overgrown, and there is no signs of tracks anywhere. How that old man got there we don't know. He looked like an old hermit. The road was impassible to any vehicles and there were none there.

We would love to know about the mining operation that took place here so many years ago, and who the old prospector was.

We eventually came to an open area where we could see off in the distance. We decided to rest the animals for a couple hours and let them graze. We had a bite to eat and looked around for anything that might be a sign as to what kind of towns these were, deserted way back in the mountains.

About 5:00 p.m. packed and decided to head for Kaslo nonstop. We were half way between New Denver and Kaslo, east of Bear Lake. We still had a fair distance to travel. Hadn't gone half an hour from camp when we saw a large animal off in the distance, approximately a quarter mile away. It was snow white and appeared to be the size of a moose. We watched it for a while and it slowly browsed its way along. It possibly could have been a lone white horse, but we took it to be an albino moose. We couldn't get close enough to know though. It was so interesting that it held us up long enough, that once we got underway we had to really push it to reach Kaslo before dark, and we did.

At 9:30 p.m. we finally broke in to an open area. It was overcast and quite dark. The first place we could see well enough with a fence and a field, we managed to get in the fence and make camp. Took care of the horses and called it a day. It was the longest day so far. Forty four miles. The rain followed us most of the way and we heard thunder in the distance for several miles but managed to keep quite dry. We are bushed and too tired to even grab a bite to eat.

We bedded down on empty stomachs and had no problem going to sleep. Our knees were quite sore and stiff from trying to keep out of the saddle at times, but no saddle sores on man nor beast. All is well except for the mosquitos. Joyce is feeling better she says, but she hadn't been feeling well all day.

May 12, 1965
Kaslo

We were up at 7:00 A.M. and packing. Found a place to wash up when a young man came over to talk to us, told us about Kaslo, and that we were on the school grounds. We had to stay in town to pick up oats, so decided to go to a café for breakfast this morning. We spoiled ourselves with bacon and eggs. We are so stiff we can hardly get up off the stools after travelling forty four miles yesterday, but we felt proud of the distance we accomplished.

We had breakfast at Thompson's Grill. It was great. Then, we tried to get oats that early. We went to the Farmers Institute and it was closed. A young man was there and opened up for us anyways. He loaded the oats for us and we headed out. We need to make one more stop to pick up horse ointment for Belva-Dears' leg, as he took the top off his cut again. It was nearly healed.

We rode on and came to the Kootney Lakes and they sure are beautiful. There were a lot of creeks along the lake, and the grazing looks excellent. We really enjoyed the ride into Ainsworth Hot springs, where we stopped for a hamburger and a quick coffee. We wanted to make sure we made the ferry to Kootney Bay from Balfour. We left Ainsworth in the early afternoon. Came to a stop sign and cars were lined up waiting for the highway department to clear some rocks off the road. We were told that they had just blasted and it would take about an hour and a half to clear the area.

Rather than stand in line behind a bunch of traffic with three horses, we were let through. We climbed up over all the rocks on the road and we were told not to go more than two miles, as they were blasting up ahead past there and as soon as they were finished they would probably let us go through. This situation was completely different to anything the highways had ever run into. The crew warned us to be careful and watch for falling rocks etc. Real nice guys.

We proceeded south, came around a corner, and two workers just told us to hang in there, as they were still clearing up ahead. About half an hour later it was terrifying. My God! Boom! The dust came down on us, and just around the corner one hell of an explosion after another. My mare just went into reverse. I couldn't seem to hold her. I looked back and straight down several hundred feet into Okanagan Lake.

My God, I thought I was going to die. Somewhere this fellow in a bright colored hard hat appeared. He grabbed the pack horse and said "What the F--- are you women doing out here?" The other two workers said nothing. We told him we were allowed to proceed, but were told to be careful. I guess enjoying all the scenery and the time past fast, not being aware, we travelled a little more than the two miles… two and a half miles. We were told, very clearly to get our mounts and get back three hundred feet and NOW. We were told, to dismount and get ahold of our animals, as there is one more blast to follow. (WELL!) We had another hair raising event, but, managed to hold them in this time. If it wasn't for the pack horse, we might have managed quite well.

After all the excitement passed and everyone got a hold of themselves, we were in for an hour and a half delay. No way could we talk these nice guys into anything different. The man in the hard hat asked us "What the hell were you thinking, didn't you see the traffic stopped?" We told him yes, but we had been told to go through no more than two miles. He told us "Get Back and Stay There! I will tell you when you can go." We heard him mutter, "those G. D. Bastards!" It was not a laughing matter.

While waiting we talked to one of the crew who came over the Purcell's in 1937, with a string of pack horses, from Fernie to Kaslo. He told us of all the bears he ran into and how he lost half his string. So, we told him how we high tailed it into Kaslo because of the same kind of story we were told before we decided to chance it. He said 'luck' was on our side. Believe it, this time of year they are out there. We laughed and swapped stories and hoped someday to have the privilege of meeting this man again.

Finally they cleared the road. The traffic went through and we followed. We really tried to get the 5:00 p.m. ferry, but missed it by five minutes. So, decided to go on to the 7 o'clock one. It was drizzling rain now and the pavement was slick. It was getting dark out and we had a two and a half hour wait. We tied the horses outside a café, got a pail of water for them each, and ran in to grab a couple of hamburgers. It was a quick trip as did not want to leave the horses alone in the conditions we were faced with, a lot of people around, traffic, raining and near dark. They were very good considering.

We got the ferry at 7 o'clock. The horses did not like going aboard. They were still very nervous from the day's excitement. Then, to top it all, the ferry had a steel decking. They had a heck of a time navigating. The crew threw some sand down for them. We could not believe it. What nice guys. It took thirty five minutes crossing. The horses were angels. The lights going across the water were spectacular, but we were extremely cold on the deck.

We reached the other side and rode up the hill. I saw my first rabbit. But not J. C., as she had hunted them as a kid. We travelled a mile before we hit Crawford Bay. A family came along in a car. A young fellow jumped out and said "Where are you going?" We told him and he asked if we were looking for a place to stay. He invited us to stay with them for the night. We gladly accepted. He walked alongside of us and the mom followed in their car. Another young fellow jumped from the car. We let them ride the horses, and it sure felt good to walk. They introduced themselves as Wally, Carl, Barry, and Ethel.

Finally got there at nine o'clock. The dad came out in the yard with an extension cord. The sons asked if they could unpack our horses and all the gear while we were taken in and fed. Later we talked for hours and found out they were from part of the country my father comes from. They introduced themselves as the Eddy Family, originally from Pincher Creek, Alberta. They also have two daughters Joy 16, and Carol, 18. They knew the Alwood Family from High River Alberta. They knew Uncle Lee, but not my dad that well. And said his brother worked for years with my great grandfather Dave Alwood. A small world it is.

After all the talking they brought a guitar out and a case of cold beer. We had a great evening visiting with them. They are great folks. They also knew J. C.'s stepfather Alphie Cyr. Before we called it a night, we all sang several songs and ate again. Went to bed after midnight. Even with the delays, we made near forty miles today.

May 13, 1965
Leaving for Crawford Bay

Up at 7:30 a.m. rounded up all our gear, and found out the horses were gone. We have a feeling the Eddy Family may know something about it, trying to get us to stay another day. We would love to, but are far behind schedule, and have to make up time if we can. Nice try guys! Soon they found our horses.

We washed up in the house this morning. What a treat. Then, the kids wanted us to drive them to school... They said, "Dad said, you can use the car". They said they wanted to show us off (Oh Brother!), every kid they knew, and that's what they did. The car was returned in an hour, and we didn't want to explain why we were gone so long.

When we got back, Mr. Eddy had a huge breakfast ready for us. Big brown farm eggs, bacon, and the works. They took several pictures and asked us to please, come see them again. We hit the road about 10:30. It was real warm and sunny today.

We travelled about twenty miles south along Kootney Lake, and stopped for noon grazing. We grabbed half an hour sleep. While packing up, some folks on the lake asked us in for dinner. We had to turn down the invitation, and explained, we had to make up some time, today and once again probably missed getting to know some real great folks. We talked to a couple of young school teachers, along the way. They said they had heard about us going to Halifax, on the news last night, and wanted to know about the trip so far.

Looks like rain and Frankie just threw a shoe. We will have to slow down the pace until I can get one put on her in Creston. Make sure we keep off the pavement, where the ground is softer. Saw two nice mule deer, and they sure aren't afraid. It's nice to be able to ride in so close to them. Going to stop and pack Frankie, and I will ride Scout until we get the shoe replaced.

During the day, around noon, we were miles from nowhere. There stood a little older lady on the side of the road. She flagged us down and said "Dears, you are the girls crossing the country, how exciting it must be." She said she had been there two mornings as not to miss us. She had read our story in the Calgary Herald. Now we do not know where they got the story from, but she seemed so sincere. We talked to her for half an hour and would love to take her with us. We believe if she was forty years younger she would be right there.

Where she came from, we do not know, but there was what appeared to be an old age home in, off the road. We are sure glad she didn't miss us after waiting all that time, as the time we spent with her was priceless. There is something special about grandmas. I lost mine when I was thirteen, and how I missed her. I asked J.C. if her grandma was still alive, and she said no.

About a mile and a half up the road, we came across what appeared to be a 'Glass Castle'. We would have loved to have seen it, but it was closed, and almost dark so we had to find a camp soon. We heard later on that a Mortician named David H brown had collected embalming fluid bottles to build this castle. (I highly recommend visiting it.)

We have a full moon tonight. Warm, and the creeks are really high this time of year. We decided to camp eighteen miles this side of Creston. The people are really friendly and we have talked to several who have heard of us travelling thru B.C.

Met a fellow who said the hay he dropped off for us the night before, is the best in the country. We believe it, as the horses made short work of all of it. We thanked him, not having known where it came from.

Clear and cool tonight, and we are too tired to have a fire. We were so sorry we never got the elderly ladies name, as we could have sent her a post card along the way. Even laughed about going back to get it, as there are those special people that stick in your mind. She was one of them. We're camping near a Provincial Park tonight. Took care of the horses, threw down our bedrolls, and we were exhausted.

May 14, 1965
Kuskonook Provincial Park

We did not stir until 8:00 a.m. We were still tired. Managed to get on the road about 9:20, and what an effort we had to put in to it. We both could sleep for a week. Its sure beautiful travelling thru the Kootneys. There was not a lot of chatter among us today. I even turned around to make sure J. C. was still awake.

We have seen deer almost every day for the past week. When you get to see them really close, one can see they are not all identical. We travelled on thru Sirdar and Wynndell and arrived in Creston about 2:30 in the afternoon. When we first arrived in town we found an old blacksmith shop which was closed out. It was owned by A. W. Irving & Son. We met these folks. They had horseshoes and knew of a blacksmith named Mr. McKay, who is eighty three years old, still working as a diamond driller and shoes horses. Prior to Mr. McKay shoeing them, Mr. Irving put a hard coat on them for ten dollars.

He got ahold of him for us. We both liked him right away. He checked them all, pulled and replaced any that needed done, trimmed up their feet, and kept saying to pay attention. We laughed, but he said he meant it. He said to us, "You got to know how to do this right" He was about as interesting to talk to as anyone we have had the pleasure of meeting. He really made sure we paid attention, and said, "If you don't, you will surely know it." His wife came down and watched with pride. He then left and went back to work. We paid him and thanked him.

The Irving's had invited us over to their home for a barbeque, chicken and potato salad. It was wonderful. It was starting to get late. We had to move on, and turned down their overnight invitation for hot baths and all. We were in the middle of town, so we rode to the outskirts. What a good day this has been.

Just as we got underway, a newspaper reporter got ahold of us and took pictures, asked about the trip, and wondered why we decided to go on this journey. I told him it was something I had wanted to do since I was a child..

It was dark before we pulled out of Creston. We were really beat, but rode on until we found water and pasture. We got permission to turn the horses out from a land owner in the area. We camped at Arrow Creek. The water is really high and it looks like the creek is ready to spill over. We have been warned, by several people to watch out for flash flooding.

We have both lost a few pounds and our knees are still killing us. Combed the horses tonight. They seem to really enjoy it and you still have to watch out for Belva-Dear as he still wants to bite. We went to bed without dinner, too exhausted. We planned on a good night's sleep.

May 15, 1965
Kid Creek

We are getting better. We rode out of camp by 8:30 this morning without breakfast. It's fairly warm. Nice country with lots of creeks (Kid-Russell-Hazel). Stopped at 11:15 a.m. for a big meal. We cooked up a chicken stew and J.C. made some baking powder biscuits in the coal. They were as good as I've ever eaten. I told her it was just the fresh air that made them taste that good. She tossed a handful of dirt at me and laughed.

Eating out in the fresh air and a home cooked meal over a campfire, what more could anyone ask for? Cleaned up camp and headed east pushing for Cranbrook at 3:15 p.m.

Around 4:30 came the rain. It came and it came, what a downpour. Glad for the rain slickers. We packed Belva-Dear this afternoon, as Scout has a slight rub spot. Nothing serious. Belva-Dear is still the roughest horse to ride. It's almost like he lands on all fours each stride. J. C. still likes him best.

We rode on in the rain until 6:30 p.m. By this time the water was running down our backs. We did not seem cold. It seems like you adapt to outdoor conditions after a while, as we find it awfully warm and uncomfortable indoors. Not while you are there, but when you leave. We stopped and had a hamburger and coffee and chatted with a few people. They took several pictures and said they would send copies home to the folks. We've met so many great people, Canadian and American.

We rode on to Irishman's' Creek and made camp for the night. It was about seven o'clock and we were drowned. All of our gear was wet. It is raining too hard to make any attempt to dry anything out. We are not cold. We took care of the horses and threw a tarp over us. With the remaining daylight, we played two games of 500 rummy, then crawled into our damp sleeping bags. Within minutes we were quite warm.

We talked about the events of the day and laughed about playing cards in the rain. The horses are in fine condition and travel well. The Moyie River is beautiful. Looks like it's going to rain all night.

May 16, 1965
Moyie Lake – Cranbrook

It did rain all night but I told J.C. not to worry as we can't get any wetter than we are. We slept well. Frankie got loose during the night, but stayed around and was grazing quite contently.

We woke up around 6:30 in the morning, stretched our aching bones, glanced through the mist, and decided to crawl out of our damp, warm sleeping bags. Gathered and packed all our wet gear and managed to be on the road by 7:15 a.m. Travelled on to Moyie Lake.

Around 2:30 p.m. we stopped for an hour to rest the horses, and make ourselves a snack. The rain was not going to let up so we made the best of it. Thankful for the rain slickers as they hold in the heat. The horses appear to be faring well and Scout's rub spot has healed. J.C. is still riding Belva-Dear.

We were on the road again around 3:30. Just as we started out it began to hail. Then it turned to rain, then to snow. The wind came up within half an hour and became quite miserable for travelling. What a time we had getting the horses to cross the bridge near Moyie.

Once on the other side, we decided to make a shelter and wait it out. Before we left our so called shelter, as hard as we tried to keep dry, we were thoroughly soaked. I made a mistake in lifting my headgear as the water ran down my back. Now I was wet and shivering. Just wet we could handle. We were not appreciating Mother Nature about then.

Saw a café up ahead and a place to put the horses. We had a quick coffee and got back on the road right away. Yes we got looks. What we must have looked like, soaking wet, rain gear on, and forgot to take off our spurs. It was still snowing and quite heavy by this time. Heading out we were looking for good grazing and some sort of shelter, which turned out to be approximately ten miles south of Cranbrook.

Our hands were numb by the time we dismounted. Tethered the horses out as the grazing looked good. Gave them some oats and water. J.C. said "Do you think they need water?" We stayed for two hours, put the tent up between two trees, and managed to get a nice sized fire going. Got some of the gear somewhat dry, enough to keep us going to the next camp. The animals are looking good. Belva-Dear had three rub spots on her back, so we changed the pack back to Scout.

It has warmed up some and by 5:30 p.m. we moved out. Folks were driving by and waving. Even though they are going fifty miles an hour and not stopping, it made us smile. Then as the rain came down its hardest, a couple stopped, said they heard we were going to Halifax and wanted to know if it was true. There was no reply. I just looked at J.C. and there was no reply there either.

They wanted to know if they could take movies of us. They stood in the rain and talked to us for awhile. Then, they left, and went back to their car. They watched and filmed us as we were pulling out. The condition we were in, they probably could not believe we could make it out of the Cranbrook area let alone ever reach Halifax. (But, they don't know us.)

The clouds are black up ahead. By the temperature, we guessed it would be snow. We are freezing cold. Up ahead we came to a motel. We inquired inside, and they said it was six dollars per night. So, we asked if there was a place we could put the horses up. He said there was a shelter behind the motel and a fenced in area.

We gave them their oats and a neighbor got water for them as our bucket has a hole in it. We packed our saddles into the motel, washed all our gear, and thoroughly enjoyed our third night indoors.

The owners phoned the radio station and they were going to come and interview us. 'Oh brother', was both our response, with grins on our faces of course. I told Joyce "I should tell them about the whole journey, then we won't have to keep the diary as its wet". We could see the horses from the window rolling and snorting.

The animals had the best grazing so far. Things are starting to look up, even though it's snowing out. We figured the weather had to be warmer or the grass wouldn't be so green. We both have lost a considerable amount of weight but feel like a million dollars after our hot showers. Yesterday, all day it snowed, cleared up, rained, snowed, and the wind never let up.

Earlier when we were asked whether it was true that we were going to Halifax, we weren't too sure we wanted to do this, as it had almost pushed our limits. While writing this we had to laugh. I asked J.C., "How can I enter this if I can't complain?" It's what's keeping us going as well as the horses are holding up great. We both discussed again about mentioning 'not quitting' and in two weeks how good it is going to be, to be in nice flat country all the way to Ontario. Being June, it will probably be a lot warmer. Checked out the horses and never stirred all night.

May 17, 1965
Leaving Ponderosa Motel

Woke up at 7:00 a.m. We instantly opened the door to get a lung full of fresh air. Phew we're all stuffed up and feel terrible. J.C. said that this indoor living is for the birds. I could not help but roll on the bed with laughter as last night those were not the thoughts when we arrived. Every night we sleep indoors this happens. We are sure suckers for punishment.

Just as we were getting ready to saddle up at 9:20 a.m. (which is a real late start for us), a fellow drove up from the newspaper and asked if we would put our saddles on our shoulders and walk back in the motel, so he could get a picture. He interview us, got our story, then, we saddled up and rode out telling of our journey and answering questions. We were unaware at the time that we were live on the air.

Outside motel with saddles

Finally, 10:45 a.m. we were out of town. Rode on until noon, stopped at a roadside hamburger stand and grabbed a couple hamburgers and shakes. As we were eating our burgers on the side of the road, along came the news cruiser again. He wanted pictures for a magazine to send from 'station to station' and 'coast to coast'. We were not looking for publicity just the journey, to live outdoors, travel and see the country.

Sawchuck. From C.K.E.K Cranbrook

Amateur Cowgirls Head For East

If you'd never ridden a horse, would you try to ride across Canada?

Two young girls, Helen Alwood, 28, of Port Alberni, and Joyce Myhon, 32, of Prince George, decided about three years ago they would do just that

They left from Clinton April 23, nine other would-be adventurers backing out for various reasons before the start.

The pair passed through Fernie last week, looking very much like cowboys, in wide hats, jeans and high boots. They hope to get to Halifax, about 3,500 miles away, by next August, averaging about 30 miles a day.

Meet press side of road

The day was almost over and at this time, all we have travelled is a mile. Back on the road to Wardner to pick up our first mail. People stopped and talked to us again. The younger kids thought we were 'neat' but they might not have thought we were 'neat' coming through the snow storm yesterday all wet and blue. You have to smile.

We finally arrived at the Wardner post office. The woman there smiled and went and got our mail for us before we even asked for it. She said she knew we were coming and she was waiting. She heard the interview on the radio, and was sure we would be there today. She told us a lot about the area and what it was like travelling to Fernie. Wardner is a beautiful place and the people sure are friendly. I would love to come back to this area another time. Sorry not to have gotten the name of the lady at the post office..

We went to a general store and several people gathered around and asked us questions about the trip. I could not answer fast enough before the next question came up. J.C. laughed and she stuttered a little, and everyone laughed, until they realized she had a slight stutter. We all laughed. Then J.C. got talking to one group of people and I talked to another group. People are really, not nosey, just genuinely interested. We do not mind stopping and talking to them all. It does take up a lot of time though, as once it hit the news, things changed.

We finally, camped at the top of the hill above Wardner.

J.C. on Scout above Wardner

So beautiful looking over the green valley. Pulled off the road and started setting up camp, when here comes a car full of people. We talked awhile then explained we were sorry, didn't mean to be rude, but had to take care of the horses and make camp. They understood and left. Great people. The kids turned and asked us if we were 'movie stars'. I said, "No sweetheart, we are just cowgirls." That really got a good chuckle from us both, but did not come until after they left.

It sure feels good, to have a good laugh, helps take the tension away. We finally got a great fire going and started cooking at dusk. The sky was red as the sun, set. It was absolutely, spectacular. Decided after dinner to lay back and when we say lay back, there are no chairs, just rocks on the ground.

Watched the fire and enjoyed the stars. We are totally exhausted. While I was over-looking the valley and combing my mare, I remembered how much I loved her. Just as we were ready to retire for the night we spotted four kids that were crouched down behind a bush watching us. I sneaked out back of them and scared the devil out of them. Said I was sorry as they screamed. I told them I didn't mean to scare them, just wondered what they wanted. They were four teenage girls just wanting to see the horses. So, I walked over with them, chatted a few minutes, and they drifted on home.

Back at the camp fire, J.C. said, "They sure can ask a lot of questions, can't they?" Just then some more people stopped and asked if we wanted to come stay with them for the night. Thank you very much, but we were just about to bed down. They sat around the fire awhile and talked for about half an hour. They left. We thanked them and later found out they were thirteen miles further east of us.

We lay there talking about how many people we had met during the four weeks we had been on the road. Today was quite hectic. It's not that we are anti-social, it is just hard making up time, especially after the news reporters have been out.

I was raised in the hills, and normally quite shy. Joyce said she was raised even further back, and the devil, she loves it. I thought about that for a moment and asked "Well where were you raised?" She replied in Wells B.C., then Prince George. She said she had a brother who was not well. This is all I knew about my travel companion at this time.

We are now slowly adjusting to meeting all kinds of folks. It's certainly breaks up the monotony of just the two of us. Thinking of it, there wasn't a moment we weren't occupied. Both of us taking care of the animals, setting up camp, gathering firewood, preparing dinner, saddling, unsaddling, lots of people, etc. so how could we use that expression. We both laughed at this comment after we wrote it in the dairy.

Made a nice stew and biscuits. J.C. makes the best biscuits on an open fire that I've ever eaten. All is well. The animals are in excellent condition. Just love the campfire, smell of food cooking, and watching the stars at night. Overlooking the valley on the hill above Wardner sure is beautiful. I will definitely return to this place someday.

May 18, 1965
Wardner — Galloway

I woke up early. Everything is so quiet. I'm wondering about the little town down in the valley. We had the rest of the stew for breakfast. There was no water left to drink. It's a clear sky but we heard thunder in the distance. Tended to the horses, packed up, and pulled out of camp by 9:30 a.m. (Hope folks stay home today.) Being on the air is what started it all.

We never travelled far this morning when two women stopped us. The younger of the two was an old roommate of J.C.'s, sixteen years previous in Kamloops. She heard about the journey, on the air, and came to see her. They were very glad to see each other after so many years. We made plans to meet them up at Jaffrey at noon, at the creek, as we needed to be near water for the horse. They brought a picnic lunch with them. They took pictures and really enjoyed their roadside visit. They exchanged addresses and phone numbers. We visited a few hours, and then started out again. J.C. said they were room-mates in the Okanagan a few years back.

The day turned out to be quite warm and J.C. was very glad to have met her old friend again. Ahead, we had planned to cross the Lizard mountain range into Fernie. We enquired and found out it was impossible this time of year, as the town people figure there is about fifteen feet of snow on the ridge. We spent most of the day finding this out. So, we back tracked to Galloway and thank you to the woman who went to a lot of trouble contacting us to try and stop us from going over the ridge because of all the snow. Thank you (K) for all your troubles.

We stopped at Galloway from 2:30 – 4 p.m. for grazing. Then we travelled on to Elko and stopped for apple pie, ice cream, and coffee. We are really stiff today. Figure it's more from being damp than a long day in the saddle. We were, asked again at the café if we were Indians, and what part of the country were we from? When we told them no, they said they have not seen anyone that tanned before. We are dark tanned, weather beaten, and proud. Our clothes are starting to look like they are more than broken in.

Sent money and cards home to the folks. The day has been great and just perfect for riding. Sometimes it takes a lot of effort taking care of the horses. We saw a strange sight. Trotting along the road, the mare came to an abrupt stop. Just as fast, she started backing up. I tried to make her go on only to find out a doe had been hit by a car, and her perfectly developed fawn was popped out of her stomach. It was a beautiful fawn, so sad to see.

Mother & Unborn Fawn, so tragic.

We started to ride past and Frankie went crazy. She ran off the road into the bush, up the creek that was full of branches, I was branch whipped, and back out onto the road ahead of the deer. She does not stop when she's afraid. I looked back and J.C. was just howling. I thought in my mind, 'asshole', and then had to laugh and rode on.

Later on we stopped and visited the ranger station at Elko. It was very interesting and we talked to several people who were visiting also. We headed out for Fernie in the afternoon, after grazing at Elko for a couple of hours.

We travelled thirty two miles today, and we're camping eight miles south of Fernie. Just before we camped we saw a small black bear on the road up ahead. The horses never paid any attention and carried on. It was the only bear we've seen.

We got an early night tonight. J.C. said I had a red mark across my face. I said, "Do you remember the runaway?" In my mind the same thought as earlier came again. I just looked at her. It must have looked funnier than it was. All is well. Made camp on the creek.

May 19, 1965
Fernie

Up at 7:30 a.m. and cold isn't quite the word. Everything is frozen, the ropes, sleeping bags, and even the tips of our hair are frozen from sticking out of our sleeping bags. Yahoo, do we ever have to get our butts in gear this morning. Peeking out from a horizontal position, it looks like a beautiful day is in the making. Boy, it's cold. Got up for a second, but quickly changed our minds. We will wait until the sun hits us.

We pulled out of camp by 9:00 a.m. and we really hated leaving the campfire behind. We have to pick up oats today and hope to be in Alberta by tonight. It's the end of our fourth week. We have seen by far too many dead deer on the road. What a waste!

After the sun comes up, the birds are singing. Spring is in the air, and oh it's good to be alive. We feel the hardest part of the journey is behind us now. We are nearly out of the mountains, the cold weather, and heading into Alberta.

A man from the newspaper met and interviewed us. Then we met the town butcher who gave us T-Bone steaks and six buffalo burger patties. He congratulated us on our trip thru B.C. Thank you Mr. E. T. Brown of Fernie (The store is still there to this day May 2013).

We were also given a case of pop compliments of Jaffrey General Store. We then stopped and mailed post cards home, and picked up oats. We have met several towns' people in Fernie. They all congratulated us and wished us well. Some said they saw us on TV. J.C. said she didn't remember being interviewed for that. While she was looking at me, I started to laugh and said "Now we ARE movie stars".

We went into a café and had a bite to eat, as we were in town to pick up supplies anyways. Several people gathered around to talk to us. They paid for our meal and gave us clippings out of the newspaper. Everyone seemed to be interested in our ride. It still amazes us. Believe me! Nobody knows we nearly gave up and went home at least twice.

We were looking for oats in town, and a young fellow said that he had fifty pounds for $1.50 and would drop them off for us on the road. We travelled a couple miles outside of Fernie. He came along with the oats for us, so we stopped and fed the horses and chatted awhile.

Scouts back is still a little sore looking, but doesn't seem to be bothering him. We put ointment on him and cut a piece out of the pad so it wouldn't rub. He seems to be coming along well, as he doesn't flinch at all when you comb him.

When we got to Fernie we were sure glad they stopped us from trying to go over the ridge. From where we are now, we can see the mountains are laden with snow. Believe me, you get a much better view of the range from here. It has rained all around us but we are still dry.

Heading out for Crowsnest Pass (near the Alberta border). A man asked us to stay for dinner in Natal. We had to turn him down as the horses had to be pastured before dark. We had a very short time left. Everyone we met through Natal and Michelle were very friendly.

We got free groceries from the grocer and more pop. People came around and chatted for a few minutes. We seriously had to push on before dark. The grazing around the coal towns didn't look too healthy, so on we went.

Natal is a coal mining town and everything in it is black. Even the dogs! We went under a crosswalk as we were leaving. The miners were coming out of the pit with the lights still on their helmets. They all yelled "Good Luck Gals", and they were all just as black as tar.

People in town said they saw us on the Lethbridge TV. We camped one and a half miles outside of Michelle, down a draw, across a creek, and into a flat area in the timber. Tied the horses up. Two cowboys brought us some hay, and they wouldn't take anything for it. We talked about horses, travelling, and living out. Real nice fellows. They said they were from the Fernie area.

We hit the sack around 10:00 p.m. It was too cold to cook a meal. When we got into our sleeping bags they were wet. Not damp like other nights, but wet. Nothing we could do. We had a Coke and a Butter Tart, and laughed like crazy fools. We wondered who would believe we were laying in wet sleeping bags, after dark, in the bush, drinking cold Coke and eating Butter Tarts. Belva-Dear was a little sluggish today so we gave him his tonic.

Laying there we knew we were near a creek because we could hear it. We knew the grazing wasn't that good but the hay would do them for tonight. By this time we had warmed up just a little. The night was blacker than the town we just left behind. The night was bitter cold and we could hear the creek running. It had been raining hard, and now it started to snow.

Checked the horses out once more and quickly crawled back into our bed rolls. We threw the tent over us, and fell asleep. We'll dream of the flat prairies ahead, and warmer weather sure will be a treat. Sleep came fast.

May 20, 1965
East of Michelle

When you are sound asleep and a cold chill runs over you, it may not be the creek had overflowed its banks. It was still dark and snowing. When it hit us, we stood up fast and were still in our sleeping bags. Did we ever move. We could not make out where the creek originally started. We were now ankle deep in water, looking for our boots. My God was it ever cold. Our gear, some of it, was floating, and some we could not find.

LOU H ALWOOD

We looked for the animals in our panic. We wanted to turn them loose and hoped they would head for higher ground, not knowing what we were doing, as we were having a hell of a time trying to stay alive at this moment. You could see thru the timber that there was snow on the ground. There was nothing dry. Not even a match to try to light a fire. No traffic on the highway, and snowing like a son of a bitch. We never panicked though, and certainly do know what it's like to be cold.

We put the wet sleeping bags over our shoulders and went through the trees looking for dry moss to start a fire. There was really no purpose to this as we were very disoriented. I was totally numb, and worried about my friend, who never complained about anything though. I grabbed the mare, tossed a wet sleeping bag over me, and rode bareback into Natal for help. Arrived there about 6:15 a.m. and rang the buzzer in the hotel lobby.

Flood

I realized it was a hell of a time to wake anyone up in a small community like Natal, but felt this was a moment of absolute need. A man came through the door pulling his suspenders up over his shoulders and looked like he needed more help than I did. He said, "What the F---ing hell do you want?" I tried to explain our situation to him, but he wouldn't listen. He just said there was no one there that could help us. He yelled again, "Are you crazy or something? Now F----- Off!"

I was mad and when I left and I'm sure the front door was left hanging on one hinge. Not because he could not help us, but the language he used. And the way he spoke to me. I nearly lost my wet sleeping bag, as it fell off my shoulders! All I could think about was getting back to my friend in the bush. The town looked dead, and there wasn't a living soul anywhere that I could see. It was only Thursday. Where had all those nice people gone that we had just met a few hours previously?

I wasn't even cold at this time, or was I just too worried to even feel it? I headed back to J.C. and it seemed like ages before I got there. Damned it I'm cold! Now I can't even make up my mind. Now I'm confused!

More flood

The whole situation surely needed tending to. There was a couple of inches of wet snow on the ground when I got back. J.C. was under some blankets leaning up against the trees behind two horses. I thought we had untied them, but they were still there. With sleeping bags on our shoulders, we got some pitch off a few trees. We remembered that in the saddle bags we should have a waterproof container with matches in it.

My God, when we saw smoke we prayed it would catch. Oh how we prayed. I ran through the bush breaking off small dead branches and lichen. We finally managed to get a very small fire going. There was no warmth from it at this time, but now if we could only keep it going and we did.

We were under a large Spruce, which helped some. Then the snow turned to rain. We kept taking turns watching the fire and fetching dry wood. Now the horses were under the trees with us. We wondered where the hell everyone was. It's 7:00 in the morning and not a single car. Phew, cold is not the word to use in a situation like this.

When you get bawling it's more than cold. We made a lean-to and tried to wrap the tent around the trees to keep the heat in and to attempt to dry out the clothes we were wearing. We got well smoked. Finally we felt like we might survive. We heard a vehicle. "My God, J.C. it's a grader."

I peeled up towards the road and the grader man stopped. He pulled back his shoulders and looked at me, and the small fire in the bush. The look on his face was worth a million dollars. He said "What the hell are you doing out here?" Stupid me, said "We are going to Halifax." He scrunched up his face and said "Halifax!" He never said any more. He got off the grader and handed me a small can of diesel. He said "Put this on that fire". We never argued. He just stood there a moment and looked at us. Then he said there was three inches of snow in the pass, looked at us again, and left.

We thanked him, and were so grateful he came when he did. We put the diesel on the fire and hoped the rain would let up. We scorched our clothing and gear. If we can get the tent over us in the branches, we'll probably stay here until the weather improves a bit.

The grader man came back. He said there was a prospector's cabin about a quarter of a mile up towards the pass on the right. He also said the door was always open, there would be no one there until spring, and we were welcome to use it. We thanked him, asked if he wanted his can back, and he said just to leave it at the cabin.

Between 12:30 and 3:00 p.m. we had our two blankets partially dried over us. We finally felt like we might survive. We sat back up against the trees, and just let the fire warm us. The animals seemed to be o.k. under the lean-to. Now and then they would snort, and turn around. We dried out their blankets, and threw it over them and gave them some oats.

J.C. is sitting up against the tree sleeping. She looks so peaceful, but doesn't look warm by any stretch of the imagination. Things started to look a little better now that we have survived this ordeal. J.C. rode up to take a look at the cabin and came back all enthused. We soon packed up all our gear, and within half an hour we were unloading it, all at the door of this beautiful little cabin about three hundred yards off the highway.

We took care of our horses first. Walked them to the creek for them to drink and put them out on fifty feet of rope each, far enough apart so as not to tangle. The grazing didn't appear to be that bad. They got right at it.

The cabin was above the creek. It had a pot belly stove, two bunk beds, a large wash tub and a table. It appears no one has been here for a while, but all their personal effects were there. The grader man stated that it was an old prospector that lived here, and that he leaves it open. He says the gentleman comes here every year, but only for a few months. We would love to meet him one day to thank him for the use of his cabin. It even has a coal oil lamp. According to a post card left here, we believe this cabin belongs to a man named Tom Branch.

We put a huge tub of water on, and boiled all our gear; sleeping bags, blankets, horse blankets etc.

Carrying water

We packed many pails of water from the creek, let it sit half an hour, and tried to let the silt settle, as the creek water was the same color as all our gear. We ran a make-shift clothes line outside, and hoped some gear would dry before nightfall. We were successful.

We forgot about our several warnings about high water, and all we lost was a couple rolls of film. We will always remember what you can do when survival mode kicks in. Thank God, we are strong enough to push thru this. It was 5:30 in the morning and we were thankful later on for the reflection of the snow, to be able to see well enough to navigate. We will sleep well tonight, warm blankets, hot meal, and warm bath. Our boots will dry for the first time in a week.

By 10:00 p.m. the blankets could come inside and finish drying. We enjoyed our hot bath, even if it was from a washtub. Made a hot meal of corn, potatoes, and the buffalo burgers we got from Ed Brown. Took water to the horses and checked the area out. They were still nibbling back near the timber. We feel we are extremely lucky to come through it all, and will not soon forget it.

The horses are looking good. Laying there, thinking about the events, J.C. said to me from her bunk, "You were crying". I said "No". She stuttered and said "Yesss I heard you" (I guess I must have been sleeping). Then we got talking about the man at the hotel walking out, pulling up his suspenders, looking at me standing there, in a soaking wet sleeping bag, hanging off my shoulders, and we both laughed so hard, we begged each other to please stop laughing. We couldn't get our breath.

In the middle of the night, we were sound asleep. I got woken up by J.C. laughing so hard she had to sit up. It got me laughing and we both laughed until we absolutely ached. I had to get up and go outside. When I came back in, she was still laughing. We both had tears running down our faces from laughing so hard. I have never laughed that hard in my life, especially not knowing what we were laughing about. We finally left the cabin door open, let the fire go out, and fell back asleep.

May 21, 1965
Prospectors Cabin

One month ago today we left Clinton full of hope, and all excited to be heading for Halifax. We are still in B.C. and don't feel we're that far behind schedule. Hoping to be in Nova Scotia before the snow flies. Laying in bed, writing the diary wondering if we would still be enthused if we had even a clue as to what was ahead when we left Clinton. We both got up about the same time and boy are we ever stuffed up. That pot belly stove was still warm. We must have got up in the night and closed the door.

We headed outside to get some fresh air. We are both very tired and exhausted today. Like we said before, it seems like we are always excited to get a chance to sleep indoors, until we do. But, we decided to stay one more night. Took the horses to water rather than pack it to them. Don't think either one of us could lift a bucket this morning. We've never been so totally wiped.

After we took care of the horses we just left the door open in the cabin and went back to bed for a couple of hours. Got up around 11:00 and we were just as tired. All the gear is fresh and ready to go for tomorrow.

We walked down to the creek, splashed our faces in the cool water, and I wondered if the Prospector fished here in the summer. The cabin is so nice and cozy we could stay here a week. We drew straws, I will mind the horses and sort out the gear, and J.C. said she will hitchhike to town to pick up a few groceries. Told her that was a good idea after yesterday I was not willing to backtrack.

The animals were being attended to. Noticed Scout's rub spot is healing well. I see there is a salt lick out here that they have been at, which we never saw the night before. While combing Scout found some more burrs in his tail. I have no idea where he picked them up.

Went down, got a couple buckets of water from the creek for the evening. Here comes Joyce with a couple bags of groceries, $5.91. Put the groceries in the cabin and decided to take a walk out back to see where this little road went, just to get out of the cabin. Spotted a newer cabin back in the timber, which appears to be occupied. The spring air is so refreshing. I'm wearing the prospector's boots as I've oiled mine and they are still drying. They are brown and probably made in about 1940, size 8/9.

We walked over to see the horses and watched a playful gopher that looked like a squirrel. We just walked and talked, about yesterday, and stretched our legs. We had a good laugh at ourselves at some of the crazy things we had done.

We were laughing so hard J.C. lost her balance and pushed me. The next thing I knew we were in a wrestling match like two eight year olds. I grabbed her head under my arm, she knocked me off balance, and when we hit the ground her face kind of crunched into the earth (as she called it later on). We got up and I've never laughed so hard in my life, just like last night. We both were bent over killing ourselves laughing.

We both just howled. We were still exhausted. Both of us laying out in the sun, and just let it all go. The fresh air was rewarding.

All I could see was eyeballs, mud and blood. Her face was scratched a little, my nose was bleeding, and the old man's sole has ripped off his shoe. I did not find that funny, so why were we still laughing. We just laid on the ground and howled. Glad no one can see us now. The past month has been quite trying and we feel the tension of the journey has now come to rest. Both of us have sore ribs from laughing, so hard.

There are a set of Elk horns here at the cabin. Never seen Elk horns before. The horses are quite frisky this morning. Wonder if they are trying to tell us something. We set all the gear out, and ready for tomorrow. Hope to start out real early, 5:00 a.m. J.C. noticed she has lost her wallet with one hundred and seventy five dollars in it.

We went back to where we had walked and it was laying there in the dirt. I looked at her scratched face and we started to laugh again. J.C. said, "What are you going to do about the old man's shoe?" That stopped the laughing for a minute, and then away we went again, just howling. I said "I ddddon't know". She gave me a funny look. I was just laughing so hard I couldn't get the words out.

She kind of half laughed and went back to the cabin. I felt the tension and didn't know how to approach her about it. Therefore, when I returned I told her we needed to talk about it. I said, "It's easy to pick up other peoples habits, I respect you totally, and would never intentionally mock you in any way. I'm sorry if I offended you J.C. I think you are one hundred percent".

She then talked about it, and how different people, tried to cure her stuttering. She found it rather annoying. I thanked her for sharing that. I asked her "Do you remember when you were killing yourself laughing? When I was on my ass on the ground with concussion? How hard you laughed. I knew it was just nerves, but under my breath, I still called you an asshole. I think that maybe we should agree to talk to each other about what bothers us, as this trip hasn't been easy, and there is still a long road ahead". We both agreed on that. This past month has been very challenging for both of us.

Back at the cabin, all was well. We cooked up pork chops, carrots and cabbage, and spuds. We really enjoyed the meal. When we arrived here, we started a new film hoping we never lost much in the flood. Cooled off the cabin and decided to play a couple hands of rummy. We both are card players (500 rummy).

Wrote a letter home and will mail it on the way. I wonder if J.C. has family, as she never sends much mail. We were eager to start at daybreak tomorrow. We thoroughly cleaned the cabin up, and left a note for the prospector, thanking him for the two day stay. We left our name and address. It's going to be hard to leave this place. The memories are all we will have left. How grateful we are, at this time, as it was a life saver. And we had a chance to get to know each other better.

P.S. Our crew cuts are growing in. We cut our hair fairly short during the tick infestation. J.C. said I looked like the Beatles, but short hair is the only answer when living in the bush. We figured the prospector to be about six feet tall by his cane and shoes. (Said I was sorry about ripping the sole off his shoe.) We finally went to bed at 10:30 p.m.

May 22, 1965
Heading for Alberta

A new start. We both are ready to go on to a new province, warmer weather, and we hear it's a flat one. Up at 4:00 a.m. J.C. made bacon, eggs, hash browns, and a pot of coffee with biscuits. Still the best I've ever eaten. I tended to the horses (they came right away for their oats), put the saddles and gear all out, and we are ready to hit the trail again. Cleaned up, and checked the cabin once more. We left a note for Mr. Branch thanking him.

We were on the road for 5:30 a.m. We figured we've gone from making approximately nineteen point six miles a day, to thirty two. We are quite proud of that. The horses appear to be in good shape and travelling well. We have eight more miles before we are in Alberta. Then we will have travelled five hundred and seventy eight miles.

As we rode away and crossed the bridge on the road, looking back, you could hardly see the cabin. Oh how we wanted to stay. It is nice country from the coal mining towns to the Crow's Nest Pass. There were deer everywhere. We just stop and let them cross the road in front of us. Most of them do not seem to have any fear. It's surprising how close they get and do not run, with the exception, the odd one runs like it's been shot at.

Up ahead we see the sign saying Province of Alberta. Just as we are leaving that area, a newspaper reporter came to take pictures. He said he was from the Vancouver Times, and could he interview us. He did not hold us up long, and we thanked him.

BC AB border

Joyce at frank slide

ALBERTA

Map of Alberta

63

We managed to get wind burned again, but glad we held off with the bandanas before we were interviewed. We travelled into Blairmore, to the Frank Slide area, where on April 29, 1903 took the lives of seventy towns people. We took a few minutes before we left. As we were leaving a vehicle pulled up and a man got out and asked which one of us is the Alwood girl? I recognized him as an old time neighbor from Cameron Heights, Port Alberni B.C. They moved to Blairmore from the valley when I was thirteen. Clay and Vi Gillis. Clay said, "It's no wonder we didn't recognize you with your cropped off hair, tanned black, and tattered jeans. I had to laugh, as he has not changed a bit. They were wonderful neighbors.

I jumped down and gave them both hugs, as it was truly good to see them again. They invited us to stop for the night, and as much as we would like to, we truly have to make time. I promised to drop a line along the way. It was great seeing them again.

We started out as soon as they left and noticed a Shepherd (dog) was following us. We tried to chase him back, but to where? He just hung back, and kept following us. We were quite concerned that a passing car may hit him. After several miles, we came into Cowley, and he was still with us. He must have jumped from someone's car at the Frank Slide, and we hope someone is looking for him.

People would stop to talk to us. We would ask them if they would pass the word on down the line to see if anyone is missing a dog. You could not call him in, he just stayed back and when we went, there he came. We tossed food out to him, which he did eat. Now we need to find an owner. Someone has to be missing this beautiful animal. We both would be proud to keep him, and I hope I'd have first choice.

We took a cabin at Cowley. The owner put the horses up for us, for four dollars. It was the Lundbreck Auto court. The man took the dog with him when he put the horses in the corral. He came back later and said the dog has rounded up all the cows from Frank to Lundbreck. Then he laughed and said he sure was beautiful. We named him Hobo.

We travelled on pavement most of the day, as the gravel along the road was too coarse for the horses. It rained most of the day and was quite cool. We talked to the proprietor, the Bowes Family. They were very interested in our trip to date. I do not think they really believe we are going to Halifax. Walked out back and checked the horses. They looked great. We will need to pick up some more oats within a couple of days. The grazing sure is looking a lot better, and we are glad to be out of the mountains.

We had hot baths, watched television, played a couple hands of Rummy, and crawled in for a good night's sleep. The cabin is quite cool which is great. We wondered about the dog. Peered out the window again, and if he was there, we were going to bring him in and feed him. We know Mr. Bowes looks like a man that would not let anything happen to him, just because the story about the cows. We had a great sleep and asked if it was possible to get a call at 5:30 a.m.

May 23, 1965
Leaving Cowley

Mr. Bowes woke us up at 5:30 a.m. as requested. We looked outside and it was raining, so we went back to bed and over-slept. We were tired, and it was 8:15 a.m. before we finally managed to crawl out. It was still raining. Got dressed and went out for break-fast. We checked the horses. Frankie has a small rub spot on her shoulder. We figure out why, so changed the pack around.

The owner had already fed them by the time we got around to moving. Then, he had his picture taken with us on his own horse. They wished us the best and asked if they could buy the packsaddle when the trip ends. Nice people.

We were only on the road a couple of hours, when guess who showed up, the dog! We rode on for another few miles decided to stop for afternoon grazing. A family came along with their horses. We talked with them for a while and they left. We were grazing our horses when the Bowes Family came along on their horses and the dog followed them when they left.

We had another soggy day. Travelled on about three miles west of Brocket. Decided to camp for the night. The country sure is different from anything we've travelled thru so far. As we were setting up camp, a cowboy came along on a horse, with a real southern drawl. He introduced himself as Percy Smith.

He said he was a ranch hand in the area. We chatted with him for a while, as he asked us many questions about the ride. We found him very interesting and we picked up a bit of horse lingo. As I checked Frankie's hoof, (as she had been limping a little), he said, "Maybe she's got a stone in her 'frog'?" I wasn't quite sure that's what he said, and tried not to laugh. He soon left. It was 10:00 p.m. when we decided to bed down. It's been nothing but rain in Alberta so far.

A lot of rolling hills in the southern area. We noticed railroad tracks running off in the grass and wondered where they were going, but never really paid much attention to them. We staked the horses out, gave them their oats, and crawled in for the night. It's quite trying to be able to put the ground sheet down, your sleeping bags on top, and the tent over everything, before it all gets wet. I asked J.C. what did that cowboy say, when I was checking the horses and started to laugh. She said, "What's the matter with you now?" I said never mind, and to go to sleep. I giggled for a while, then fell asleep. (Frog?) What part is the frog?

May 24, 1965
Leaving Brocket

We were on the ground under a holey tarp, which was a pup tent earlier. Now… frightened horses suddenly awakened us. It sounded like they were on the run, but we could not see them. They ran passed us and were gone. In the black of the night, pitch black, all you could see was a huge circular light coming straight at us… from nowhere. We never heard a thing. WOW! Cripes, our hearts nearly stopped. Then it made a slight turn. They blew the whistle then a light was right on us again. Oh My God! It was 4:30 a.m. and it appeared to turn, and the light was gone.

We were still half sitting in our sleeping bags. I thought we were goners for a moment. When the horses stampeded like they did, J.C. said "The poor horses", and I managed to choke out the words "To hell with the horses, were you there?" Once the train had passed, we could see nothing at all. It was blacker than the inside of a cow. We had to feel, for the sleeping bags, to crawl back into.

There was a real downpour all night, and you could hear the train whistle in the distance. We prayed the horses weren't back on the tracks. We managed to find enough bedroll to lay under and waited until daylight to see if we still had horses. There was water on the tarp and the bedroll was soaking wet.

Daybreak came and J.C. was up running around and limping. She thought one of the horses might have stepped on her when they ran, as it was swollen. I headed over the knoll and way off in the distance, probably about a quarter of a mile away, and they appeared to be all together. I called out not knowing what would happen, hoping they wouldn't spook. They appeared to be coming back this way. As they got closer, I recognized the mare. The other two were following her. They were all tied together. I asked J.C. how that happened as we always stake them separately.

Only that night, she said she decided to tie them closer together. Then she said, "They all have their own rope still", and then she said she tied them all onto the other rope. I never understood a thing she was saying, and at that point, I didn't care. They came back so it worked. I said, "Well that worked, what did you say you did?" She kind of snapped and said "Forget It!" I could tell her ankle was bothering her. She was sitting there trying to put her boot on. I said, "I thought you slept with your boots on?" I got no reply. I could tell she was in pain.

Note: When we found the horses, it was 5:30 in the morning and they were heading back. Scout was still snorting and appeared as if he still wanted to run. We finally gathered all our gear together and headed east at 7:15 a.m. heading out for Fort McLeod. This is not the best morning we have had.

We arrived around 2:30 p.m. and were starving. Tied up at a café and out back got water for the horses, unloaded them, and used the tarp to cover our gear. We then went inside and had breakfast. I had sore ribs and Joyce's foot is quite swollen. I must have hurt my ribs when I jumped up during the stampede. No complaints are allowed.

I had a hot pork sandwich and J.C. had hotcakes and eggs. When she went to the restroom, I swapped meals. She sat down and ate. Halfway through she looked at me and said, "I thought I ordered hotcakes and eggs?" I had to laugh, glad she is good-natured. She told me it was not funny, and she enjoyed the hot pork anyways.

A woman from the museum came and took our story, pictures for the local paper, and paid for our meal. While we were at the museum two men came up and wanted to know if they could have their picture taken with us. They asked if we would mention them in our book, as 'The Two guys from McLeod'. We enjoyed touring the museum with them. It was a great break from the weather, as it was still raining quite hard and didn't look like it was about to clear up soon.

Fort McLeod

We rode on until about 4:00 p.m. It started to look like it may clear up but with rain clouds still all around. Its predicted rain for all of tomorrow. We will ride on and hope to get near Lethbridge tonight some time. I shouldn't have said anything, as now here comes the rain. The wind has picked up and it has really cooled down. The horses don't seem to be too happy about walking into it, but are still keeping up good pace. Their hooves are in great condition. We check them quite often and we now need to pick up oats for tomorrow.

We stopped along the highway and phoned home. No one there. It's the 24th of May and always a big day in Port Alberni. Just a little bit homesick. Love you little girl. (Sniff).

Cold and forty mile an hour winds all day. The sky is getting really black and the country is so flat now. J.C. said it would be terrible to be caught in the thunderstorm out here with three horses. The wind picked up and it was getting blacker. We stopped at a nearby farm and asked the woman at the door if it was possible for us to put our horses in their barn or out back until the storm passed. We could see the lightning coming in fast. She looked at us and said, "NO WAY! OTHER INDIAN BOYS HAVE LEFT THEIR HORSES HERE ONCE BEFORE and we were stuck feeding them."

We started to leave but not until I said to her that, we were not boys, but two women crossing the country and just looking for temporary shelter. Thank you anyways.

Well we were apologized to and taken in right away. She said, "I have never seen white people tanned like that before. Once you're taken in, it's hard to take. She apologized again." She asked us to put the horses out in the barn and please stay. She then phoned the newspaper, called her family, and took pictures.

She introduced the family as the Millwards. Frank, Dorothy, and twin sons Don and Ron. Later that evening we were invited to go with them to the Monarch Hotel for a cool drink. We checked in on the horses, and they were good for the night.

We stayed until closing time and decided to take a room. We had met and talked to so many people from around the area and had an enjoyable evening.

It did not take long after the hot shower to fall asleep. It had nothing to do with the extra brew. The weather sure did come rolling in. I had never heard lightning that loud before. So thankful to Dorothy for letting us put the horses in the barn.

May 25, 1965
Monarch

How many times do I have to say, this indoor living is for the birds? Up at 9:00 a.m. raining, blowing and cold. We went downstairs for breakfast. No breakfast, just hamburgers. Then we remembered that the Millwards, who were taking care of our horses, had invited us to come for breakfast in the morning. Oops. J.C. said it was good someone remembered.

We arrived to bacon and eggs, hash browns and the works. We laughed and talked about the previous day's events. The hotel manager thought we were 'wild', not 'cool', but 'wild'. Dorothy said, "That means he likes you". Well we like him also. All the folks we met yesterday were great people. It was like being at home with good friends, as they made our stay very pleasant. Mrs. Millward called CHEC Radio and the announcer came in his mobile unit. We talked to the folks in Lethbridge and surrounding areas. They asked questions and we told our story to date. It sure was different and interesting. The announcer whispered "Please be discreet", as we were in someone's home in Monarch. Just after he left, the phone rang. It was their son calling from Claresholm wanting to know what was going on, and were they o.k. All he had heard was his moms name and Monarch. He was wondering why she was on the radio.

That was it; we'd been there all day with the family. Last night we had listened to the 'Liston-Clay fight', and could not believe Clay knocked Liston out in one minute. I grew up watching my father Dewane Alwood, from Caley, Alberta, listen to all the fights. He was a western Canadian Champion in his weight, in the 1930's. We, were interviewed again that evening for the Monarch paper. When they left, we started out and camped just outside of town for the night.

It was nerve wracking for a few minutes. Lightning cracked near the bridge as we were leaving their place, the mare just laid down, pack and all, and Joyce said I was hiding under my slicker waiting out the storm. This is the craziest country as storms can come up with such short notice. We are not used to this in B.C. Soon, it appeared to be letting up a little, so we headed out for under the bridge. The horses are down in a hollow area grazing. We are praying the lightening won't strike as the horses have steel shoes on. It's quite a scary time; it's so far between farms or ranches.

Ready to hit the trail

May 26, 1965
Leaving Monarch

We left the Monarch area and arrived in Lethbridge around 2:00 p.m. We ran into our yesterday's reporter (angel). She stopped just to say hello. Then, the city police came with lights flashing, pulled over, and asked us for our licenses. Of course, this made Frankie act up. They smiled, got out, and chatted a while. Said they were really interested in our trip. Both really nice guys.

It's a real hot day today. What a relief, as it's been nothing but rain all through Alberta. There are not a lot of places here to find water for the horses along the highway, which is a must. Therefore, we may have to travel into a ranch now and then, to get it. We pulled into the Alberta wheat Pool for oats. They loaded us up and said, "Compliments from us all!" We gave the horses water there, chatted awhile, and then headed out. Real swell guys to talk to.

The grass sure is lush and green, good grazing for the horses tonight. They have been travelling very well. Even though Scout acts up now and then, he really isn't that much trouble. It was 8:30 p.m. when we camped in a farm field. There were about a dozen square boxes. Looked like old beehive boxes, but no bees around. We decided to make camp for the night in this partially fenced in area. We managed to get sun-burned again.

It's hard to find water and we have to fill our canteen again. Noticed we just have the one now, as the other one is between here and somewhere west of the Rocky Mountain range. We will sleep well tonight as it's been a long day and we are too tired to eat. Crawled in and was asleep within minutes.

May 27, 1965
Somewhere East of Lethbridge

We had no idea that those boxes were active beehives. It was very early in the morning, when we heard bzzz bzzz. Lord! It took some time to grab the horses and try to flee. They were uncooperative believe me. We grabbed one horse at a time, while the other one swung a blanket. Three times, we did this but never got stung. Hard to believe. Never thought we'd get out of this situation and still have all the animals. Then, there was our gear to retrieve. Are we ever glad we didn't have an audience, as we'd never live this one down.

Why they were not active last night is a mystery to us. The more we swung the blankets, the more they came. Believe me, it was a very frantic moment. It started to rain, which seemed to help. Looks like it's going to clear up ahead, though. There were still bees around so we moved them another fifty yards, and then went back for the gear.

We were starting to pack up when we heard "Hello, Sundown Hank is the name". He pointed to his huge van that had it written across it. He was dressed in very fancy western attire. He shook our hands and introduced himself. He had heard our story on the air in a café and hoped he would run into us along the way. He talked a while and said he was going to go across Canada in a covered wagon in 1968. He wanted to meet with us and ask about our experiences. He wondered why there was so many bees. We told him it was too long a story, and laughed.

We really enjoyed his company and wished him all the best. We headed out again and stopped to graze the horses this side of... (Lost track) for noon grazing. So many people are stopping to talk to us and it's taken several hours out of our day. They mean well, and are genuinely friendly. Just very interested, as we would be also. We figure we get behind about two hours a day. The biggest problem is the horses standing by the highway as traffic buzzes by. Frankie does not need an excuse to go down, noises and honking horns really scare her.

Starting out this afternoon for Medicine Hat, and hoped to be in Saskatchewan by Sunday. It sure warmed up this afternoon, flat, dry, and with the wind, dusty. And no water for the horses. Belva-Dear has a rub spot so we are switching to Scout. We found out it was from the handle on the water pail causing it all. So we removed the handle and problem was solved.

We camped six miles this side of Grassy Lake, and were excited a lake was coming up. Prior to stopping, we gave the horses a bucket of water each at a service station off the road. Maybe we can have a bonfire if there are campgrounds at the lake. Tonight we will have a can of ravioli, corn, and water for dinner. People still ask us if we are Indians. I finally told them I was, and all our family is from the states, which is true.

A fellow from the Herald has stopped us at Tabor. Outside of Petries Restaurant. They invited us in for dinner, but we had just eaten. Oh how we wished we hadn't. We did have a tall cold lemonade though. J.C asked where we could pick up some more sunscreen. I said that it is not that easy to shop on horseback. J.C. said she thinks we have earned the right! Everyone got a good laugh out of that.

May 28, 1965
Grassy Lake Area

This morning we had a can of Irish stew with water and yes, it was good. We sure miss the big campfires, which you can have in B.C. A cowboy stopped and chatted a while with us this morning. Said, he was from here and was interested in our journey. He was helpful in telling us about the area ahead, and asked what route we were taking. We asked how far it was to the lake up ahead. He just smiled and said "What lake?" Very sorry I did not get his name.

We met a family on horseback this morning. The Phillips Family, Bob and Donalda and their two kids" from Grassy Lake. They invited us to stop in for coffee when we get there. They looked so neat on horseback, dressed in western gear. They gave us a picture of themselves with their address on the back, and said to keep in touch.

We finally pulled out at 8:30 a.m. We really have to make up time today. We thanked them for their invitation. They are really nice people. We travelled a couple more miles. Three women stopped us and wanted to know if they could join us the rest of the way east. We declined the offer, as we found that three horses were already a handful with the traffic but thanked them anyway. The first time we had people wanting to travel with us, they were more into a party than anything. This is the second time someone has wanted to join us. Another time was 'could they travel along in the vehicle and do the cooking'. It was very thoughtful, but… THIS IS OUR JOURNEY. With the wind and the heat, we were exhausted. We had water for the horses, and decided we would pull in for the night. We would get an early start in the morning.

May 29, 1965
Heading for Medicine Hat

Leaving camp at 8:00 a.m. It's supposed to go up to 75 degrees Fahrenheit, and overcast. I asked J.C., if I look like leather too. I got that 'Myhon stare'. "Yes you do." Then she laughed.

We rode twenty-one miles this morning and decided to stop and graze the horses for a couple of hours, as there was water in the ditches off the road. We are going to ride and try to get near Medicine Hat tonight. Hope to be in Saskatchewan soon.

While grazing this afternoon another storm was rolling in. We tied the horses to a dip off the road. They did not want to go. It is no time to be heros boys, we had our hands full. Believe me. Did it ever Rain. And lightning was near... We headed for cover fast, and where do you find cover on the prairies.

Weathering storm

After twenty minutes it seemed to have passed. We are ready to start out once again. The rain has cooled it down some, making it comfortable travelling. We started out and a couple stopped us and asked for our autographs. It took us by surprise, for a moment. We never responded, we just looked at them. The young boy said, "Can we please have your autograph?" We had to smile. Thank you, we told them. Someone believes we are going to make it. We are pretty sure most of the time, but have to be positive all the time. J.C. said later, "Remember we were asked for our autograph once before at the Frank slide by a fifteen year old girl?"

I had totally forgot as there were so many people around that day, and meeting our old neighbors with a lot of questions, and the dog following us. I thanked her for reminding me. Yes, I did recall after talking about it that night. We were about to camp when a dog came up over the bank and spooked the horses. They all took off again. What a ride! They are so easily spooked. A little hard on the back, that sudden jerk, but all turned out well. Made good miles today, so decided to pull in and camp for the night.

J.C. hiked into a café to pick up sandwiches while I set up camp. She was gone over two hours. Yes, I was worried, as it was getting dark. I hate feeling that way. I remember well being the oldest of four. I had to be responsible for my younger sisters while mom worked.

She finally got back and said the place up the road was closed so she hitched back the other way. She is quite brave. Personally, I would go hungry first. She said I worried too much. I told her that was true; I am not a risk taker. She howled and said "Then what are you doing on this trip?" I said, "Well you never know what the next day will bring so always be prepared." That got us laughing again. We did make an agreement, to stay together, means to stay in sight.

May 30, 1965
Walsh

Up at 5:30 a.m. the birds are singing and it looks like a great sunny day. Left camp at 6:45 a.m. We love the early mornings as everything smells so fresh. We are heading for Saskatchewan. I told J.C. that you cannot beat the wide open spaces, a good companion, and a warm sunny day. I got no comment from behind.

I called home just the other side of Medicine Hat. It was good to talk to mom again. All is well at home. Mom is keeping all the letters to go with the diary re our journey. Mom said to say hello to Joyce.

Travelling along the highway, the mare started to dance, and was not going to go forward. We had to make a slight detour as there was a huge dead snake laying on the road. Do not know what kind it was, but it looked dead. That did not matter, we were off and running again.

Prairies

Stopped for noon grazing just this side of Walsh, near the Saskatchewan border. J.C. is not feeling well. It's a good time for a rest. She is quite feverish and pale. I set a blanket draped off the fence at the side of the road. She crawled under it and had a nap. I checked her about an hour later. She still looked quit pale. I suggested stopping for the night, but she said if she ate, she might feel better. I had made up some liver, onions, and bacon. She ate and insisted she was feeling fine. We cleaned up, packed up, and moved out. She said she wanted to go ahead, to pick up some ginger ale. She's a pretty determined woman some times.

J.C. was riding Scout, and there was a pool of water alongside of the road. He went down for a drink with her on him. He sank belly deep in a hole. It was quite frightening for a moment. She managed to jump off him and he came out o.k. With her not feeling that good, it was no time to laugh. I'm sorry, it's just nerves I told her.

Horses watering

We only rode another eight miles when we decided to stop rest up, and get a good start tomorrow. There was no place to stop for pop but J.C. says she's o.k. We're approximately six miles west of Walsh. Took care of the horses. Found that Belva has a lump on his lower jaw, which we will watch. There was a place we could get thru the fence and tether the horses on the other side. The grazing look good, and there's water.

Bedded down early. Joyce is not feeling well. If she's not better by tomorrow, we may have to seek medical attention. Looking back, where would you find a doctor out here. She is very stubborn about that. I asked if she wanted to see a doctor, but got a very firm NOOO! We have run into two vets along the way so far, so we know the horses are doing well. We are down for the night at 10:00 p.m. It was windy and cool, with a million stars. Sure helps with the mosquitos. I lay there looking up at the stars until I drifted off. Wondering "WHY" I needed to make this journey. I always felt, I would one day.

May 31, 1965
Heading for Saskatchewan.

J.C. found a tick on herself this morning. It was full of blood and partially under the skin. She is quite fevered. We have heard they can be quite dangerous, as they carry Rocky Mountain Fever. She must be feeling better, as she has a good sense of humor, as she said, "please don't shoot me". Belva-Dear, his lump is twice the size. J.C. said to get a vet, he can take care of them both at the same time. (What a pair.)

It's clear and windy. Looks like it will be good day for riding. Frankie also has a tender spot. It is almost healed and doesn't seem to bother her. While I'm waiting for the crew to feel better, I decided to comb the horses. Glad I did, as there are a few more ticks we missed. We have to keep away from the sage or wherever they come from.

About an hour later, J.C. said she is ready to go. We are on the road again, and heading for Maple Creek. A woman stopped us. She got out of a 1959 Buick, walked over, and said she would love to give us a bag of groceries for dinner. She was visiting her daughter, who was being ordained in Swift Current Saskatchewan. There she heard of our journey and was on her way home. Her daughter will preach in Hubert Saskatchewan. And said, she had all this stuff left over, lettuce, tomatoes, pickles, bread, roast beef, oranges, and cake. They took our pictures and gave us their address. They introduced themselves as Mr. and Mrs. Sasse, Mr. Doug Eves, and Mrs. J Snow, all from Milk River. We thanked them, and we really enjoyed talking to them. As soon as they left, we ate the cake right away.

We never got too many miles chalked up today as J.C. is still not well. The horse are doing great, and we will pick up more oats the next couple of days. We are stopping tonight at Maple Cree Junction. It was great seeing the Saskatchewan border. This morning.

SASKATCHEWAN

Map of Saskatchewan

June 1, 1965
Maple Creek Junction

Up at 7:00 a.m. It was windy, quite cool, and cloudy. On the road an hour, stopped and picked up eleven dollars' worth of food, oats, and four horseshoes with nails. We stopped in for a coffee, we were talking about the events of yesterday, and met the two easterners that we had met the previous day. They were having an argument. She said to her husband that the tracks alongside the road they had been following for miles, were horse tracks, but he said he was sure they were moose tracks. She said," what moose would walk that far, from the last town to here. Then he said, "well he hadn't heard of our journey". We all just howled. They took some pictures and we were still laughing. He said they were glad we hadn't gone off the road somewhere, as then it would have remained a mystery, and they still would be arguing. She rolled her eyes and didn't say anything. You really needed to hear the conversation to appreciate it.

We travelled on to the other side of Piapot and it is still quite cloudy. Frankie is travelling well and J.C. is still not feeling good. Made roast beef sandwiches for lunch. J. C. ate and said she felt better. We had bought a couple of bottles of Orange Crush, since I hadn't seen this brand since the 1940's in Port Alberni.

We travelled seven miles past Piapot, and camped for the night. J. C. is still not feeling well. Will see how the next few days go. If not better very soon, we are going to see a Dr. I read her the story of our journey from the Star Weekly in World News. Someone dropped it off for us.

Made camp and tended the horses. It's too dark to read anymore. We went to bed about 10:40 p.m. being sick and a little cranky J. C. bounced up in the night and said, "I'm going out to bury your 'shite' as it stinks." I could not stop laughing. I said "It must belonged to the horses, because it is not mine!" I added "What a long day hey". No reply.

Grocery List: Cards, T.P., Chili, Bacon, Margarine, Stew Meat, Turnip, Carrots, Onions, 5 lbs. potatoes, Flour, Salt, and Rain slicker.

June 2, 1965
Leaving Piapot

Up at 6:30 a.m. J.C. is still not feeling 100% but wants to go on. We are making for Swift Current. Leaving camp at 8:30 a.m. Had to put two nails in Scout's partially worn shoe. Sunny and looks like it might be a good day for travelling.

Come noon J. C. says, she still was not feeling well but she'll be o.k. to go on. We grazed the horses at 1:30 p.m. Got a nice fire going. Boiled and washed all our clothes, and had a bath in the lake. When I took my jeans off, J. C. just howled. I made cut offs from my old jeans. She said. I really needed to tan my legs, as my face is nearly black, and my legs were snow white. She told me that was too much for her to look at. I assume she may be feeling somewhat better.

Its starting to cloud over again and quite windy. We've seen loads of rabbits in Alberta and Saskatchewan, as well as a lot of deer and antelope. The antelope are creamy with white rumps and black pronghorns. Several people have warned us to watch out as they can become quite aggressive. OH goodie. What's next?

J. C. went and laid down right away. I felt she needed to see a doctor soon, but she's stubborn and says she will be o.k. I asked her if she thought we could carry on. She said she didn't know. That really shocked me, and I felt panicky and sick, thinking it may be over. I'm so sorry she's that sick, but she won't see a doctor. I put another blanket on her and just let her lay there for a while.

We have never brought it up, that if one of us had to drop out. What, would we do. (It could happen.). She slept for a bit, then sat up and said she felt better. To me she did not look well at all, but she said we can't give in. I told her we were going to look for a motel tomorrow until she is back on her feet. We will take one day at a time, and make more stops. I suggested J.C. see a doctor, but after getting that look, I won't ask her again. I combed the horses down, and checked their shoes.

We were starting out at 3:30p.m., when two guys stopped and wanted to know if we wanted a drink to brighten our day. We thanked them, but no thanks, and they left. Just then another car stopped, and gave us half a sack of oats, he said, they were 'whole grain' so feed them less. We are sorry we did not get his name.

We arrived in swift Current at 6:30 p.m. and decided to camp early and finish drying our clothes. We are carefully watching our funds, as it,s a few day's to our next mail pick up.

June 3, 1965
Swift Current.

First thing we hard on the radio this morning was that the Astronauts are taking off to walk in space. We were up at 8:00 a.m. Cloudy and quit cool. The horses are looking good, but Belva- Dears jaw is still swollen. We will try to see a vet in the next town if possible.

We were only on the road about an hour when we had to stop and pull in for cover, as the rain was very heavy. The winds were about sixty mile an hour and very cold. We had a hard time riding into it. We came to a motel and enquired for a place for the horses. The owner said they had shelter for them out back and out of the wind. J.C. realized she had lost her saddlebags and had to go back to retrieve them. I got the horses out back and settled. The motel with the horses, was only eleven dollars for the night. J.C. returned, she did not have to go far to retrieve her gear.

By the time we got the horses taken care of, we were soaked to the skin, and extremely cold. Got in, grabbed a hot shower, changed, and went to the café to eat. It was $1.90 for two order of fish and chips with drinks. The motel and the meals are the most expensive on the trip so far, but thoroughly enjoyed both.

I have to pick up a new hatband today, as J.C. lost mine when she took it off to put my Stetson on the heater to dry. It was never, found again. I had to take the insides out to make it fit. Now it is too large. Next time it gets wet, I will have no Stetson. I need one to keep the rain and the sun at bay. (If none of this makes sense, please pretend you didn't read it.) What a day this has been.

Hope to catch up soon. J.C. is feeling a little better. What a day. We had a late start today and decided to call it an early night. Still cloudy and very cool outside. It's more like February weather, and been lousy all the way across the Prairies so far with the exception of a few days. We played five hundred rummy, watched TV. J. C. fell asleep and slept through the night.

June 4, 1965
Walldeck

Leaving the K- Motel at noon, and we are making some time today. We will stop and graze around 3:00 p.m. We made it to Walldeck, eight or so miles out of Swift current, and gave the horses the last of their oats. We hope tomorrow will bring better grazing.

A man stopped and talked to us, said he was a Veterinarian and was wondering how the horses were doing. He gave us some ointment for Frankie knees. He looked at Belva Dear's lump under his chin, and said,' all we had to do, was alter the halter'. (He was a, packhorse, when he, was led, he pulled on it.)

We pulled out about six p.m. J.C. lost a blanket and her canteen. I got off Frankie quite fast, when she stepped in a gopher hole, she went down on her face and rolled on her side. Phew, it sure scared me. When she went down, I thought she had broken her leg. She jumped up very quickly and didn't appear to be hurt at all. I can still feel the gravel.

Travelling into Hebert she didn't seem to limp at all. We picked up new blanket for Belva-Dear. By the time we pulled in it was starting to get dark so we made camp. All was going well until I found more ticks on Frankie's teats. As I was checking her and pulling the tick off, a truck backfired. She kicked at me, That was not like her.

We took twenty- two ticks off her belly area. The worst we've ever seen. We were wondering if it is always like this. Yet, they say it's the coldest May they have ever had in thirty two years. They also said they had snow yesterday in Regina and Winnipeg, and it's June. This doesn't seem to bother the ticks though.

Took care of the animals, washed up, grabbed a snack, and it was sure hard bedding down thinking about all the ticks. I'm glad J.C. has the extra blanket tonight. (We feel the tension, and we are both working on it.) J.C. says she's feeling a little better. (Thank you Lord.)

June 5, 1965
Hebert

We were on the road at 7:00 a.m. on the outskirts of Hebert. We figured we made thirty miles yesterday, and never started until noon. Two Swift Current Newspaper men stopped to interview us. Again, we were asked, "WHY" we had decided to travel this way? As they have heard from some of the news clippings, and on the air, about the journey.

It is sunny and clear but still quite cool. The horses seem to be moving out well. I am very surprised that Frankie is not limping. She doesn't seem to have any effects from her fall. I sure do! J.C. said it was quite funny to watch me 'mount' this morning. Two hops up, one hop down, GROAN,

Looks like a great day. On our way, we picked up oats from a farmer. He said we also have grazing rights. Just then, a man from Thunder Valley Ranch stopped and gave us his card. He said he would like to invite us to lead in the Farmers Rodeo Parade in town tomorrow. Their names were Jack and Marion Hamer, from Central Butte Saskatchewan.

There were tons of mosquito as we pulled into camp for the night. We were quite sun burned, and very tired. We have to pick up something to spray the horses. We put liniment on their legs hoping it would help some. Took care of the horses and bedded down early without dinner, trying to keep away from the mosquitos, and it is almost impossible. They are almost unbearable.

When were bedded down with the blankets over our heads, I say to J. C. that Jack and Marion Hamer are the exact names of my mother's relatives. Not being related, what a coincidence. I got no response. She was already sound asleep. We have to flip the sleeping bags now and then to try to get some air, without letting the mosquitos in. (This is not good.) I don't hear anything from the horses though. That's a blessing.

June 6, 1965
Heading for Moose Jaw

Up at 8:00 a.m. Sunny, but the weather forecast calls for thundershowers tonight. We have to be prepared for it. When we hit the Manitoba border, we will have travelled over two thousand miles. We should arrive at the end of September or mid-October as planned. We are heading for Moose jaw today. The thunderclouds are starting to roll in already. We rode about an hour and we are heading for shelter fast.

Made a quick stop at a store to pick up two dollars' worth of food. When there, there was a message left for us. Two men called ahead to see if we needed oats. They were sending them to us while riding along the road. How thoughtful. We were so sorry that we never got their names. While travelling along the highway Frankie nearly stepped on a nest of eggs in the tall grass.

When we stopped to water the horses we ran into a red wing blackbird nest, and boy did she ever get antsy about it? She dove at us several times, and believe me we moved out of there fast. We didn't realize how fast they could be.

We both got a lot more wind burned today. We decided to pull in and camped about 6:30 p.m. Keeping the tics off the horses can be quite a chore when the mosquitos are so bad. J.C. takes ticks off herself, and never complains much. Except she did say, "Why don't you get ticks on you?" I don't know. I do understand that they are bad this year. Never seen anything like it. Actually I have never seen ticks before this journey.

Had a fairly, good day today, but travelled a little slower. It's hard riding along the highway, as so many people stop to talk to us. We decided to camp for the night this side of Moose Jaw. It looks like we got lucky, as the thunderstorm seemed to have passed. We made camp then took care of the horses, and then we were down for the night by 9:30 p.m.

June 7, 1965
Outskirts of Moose Jaw

Up at 6:30 a.m., got a good fire going and had breakfast. Packed up and started out for Moose Jaw, and arrived near noon. We went on to travel twenty- four miles past and decided to stop and graze the horses.

The Moose Jaw times stopped to talk to us as we were pulling in. We spoke to a woman from the tourist bureau. They brought us out a hot meal, chicken, potato wedges, and salad. We had a wonder full time visiting with them. When they left four other vehicles pulled up to chat..

A Policeman stopped to talk to us, about the trip. He had a young man with him from Australia, about, twenty- six, looking for a ride to the coast. Well, the look on his face, when we offered him a ride, was priceless. He said, no, no not on horseback.

MOOSE JAW TIMES-HERALD, TUESDAY, JUNE 8, 1965

Moose Jaw Times

Another car pulled up filming as he came towards us. He said, "Which one of you is from Port Alberni?" I told him I was. He asked my name. When I told him, he asked if Dewane was my father. He said he knew him well in Clinton and introduced himself as Jack Peterson. Then he took more movie film, shook our hands, wished us the best and left.

It's nice chatting with people who know your family and friends.

Several people have asked us if we are travelling with the covered wagon. We told them we had heard there were two men in a covered wagon, and heard they were about a month ahead of us. We also heard they are from Alberta, and travelling east. Then again, we thought about that song, 'Four wheels on your wagon'. Now our goal is to pass them singing it as we go.

We've decided to rest the horses for a couple hours, as they seem restless, and to check out Frankie's knees. It is good to know there is no swelling, and she heals well. We got a pail of water for them before we went into a nearby café in Bell Plains. We had a cheese Burger with the works, with coffee, for thirty cents each.

We met and chatted with a woman from the café and learned a lot about the area. Before we rode on, we swapped the pack to Belva Dear, as Frankie does not pack well and spooks too easily. I enjoy riding her regardless of the spills. I just have to be more alert.

It is still blowing and quite cool (but no mosquitos). We managed to make nearly forty- five miles today, which is the longest day so far, since entering Kaslo through the mountains in B.C. The horses are doing amazingly well. Frankie stepped in a hole in the tall grass, and nearly went down. We have to travel closer to the highway as the gopher holes are hard to see in the tall grass. It makes it a little harder on all of us, as nearer the pavement, people blow their horns or wave. Even though they mean well, Frankie does not seem to understand. It puts her on the run every time. It's the second fall for the mare, but she has no swelling and doesn't limp. She is amazing. As well, J.C. says she is feeling much better.

We will pull in and camp outside of Belle Plains, which is half way between Moose Jaw and Regina. The grazing is great and we were down around 9:00 p.m. All is well.

June 8, 1965
Leaving Belle Plains

During the night, the horses seemed a little more restless than usual. I sat up and checked them once, and a little later on, they were still snorting and still seemed restless. When I got up to have a good look. It looked like a small fox, but ran too fast. So, I made sure I covered the sack of oats just in case. They seemed to calm down after that.

Up and on the road close to 9:00 a.m. It's sunny and still a little chilly. Where is summer? We gave the horses a good combing before packing up and everything looks great. They cleaned up all their oats last night and most of the grass around.

We hope to be in Kenora Ontario in a week. There we will pick up our next mail and take a break. We all could use a good time out. The journey has been very exhausting.

This afternoon we stopped at an amusement park to pick up hamburgers. A whole bunch of kids really got a kick out of the horses. There were quite a few of them, and we had to watch that none of them got too close to the horses, as they would kick or be stepped on. There was a couple dozen of them and it looked like they came out of the woodwork. Our hands were full. Believe me. I hollered out "If you all line up, you can take turns petting the one you like best. Of course, there was the odd one who liked them all. I think it was the parent's idea. Then, there was the picture taking.

We moved out of there ASAP, on into heavy traffic. J.C. asked, "Did we eat?" She said, she thought she laid her hamburger down on a table. Did we eat? I changed the subject. I figure we will be half way in two and a half weeks. They say the weather is to improve, (I don't know who 'they" are, as we've heard that since we entered Alberta). Oh well, one day at a time. What do you mean did we eat? No answer.

We are down to sixty dollars. I told J.C.not to worry as our energy was spent, also. I just got 'that' look. We both need haircuts badly. J. C. says we will get perms for the horses, then, laughed as she meant us. Then she started to laugh, and laugh, and laugh. I could not figure what was wrong with her. She managed to get out "Energy spent!"

We noticed we are getting tired a lot more lately, but the horses seem to be travelling well. We are just at a slower pace, even though we are making about forty miles a day. The horses are taking vitamin drops given to us by the Vet. I think we need 'Geritol'.

You should see the face they make when you put the drops under their lip. We are out of film right now, but have to capture that. Oh brother.

We travelled off on a side road, saw two horses. One was a Shetland pony. It seemed like he wanted to fight, so we put the run on them. They apparently broke loose from somewhere as they both had ropes dangling off them. We should be half way to the twin cities, Fort William and Port Arthur, as we are heading for McLean tonight.

The wind has come up. It's quite strong and cool. We decided to stop earlier this side of Bolognaise and made camp for the night, as Scout did not appear to be traveling too well. Another good reason to stop. We figure we made nearly forty- three miles today. Scout would not take his oats tonight, but he drank his water, nibbled a bit, and laid down. He appears to be sweating a bit, where the others are not. We put a blanket on him, and gave him more vitamin drops.

We made a nice fire and had an early dinner. We talked about all the events of the day, and all the kids. J. C. said she was starving, and I asked well didn't you eat? She said that when she laid her hamburger down, one of the kids took a couple of bites out of it, so she left it for them. Had to laugh at that.

We hear the Astronauts are doing fine. We are going to bed down around 10:45 pm., and make plans for tomorrow. Sure hope the weather improves, and we will stop another day if Scout is not feeling better.

June 9, 1965
Bolognaise

Up at 7:45 a.m. Scout is eating his oats this morning and seems quite normal. No breakfast or campfire this morning. We're just going to start out and see how it goes. It's the end of the seventh week tonight. We feel we are making good time, and if all goes well we should be in Ontario in sixteen days. (We are one week from half way, (what a journey it has been.)

When we hit Kenora we have decided we will camp for a week, and truly give the horses and us a good rest. We'll have them checked out by a vet before we start the second half of the journey. We both really need this stop. My knees, are still swollen from the fall off Frankie. I am having a hard time getting back in the saddle, and J.C. has not recovered one hundred percent from when she was sick, but we both still agree to carry on.

It's sunny and there is quite a cool wind. We just heard on J.C. little radio that there is more rain predicted for the next two days. We have never seen so much rain and lightning in such a short time as crossing Alberta and Saskatchewan. We talk about it often. When you are out in the open, and there is nowhere to go, believe me, it can be quite frightening. There was only two days crossing Alberta and Saskatchewan where it did not rain.

It took a toll on us for a while, as it was very hard handling the horses when the lightning spooked them. Even though it was most spectacular at times, it is amazing how quick you can move if you have to. If, this is a typical prairie living, it would not be one of my favorite places to live. Talking to people we have met from the prairies, they say they absolutely love it, and would not live anywhere else.

My father came from Cayley Alberta, and when he moved to Vancouver Island, he did not like the mountains. We met one woman from Alberta who also stated that the 'only' thing she hated about B.C. was the mountains. I said, "Well do you like deserts, orchards, miles and miles of beaches, the ocean and lakes? She said, "Why, do they have that in B.C.?" I told her yes and she just said, Oh. And I really do believe, that each province has beauty of its own. Except, for the prairies during a thunderstorm, on horseback.

Later on, a Policeman stopped and chatted, and gave us helpful hints about what's ahead of us. He said he has arranged to have some oats dropped off for us just off the road tonight, and said there would be a marker for us to see. Just then, he had a call out and would have to go. Thought it was nice of him to do that, and to take the time to stop and let us know. As Canadians, we are great people.

We stopped for lunch at McLean. After, we watered the horses and staked them out for a couple hours, outback in a field behind the cafe. We went inside and had hot beef sandwiches. A man came to the café, and gave us two dozen fresh buns.

The same Policeman met us again. Driving by, He flashed his lights and yelled over his loud speaker, "Good luck girls!" He waved and carried on. That made a few cars pull over. We got a good laugh out of that. By that time, we were ready to move out. The rain let up, it was warmer, but still windy, and the wind can sure dry you out.

All is well but Scout still seems to be a little sluggish, so we are taking it easy the rest of the day. I suspect he is the one that got into the new sack of oats, and ate more than his share last night. Noticed I still have that cactus thorn in my right index finger. Souvenir of .B.C. Yes, it still bugs me. J.C. has not complained about her thorn. Hmmm.

We find the water very hard in the Prairie Provinces. We cannot wait to be back in B.C. to have a nice warm bath in soft water and a nice cold glass of our spring water. No one can tell you how much you can miss it. We would even give up a night indoors for it.

We got half a sack of mixed oats from a farmer. He said, it was mixed with barley. It was very thoughtful of him. He did not stop long enough to give us his name, as there were two cars pulled up talking to us at the time.

This afternoon it was hard to get in a good days ride, as we met several people along the road. The country is very flat here, and when traveling along there are no outhouses available. How do you explain to people why we threw a blanket over the fence in the middle of nowhere? It's worse trying to crawl through these fences. It's beautiful country though, and the people have been wonderful all along, except for the tooting of horns. Frankie hated that, and like I said before, she is off and running.

We put another nail in Frankie's shoe today. It looks like it will be good until Kenora, where it will be time to trim and re-shoe them all. Stopped and gave Scout a couple of drops of Doctor Bell's with a half a pail of water. We both are exhausted this afternoon. I'm not sure, but it looks like J.C. has fallen asleep in the saddle. Time to pull in.

Looks like a good grazing spot just off the highway. We layed our blankets out and had a quick nap while the horses grazed and rolled. It's the end of our seventh week, and we're nearly through Saskatchewan. We travelled on to near Sintaluta, and pulled in off the road and camped for the evening. We played one hand of Gin Rummy and we are down for the night at 10:00 p.m.

June 10, 1965
Sintaluta

Starting our eighth week. We are two and a half days ride this side of the Manitoba border. Wow! It's sunny and windy as usual. Looks like a great day for riding. We are leaving the camp about 9:00 a.m. We never stirred during the night. We just went to bed, no meal, no campfire, but slept well. One thing about the wind, is that it keeps the mosquitos away.

A Newsman from. C.B.C. Interview us about the journey and took pictures. He said it would air Tuesday or Thursday. A couple stopped and said they were from Banff, Alberta, and as soon as we get there could we stop and stay with them. It took us a minute to realize what they said, so we laughed and asked, "Will that be after we get to Nova Scotia?" They just looked at us, not realizing we were travelling to the east coast. The man went back to his car and got their four kids. They all wanted their picture taken with us.

The wind was light but warm this afternoon, and it was getting late. We had to travel on to be able to stop before dark, as there was too many gopher holes to watch for. The ground was soft and muddy, as there was too much rain. We have to travel a lot closer to the main highway. The mosquitos were extremely bad tonight, and Those darned horns, blasting and tooting.

Before we pulled in for the night, we met people from Pigeon Mountain. They asked if we would come and stay with them, but they were miles off the road. We thanked them and explained we had to move on. We rode on to the outskirts of Grenfell and camped for the night.

June 11, 1965
Grenfell

We woke up at eight o'clock in the morning. Didn't want to get up, but we knew we had to get on the trail. It looks like it's going to be another perfect day, warm with no wind so far. The horses seem to be doing well. A woman came and took our story, said it would be for the Grenfell Sun.

We grazed at Broadview at noon. Horses look the best I've seen in the past week. The air is very hot and dry, and the mosquitos know when to come out. And boy do they ever. Along the route, we drank several pop, as believe me, we really don't like the water. We stopped at a store to get a bucket for each of the horses. J. C. weighed herself, she is one hundred and thirty three pounds, and myself, I am now one hundred and forty pounds. I've lost twenty four pounds. The horses have lost weight also. The owner of the store says, he does not have a scale to weigh them but a woman in line said we could try the meat market.

We were near the highway, as off the road it's too dangerous for the horses, too soft and unpredictable with all the rain. There has been that much rain, after three days, the sun still has not dried the ground. It's only two thousand mile from the west to here. Ohhhh! Only three thousand odd miles to go, and another seven hundred and twenty six miles we will be half way. We decided that we are not going to look at the figures anymore. We know Port Arthur is about half way. End of story.

This is a long, long journey, and the longest either of us have ever taken in one big country. We could sleep for a while after just thinking about it. We had to laugh, let's get at it.

Scout has lost his front shoe, and the rear one is loose. We'll have to take care of it right away. We were going to do it in Manitoba. Decided to get at it, pull the back shoe now and put a new one on right away. We hope within three or four days to be into a more wooded area and start having our own cooked meals again, as wood is hard to find on the prairies, and fires are not a wise decision on the side of the road, in the grass.

The weather forecast for the next week looks very good. Because of the lightning and heavy rains, we have been eating on the run, picking up fast food. It's costing us too much. Most of all we enjoy the campfires and our own cooking. We are both good cooks over an open fire.

We have seen several rabbits along the way. They seem to be bigger than and not as streamlined as our B.C. rabbits. People are stopping us for autographs, saying they had seen us on TV last night. Said they are from Nova Scotia, and will be looking to meet us when we get there. It was nice talking to them, and great to hear that people are starting to believe we will make it. Believe us that really feels good. There have been more than a few days, we seriously did not know if it was still possible, but will not say the 'Q' word.

We are going to make camp for the evening. The horses have missed their oats for the first time, but the grazing is good, and there is water. We are going to take half a day off on the 12th. We are near Wapella. We only did sixteen miles today. Stopping for the evening, as there is water.

June 12, 1965
Wapella

We travelled two miles east of Wapella this morning and made camp. There is good grazing and water. Tossed all our gear down and took care of the horses. When we came back to our gear, we realized we were on an Ant Hill. Boy did we ever move our stuff out of there. Moved it all to another location very fast.

Started to set up another camp. Holy cow it didn't take us long. We were on another ant hill. J. C. yelled "Happy Birthday!" You're not funny. Finally found a location to set up camp. Hitched the tent to the top of the fence, and angled it down. Tossed our sleeping bags under, and prepared camp for the day. We had to trim and put a new shoe on Frankie. J. C. trimmed and put a front shoe on Scout. She asked me to look at it. It was a perfect job, and looked great. I let her know, that I could not ask for a better companion. Yes, we have our moments, but know it is just tension.

We just loafed around all afternoon and took it easy. It was a great feeling to do so. The grazing was excellent and the water was right there. The camp was set up and we are going nowhere today.

It was later in the afternoon when two young people came around in two different cars, spinning their tires and yelling. They were going to let the horses loose. Boy that made us feel uneasy. We were only about thirty yards off the highway. I said, "Those young bastards." It scared the horses. J.C. thought I was going to go after them, but I was just letting them know I was jotting down their license plate numbers. They spun out and left. It left us uneasy just the same. J.C. asked if I'd really go after them. I told her I really did not know what I would have done if one of them got out of their car and tried to approach the horses. And, I hope you are here.

We kept watch for a while just the same. It's the first problem we have had on the trip and we were not prepared for it. We will be after this. Believe it. Too nice a day to keep worrying about it for now.

The rest of the day went well. Joyce saw a farm several hundred yards away across the tracks, and went and got some oats. We had chili for dinner over a small fire, and orange pop. Laid back and relaxed, and just at dusk I caught a firefly. It kept flashing on and off, off to the side of the tent. J.C. said she had never seen one before, and started to laugh. What will people think if they see a flashing light in front of the tent at, night. We laughed silly, as we were so relaxed and tired. I will pretend it is a candle on my cake. You did make one, didn,t you?

We also found out that the little animals that we saw are striped gophers. They were quite cute little fellows. It's cloudy but quite windy, and we are very thankful for it, because of the mosquitos. We tucked in about 9:40 p.m. Those guys were still on our mind. J. C. said, "What are we going to do if they come back tonight?" I told her I really did not know, but do not think they will as I wrote down their license plate numbers. Just for safety, I think I am going to get the rifle out. We will not let anybody hurt our horses. I will blow their tires out first. J.C. said," really". Then, said, something else.

It didn't take us long to fall asleep. During the night, the 'nightmare' came back. We both sat up the same time. I could see it was a bright night through the crack in the tent. It sounded like only one car. Someone opened the door of the car. I was trying to look out of the tent. I heard the horses whinny, sat up and grabbed the rifle. Just then, the flap on the tarp opened on the end, and a guy yelled "Let's rape them!" He crouched down to enter the tent. I was on my knees with the rifle, and was so angry, that with all my force, I rammed the gun towards him and hit him.

I yelled "You Bastard!" At that moment, I REALLY meant it. I came through the opening of the tent. He was reaching for the dirt, and backing up with his heels digging in. He was as white as I've ever seen anyone in all my life. He looked absolutely, terrified. I must have rammed him up the nose, because there was blood running down his face. The noise that came out of him, I'm unable to describe.

He scrambled as the car was taking off fast. I put a shell in the chamber and fired in the air. I believe he thought they were going to leave him. I ran towards the road and got their license plate number. It was a Saskatchewan plate with six numbers on it, possibly a 1965 light green dodge. I actually to this day have the plate number. Phew. Anyways they spun out in the gravel and the horses were really, spooked. We calmed them down, and yelled as they drove away, that I had their plate number.

By the age of them, I believe they were in Dad's car, and do not believe that they will return. The journey now has become slightly more challenging. Neither one of us ever suspected anything like this to ever occur. It appeared that there was a boy and a girl in the front, and three boys in the back. The boy came from the back seat, as, that was the open door. I can still see the horror in his face and the blood. I'm sure the barrel split his nose. I never dreamed I would ever do anything like that.

June 13, 1965
Wapella

Checked out the horses this morning at daybreak. Found a large gash on the mare's forehead above her eye, and a beer bottle on the ground. That really angered us. No wonder she kept snorting during the night. Damn it anyways! We decided to take another day here, as the grazing was perfect and the water is handy to wash our clothes. I Believe, we are now prepared for anything! I howled as Jay walked to the bush, broke off a large long switch, peeled it, and set it by the tent. Boy, I know she could use it too! I made sure the mare's wound was clean and salve applied. She certainly didn't like me touching it.

We had biscuits, coffee, and canned fruit for breakfast. Later on J. C. went over the fence into a swampy area with a bucket, to milk a cow. Well, the cow was having nothing to do with that. It sent her running for the fence. So, away she went with the bucket to try again.

I was killing myself laughing, when she stumbled near a red winged blackbirds nest. I have never laughed so hard in years. Here she comes flying through the swamp with this bird diving at her. She was swinging the bucket and running for her life. The blackbird was coming just as fast. I ran and ducked under the tarp. Never seen anyone clear a fence quite that fast, but she did snag her jeans and ripped her leg a little.

It rained for a couple of hours but we are just having a lazy day (what's next?) We had clothes on the fence hoping they would dry. We quickly gathered them up until the sun comes out again. Now here we are laying under a tattered tarp, reading two books we found somewhere along the way. Reading and sleeping.

A good restful day. J. C. said I was sleeping and I sat straight up, and said to make sure the gun was handy. She said she thought I was dreaming. We both started to laugh until tears were running down our faces. Then, I realized I really was crying...

We got up and put the clothes out on the line, and moved the horses over a hundred yards and in the fence. We talked about not camping so close to the highway again. Then we thought, well back off the road could be more dangerous. This has obviously made us more aware of our surroundings. It was a great day though.

We got water boiling, and managed to get all our gear, pots and pans dry. The horses all look great. Put Vaseline on Frankie's gash, as it is bleeding and quite swollen. Damn it! I was mad all over again. Well that was a birthday, I will never forget.

We slept half the day. Had the rest of the chili and biscuits, and still managed to get a good night's sleep. Woke up early just before dawn, and talked about the problem we had with the boys. Is it the right thing to report since I fired a shot? We decided no, we could not afford to have it hold us up. We didn't want it to hit the news, so we just forgot about it and kept the license plate number in the diary. (Thinking back now, we should have reported it. It would have been the right thing to do. Somehow it did leak to the news about a week later.)

June 14, 1965
Leaving Wapella

We were up at 8:30 in the morning. Joyce went to get the horses ready for the day. They weren't ready for that, and they took off. Appeared to be quite frisky after a day and a half off. They didn't get too far, as they are all tied together. She untied Scout, stepped on the rope, and got drug several yards through the wet grass. Oh my, I felt that, and I do know how it feels. I told her 'that' was not a laugh, it was just a sound that came out of me, I mean the sound and now I'm not funny. (Now I'm stuttering). Well that look I got, I'm not sure what it meant.

We are leaving camp about 9:40. It's quite cool and cloudy. They call for rain again today. We've travelled very well this morning. Travelled on until noon, then stopped for breakfast at the 'Red Jay'. A man named Mr. Bain gave us each a pen.

We carried on to approximately six miles this side of the Manitoba border, and stopped for noon grazing. When tethering the horses out, we noticed a slight lump under Scout's one rib. We will watch it carefully as I feel it may be just from the pack. We will pack Belva Dear this afternoon just to be safe.

The horseflies are bad around here. A local farmer told us, that it is the worst year they have ever known.

Oh do they ever bite, ooo God do they ever bite! Now we may have a problem with the horses. As we heard, that Manitoba was not as bad as Ontario, and are very bad there. OH LOOKING FORWARD TO THAT. Well, how, can they be any worse, we wondered. (Not bad is o.k., but horrid?) We really have to think about what to use on the horses.

Arrived in Manitoba, sunny and windy. We saw quite a few fireflies. And night time they are so beautiful.. they mesmerize you. You could just sit and watch them for hours, if it was not for the mosquitos. God, the bugs are horrible. Now we just found out, we have to pay for drinking water in this part of the country. Just when we need water for the horses!

We've done twenty miles this morning. We are watching our money as we are down to about thirty dollars. It has to do us until Kenora, Ontario. We found out the clocks went ahead last night.

We've met several people from Nova Scotia, and some of them have left us their address, to get in touch when we get there if we need a place to stay, or just to visit. We pulled in at Elkhorn, and decided to camp early. Lately it's been the same every day, problems with flying 'everything'. I even threw my canteen when I tasted the water in it. I filled it in a café at a gas station. J. C. said. Isn't that the last of the water? Yes, and thank God. The wind has picked up a little which is certainly helping. We decided to call it a night at about 9:30 p.m. We entered Manitoba this evening.

MANITOBA

Map of Manitoba

June 15, 1965
Leaving Elkhorn, Manitoba

Prior to leaving Elkhorn this morning we rubbed some salve on the horses bellies. We were, given another small pail of that salve from a rancher yesterday. He did not stay around long, as the bugs were bad. He said it would help some. When we put blankets on them when they are grazing, they don't stay on at all. They usually roll when we first tether them out.

We have to pick up more bug repellant the first place we come to. We've even talked about traveling at night if it get any worse. Then we thought about having to stand around all day, which would be worse.

We've made twenty miles today. We are stopping for noon grazing. We got water for the horses and we were given some more oats by a farmer. We asked him about the black flies hoping to get better news. He said he's afraid they will get worse before they get better. We were waiting for him to say he was just joking. He just looked at me staring at him, shrugged his shoulders then left, swatting at the bugs. The worst ever? This is not good.

We managed to pick up some more bug dope, sprayed them, and tucked a blanket under the horses saddles back to their tails. We used branches to sway back and forth along the horses, to try to keep the flies away as we rode on. We had to be very careful on Frankie. We sprayed their tails and mane, and they hated that. We hoped it worked.

We met a local rancher. He said they had to shut down their riding stables because of the infestation this year. We believed it! It is now time to put on long sleeves and bandanas. Without the salve, the spray and the branches, we would have been done. As it was, it was very close for decision time. We will see what tomorrow brings.

We rode out, as it is better to move than stand still. We were waiting to come into a town called Rutledge. We passed it somehow. We kept waiting as we rode on. We were seven miles out of Virden. Then, fifteen miles later, we were in Horse Lake. We got some salve from a farmer. We got some water and gave them their oats. Asked the farmer about paying for the water, and he said the water was bad this year because of the amount of rain they have had. We rubbed the horses down again, he wouldn't accept any money

Travelled on a few more miles, and pulled in at 7:30 p.m. We decided to stop for the evening. Bedded down around 9:30 p.m. We were exhausted. We could not hear the horses at all during the night, but did realize it was raining. Here we complained about the wind a few weeks ago, but would give anything to have it back now. Dear Lord, we promise not to complain.

June 16, 1965
Brandon

Everything looks quite damp this morning but no bugs. Love the rain and the wind. YES! We had to move our tarp (tent) as it was under a tree and for some reason we were getting wetter.

We did not get up until 9:00 a.m., and when we were getting dressed, J. C. found three ticks on her. She was not a happy camper. I had one on my arm. Now, we have to check the horses. Can't seem to find any on them. It might be the salve. God they are horrid little beasts. Just not what we need with all this horse biting flies and mosquitos.

We kind of felt it may be the end of the journey. We really need to talk about this. What about the horses? We certainly have a lot of concern for them. If they have to shut down the riding stables, and cannot rent their horses, that says a lot. The tarp (tent) and the gear is in bad shape. To HELL with it, we are pulling out today. We are going to take one day at a time. We will make this journey somehow.

On the brighter side, Manitoba is a beautiful place, so lush and green (more like B.C.). Belva Dear threw his left back shoe. I will have to trim him and apply another one this morning. We are going to have to pick up more shoes in Kenora. The wind has picked up quite strong. Good time to put the shoe on Belva Dear now, before we pull out.

We pulled out and rode on until 2:00 p.m. We applied a little salve to our faces, as the wind is quite strong. Got a bit sun burned. Stopped for an hour to graze the horses. The first time I have seen all three of the horses lay out flat, and I wish I had film. We decided to join them. Two young fellows stopped to talk to us while we were resting. They chatted a while. They left and said they expected to see us in Dartmouth. We said, "You Bet!", and fell asleep.

We travelled on to near the outskirt of Brandon. It was getting late. We pulled in off the road, up a bank. We could tether the horses to a huge six- foot fence that was up there. It looked like we were at the back of a drive in theatre. We spread out our gear and sleeping bags. We knew there would be a movie on this evening, and we were sure going to have a good view.

After we were all settled in, leaned back on our saddles, and watched a movie. It was dark out, a little windy, and hardly any mosquitos. There was no sound, but quite entertaining. An elderly man came along and asked if we knew we were on private property. We replied yes but we were on the other side of the fence, would you like us to move. He looked at the horses, then left. I guess he was security. We thanked him as he walked away.

We were outside the fence on the highway side, and wondered why we were on private property. He may have had some time waiting for us to move anyways. The horses seemed to be grazing fine. Passing cars could see the movie also. The movie came on, and we watched Sandra Dee, in 'Summer Place'. Half way thru the movie, the most spectacular thing I'd ever seen J. C. said it's the northern lights. It was the first time I had ever seen them. WOW! They were spectacular. Joyce said she had seen them before, but I was very impressed. I enjoyed the light show better than the movie.

Checked the horses, tucked in, and slept sound. Did hear passing cars toot the horn a couple times during the night. That was all. We found out we were camped ten miles off the Douglas Highway.

June 17, 1965
Leaving the Theatre

We were exhausted, windy and warm. YES, all Is well. We are up and ready to roll at 8:00 a.m. We slept in after our 'night out at the movies'. That got a chuckle! The wind was really howling, ooohhh how we loved it.

We stopped for noon grazing at a campground, as the horses were having a hard time walking into the wind. It can be quite exhausting. We have only covered fourteen miles today. There was good grazing off to the side of the camp shelter, and a bit out of the wind. Here is where we will spend the rest of the day, as there is water for them.

We checked them out, combed them down, and all they wanted to do was graze. We sat at a picnic table and talked to several people who were interested in the horses and our ride. A young man, approximately 12-14, came over with two plates of food for us. He said his mom would like to know if we would like dinner: green beans, mashed potatoes, sausages, two slices of bread and watermelon. We thanked him very much, and he left back to where they were camped. We ate the dinner, and thoroughly enjoyed it.

Checked out the animals, and went over to thank the family. They were down for the evening. We sat around a nice fire. A few campers came and joined us. They took pictures and said they would send them along. Then we met a family from Kentucky with a neat southern drawl. They wanted to know about our journey, and said they were going to tell everyone in Kentucky about us. They said we were 'dunky', and that they have more alligators than horses.

A woman at another campsite called the television station, and said to tell us they would see us tomorrow. I put a shoe on Belva Dear, and had a few spectators. I'm glad he was very co-operative. We slept on the cement floor of the cookhouse, and found it quite comfortable. We managed to be in bed before eleven. It had just started to rain. The horses have trees to go under.

June 18, 1965
Leaving the Camp ground

We were up at 7:00 am. Looked over at the campsite where the folks were camped that brought us dinner last night. They were gone. We never got the chance to thank them. If you ever read this book, we thank you with all our heart for the wonderful meal that we were so grateful for, and sorry we missed you.

We made breakfast in the cook shelter, packed up and were on the trail near nine. We only travelled about eight miles when we met an elderly man. He said he worked for the highways department, and he just buried a deer. Said he had another one to do. We told him we would help him. We didn't get the words out when the mare would not cooperate at all. She was already taking off. We wished him a good day, and had to move on. We were just as glad, as the wind was blowing the wrong way, and it was the smell.

The wind is quite strong and almost feels like it could snow. By this afternoon, our faces looked a little swollen from the wind. As much as you try to cover up, the weather still wins. J. C. said, "You can't wrap a blanket around yourself, people will think we are Arabs." At least we can still laugh when we look at each other. Sometimes we actually howl and don't even know why. How funny can a sunburn be? It has to be the swollen face. I told J. C. she, kind of looks like a basketball, with slits for eyes. I know, I am not funny?

It would be great, if the rest of the journey was not such a challenge .The journey I dreamed of as a kid, none of these things were in the picture. Still. So many people ask why we decided to travel across Canada on a horse. We purchased four dollars and seventy cents worth of groceries this afternoon. Then we pulled in off the highway for an hour to let the horses drink and graze.

When we pulled in, and the horses were drinking, we noticed the horse flies were back again. We only let them graze a short time and headed back out. We cannot wait to camp tonight. Turned out to be quite a hot afternoon, as we had not expected, as it was very cold when we left this morning. Such a change in a few hours.

Just as we were heading out a man stopped us along the highway. He walked over, looked at the horses for a minute or two, and said "Not really!" in a loud tone of voice. He then left. There was no other conversation. We did not know what that meant, so replied "OK". Well we held back until he was back in his vehicle and pulled out. We just looked at each other, silent stares, exhausted, too tired to even laugh. I think. I said, well that was different, and we carried on.

We made thirty- five miles today considering the conditions. We pulled in the other side of McGregor and set up camp. Gave the horses their oats. We will have to pick up more oats and horse- shoes soon. We never even bothered with dinner. We picked more branches with leaves on for tomorrow, to rub back and forth on the horses and keep the horse flies away, as travelling the blankets do not work very well. We were down for the night by 10:30 p.m.

June 19, 1965
Leaving McGregor Area

Up before 8:00 a.m. Neither of us got a great sleep last night, as the mosquitos nearly drove us mad, and the cold seems to affect my injured shoulder from the fall I had on Frankie a few weeks ago. But! there were no complaints allowed. If there were, we would be complaining all the way to the east coast. That was, part of our conversation we had last night. I thought J. C. said that I was a thorn in her ass, until she grabbed her bottom and grimaced. Well I could not stop laughing. She thought I was coming unglued, until I explained what I thought she had said. It was that souvenir from Dead man's Creek, and I told her she would need a vet for that. I told her I thought she walked funny, but I had thought it was from her swollen ankle.

Sometime, during the night we decided to move out in the open, away from the trees where there was a little bit of wind. God, wish we had thought of it before we bedded down. Now we understand why we didn't hear anything from the horses, as there was no mosquitos out there.

Had no idea what time we were on the road this morning. A car pulled up and we met these people from Wapella. They signed our diary and asked if we could drop them a line when we reached the east coast.

They signed their names as Mrs. Hilda LaValle, Miss Joan LaValle, and Miss Caroline Gessell. They were very interesting to talk too.

We still find lots of ticks, and every day we check the horses and ourselves. We stopped in Portage la Prairie for noon grazing near a drive in theatre. I put a shoe on Scout while Joyce hiked to town up the road a mile. She came back four hours later with a man, two kids, and two old horse- shoes. We visited a while and they invited us to stop in for dinner when we pass their place up ahead east of here.

We headed out about 4:40 p.m. We passed the farm, where we were asked in for dinner, but it was already quite late and they were some distance in off the road. We chose to go on while we still had daylight left. It was getting quite late when we came to an Esso station. We made a stop to get a couple pails of water for the horses. The owners came out and invited us in for dinner. They said they saw us going thru Alberta and said they knew we were coming their way. We had pork and hot beef sandwiches with salad, and ice cream for dessert.

I realized it was dark out. We thanked them and said we had better get going. They said a couple hundred yards past the service station was a good grazing area. We thanked them. We were camped near Headingly.

June 20, 1965
Leaving for Winnipeg

Got up at 5:00 a.m. Then drug our gear back, into the bush, covered up and went back to bed. Both of us could sleep a week. Joyce found ticks on her, and one was stuck on her foot. They are horrible. Can't wait to get out of this part of the country. I can see where it would be beautiful by car. J.C. asked again, why don't you get ticks? I told her, I was O Negative. I'm not funny again.

Managed to leave camp by 9:20, heading towards Winnipeg. The horses still don't seem to have ticks on them. I told J.C. she should try the salve. If there is anything we've learned, you don't spray under a horse, or put your slicker on while you are riding.

It was 10:30 by J.C.'s watch. That quit. So, we stopped to graze for a couple hours as there was water here for the horses. We played a couple hands of rummy, as it keeps you awake. J.C. says she does not want to lay down, as the ticks may get her. Now Frankie threw a front shoe. We will have to get it replaced tonight when we stop.

We made a quick snack then headed out for south Winnipeg. There I put the shoe on Frankie. A group of tourists stopped to talk and asked us about the trip and how far have we come. Too far is not the answer, until we laughed and found out we were just out of Headingly. I think we went in a circle. We must have taken the long way towards Winnipeg. Oh brother, anyways we are going to go around Winnipeg tomorrow.

We decided to stop and try to figure out where we are. We just got the animals taken care of and a guard came and said we were on prison property and would have to move. Oh brother! He told us that if we cross over to the other side of the fence that it would be o.k. We moved the horses and the gear across to the other side. He was very nice about it and said he was very sorry. This will be another night, in the Winnipeg area.

It must be a fair sized city as the light are spectacular. The horses are travelling well, and we are only a few miles away from our planned stop in Kenora, Ontario. We need to get some of our gear cleaned up and repaired, wash all our blankets and get the animals checked out by vet to make sure they are really as good as they look. I believe we could use a good tonic ourselves, like 'Geritol and Tylenol'. We are still camping in the city lights of Winnipeg.

June 21, 1965
Leaving Winnipeg Area

Up, saddled, packed, and on the road by 8:30 a.m., heading for the other side of Winnipeg. We only have five days if all goes as planned, before we pick up our mail. Will be quite excited to hear from home.

We have camped on highway number seventy- five, just outside Winnipeg for noon grazing, and had to put another shoe on Frankie. So many people have stopped to talk to us this afternoon, that some of them are actually chatting with each other. It's like a convention meeting, but we really enjoyed them all. An older couple brought us milkshakes. Boy did we enjoy those milkshakes, and their company. Great folks.

Later on another couple stopped by with a three year old. In the grass was a small bird trying to fly. The father said "Kevin catch the birdy". I said "OH NO! You're not going to do that!" The man said, "Well it was just a bird", I said "no, please no." We were pleased to see them leave. We wondered later on if it was a baby bird, or just an injured one. Anyway, we left it alone.

At first, we were watching out for gopher holes, but now birds' nests. We have no other choice of travel except on the edge of the pavement. Believe me that is not good either. It rained quite a while this morning. If it helps the mosquitos, that's fine! They do not seem to be as bad as last week.

There doesn't seem to be any campfire material around these parts, and we love our campfires. We must have travelled a good twenty- eight miles today as we cannot see the lights of Winnipeg anymore. It's a good way to travel, no clock, tattered map, and a little rain. I can tell my buddy is exhausted, but never complains.

Pulled in for tonight back off the road somewhere along the highway east of Winnipeg. We found a little wood, and camped down in an area off the road. We had a small bonfire and roasted garlic sausage with beans. Good grazing for the horses. Called it a night.

June 22 1965
Off of Highway 75

Up at 8:00 am this morning. It looks like it might be a good day. It sure got cold last night, and we woke up because of it. The horses are doing and looking well. I think Scout is getting too many oats as he's becoming very aggressive and cranky. He kicked at me three times this morning while I was packing him, which he has never done before. The third time he glanced off my ankle. Oooh my God that kick was painful. He got a good swat for that.

We headed out along the highway, and it looks like it may rain this afternoon. Not sure how many miles we've travelled this morning but we are somewhere east of Molson. There are many birds in this area and we've seen a lot of moose crossings.

Turned the horses out for noon grazing, made ourselves soup and sandwiches, and it just started raining again. Under the tarp we went, and played cards, 500 rummy, while the horses grazed. My ankle feels quite swollen from the kick, and I'm glad I didn't take my boot off. We sat and made a list of some of the thing we are going to need when we get to Kenora, Ontario.

Our saddlebags are starting to show a lot of wear. We talked about possibly selling the pack- horse to a good family in Kenora. I knew I was keeping my mare Frankie, so asked J. C., which one would she keep. She said Scout is easier to ride, but Belva- Dear is less work. She thought at this time she would keep Belva- Dear. Scout is one of the hardest to deal with and seems to be cranky with the other two quite often. We figured if we cut back and only had the two horses, it would be far less stress on us. We both understand it will be a hard decision to make, but we will make sure he gets a good home if we do sell him. Another reason for our decision is that horse shoes are hard to come by in this part of the country. Belva Dear is going to need another shoe soon. We will check her out tonight when we camp, as we may have to travel a few mile before we can get another one. We actually have one more shoe, but no nails.

We can't wait to get our mail from home and to hear all the good news. I sure miss my daughter this morning. Two girls from Amherst, Nova Scotia, stopped to chat. They said they talked to the two men with the covered wagon, then said they know we are coming and said to say hi. We told them that we have sent a message ahead to them also.

We sat on the side of the road with the girls. They gave us a drink of Southern Comfort and chatted awhile, said they were heading to Calgary to work. One said, she owned a place back in Amherst and left their address with us. They told us when they left this morning that they nearly hit a moose as it ran across the road in front of them. Sounds like we're coming into moose country.

As we were packing up, the horses had all rolled in the mud. It took some time in cleaning them up. Back on the road again, we talked to some more travelers passing on the news that the 'Covered Wagon Crew' are laid up in Port Arthur awhile, as one of their horses is lame. Now we will catch them sooner, probably in three to four weeks.

Hate to mention it again, but the mosquitos are driving us absolutely, crazy. I'm sure they hum they are so thick. Not too bad when you are travelling, but when we pull off the road to give the horses a drink, we are totally covered in mosquitos. We are going to have to figure something out for this evening. Staying on the road travelling until camp tonight.

We tried to graze in a wooded area off, the road, but it looks impossible. I cant explain how bad the mosquitos are. It looks like it's going to rain again. We are actually praying for the rain now, where three weeks ago we cursed it.

It was getting late in the afternoon and we decided to camp just this side of Sandilands Provincial Park. By this time, it was almost too dark. It started to rain, so we decided to go into the park. There was a pump where we could get water for the horses. We gave them their oats, quickly combed them down, and tethered them out. For some reason as we were setting up our camp (at the back of the entrance shelter), the mosquitos were not that bad. It didn't take but minutes to get into the sleeping bags, we were not taking any chances.

June 23, 1965
Travelling

It rained quite hard last night and I think every *** Damn *** Mosquitos came into our sleeping bags. Believe me. We cannot explain how bad they were. AND MY ANKLE IS SWOLLEN AND VERY PAINFUL. I remember soaking it yesterday until the mosquitos got too bad, I could not sit any longer. J.C. was mumbling something, then, she started to laugh. I asked her, what's so funny, she said," NOTHING". We put all the bug spray on the horse blankets and J.C. has one wrapped around her. I started to laugh, till there were tears, J.C. said, now what's wrong with you. I said, NOTHING?

Woke up around 3:00 in the morning and it was quite chilly. For some reason, there were no mosquitos. The stars were so bright and beautiful. I've never seen so many stars, and the Milky Way was spectacular. Usually you can't see the stars through the Milky Way, as it always seems to be so cluttered. It was sure peaceful. How we enjoyed the coolness of the evening.

We have been on the trail for three months now, and honestly, it feels like forever. If I haven't complained today, let it be now. My ankle is throbbing. Don't know what time we got up. It's kind of nice not having a watch. The mosquitos aren't that bad, so we are going to relax, make some breakfast and let the horses graze while we are still at Sandilands Park. J.C. is not feeling too good this morning. We made some good coffee, and she said she feels better, after we ate.

Went to get the horses ready to ride out this afternoon. Frankie's belly is bloody. Damn, we are going to comb her, clean her up, and put more salve on her belly,. We're going to spray the blankets first, and try to strap them on behind their saddles. Believe me this is not an easy task. Then we will try to deal with our own battered and beaten bodies. If we can take good care of them until we hit Ontario, we will make a good decision then. Being stubborn or what, but we can't give up now. We both are very strong willed, and we will make it.

There seems to be thousands of mosquitos. If you don't wear your bandana you just suck them in when you are breathing. Bastards! A farmer stopped and told us he'd seen us yesterday. He brought us some spray for the horses and gave us some oats. He said they were from the Falcon Lake Riding Stables. He also gave us two shoes and nails, and made sure they fit. Real nice guy. Thank you.

He said they had to close down their riding stables for the afternoon, as the horse flies are that bad. He said he didn't know how we did it, but we told him what we do with the Vaseline and the blankets. We carry a branch and slowly keep it in motion on both sides while we are travelling. He said, one day he thought his horses were going to go insane. (Like all other people along the road we've heard, he's never seen them this bad). I just said "Yes there were two women riding in the same state of mind". Not as bad while you are moving.

There doesn't seem to be much we can do. As long as the horses are willing to keep going, and are holding up well, we will try to keep going until we hit Kenora, Ontario. He wished us the best, and thought it was quite remarkable that we were still able to carry on.

We are now camped about eight miles west of the Ontario border. We have two dollars and fifty cents left in our jeans. Still have groceries and oats, and we are doing o.k. It's after dark now and the horse flies have died down, but the darn mosquitos are out in full force again.

We combed the horses and gave them a light bug spray. They have had their oats and water. Scout and Belva Dear are grazing, and seem to snort only now and then. Frankie is still eating her oats. It's quite dark tonight, and we are very tired. We just grabbed our sleeping bags and crawled under the tarp for the night. We are just camped on the other side of Falcon Lake. Haven't seen any ticks lately. A guy asked us today if we knew there was no left or right for horse shoes? (We thanked him) Oh Boy....(Why?) This is a very trying time. We can not wait to stop for the week in Kenora for a rest for us all.

June 24, 1965
Leaving Falcon Lake

7:00 a.m. Windy as the devil, and I have to put a shoe on Belva Dear this morning before we start. With this wind it might really be fun. Well, it turned out to be, quite a trick and dangerous, but I completed the job. He now has a new shoe.

We rode on until noon and noticed the horse flies were gone. We are seeing something that is crawly, caterpillars and different kind of flies. They don't seem to bother the horses though. They don't look like ordinary flies. What now? There seems to be quite a few of them.

We talked to people today and they told us they have actually imported these flies from Italy to take care of the mosquito problem. Really? We thought, REALLY. never seen these flies before. We are just on the outskirts of Kenora, taking shelter for the night, and didn't record where.

Set up camp, checked the horses out, and with the wind it's nice to know there is going to be a night free of mosquitos. We gave them all a good combing. Checking our groceries. Made up a grocery list and wrote a couple of letters home while J.C. had a nap. Our money should be in Kenora tomorrow.

We are almost half way. It will be so rewarding to stop for a week in Kenora, find a place for the horses and get our gear all together. We will sell one of the horses, and send the pack- saddle and unnecessary gear home to Moms. It's hard to think of having to part with one of our horses. I wear my emotions on my sleeve, where J. C.

never seems to show how she feels about things. She seems to hold it in quite well. But it is a decision that has to be made.

If the wind could only keep up until we get past all the mosquitoes, flies and other annoying species from Italy, it will be a blessing in disguise.

Scout, J. Myhon, Belva-Dear, Frankie, L. Alwood

ONTARIO

ONTARIO
One inch equals approximately 51.3 miles
RAND M?NALLY & CO

Saddle-sore novices
reach halfway mark

SAULT STE. MARIE, Ont. (CP) — Two B.C. women who left Clinton April 23 bound for Halifax on horseback have reached the halfway point.

Helen Allwood, 29, a grader in a Port Alberni plywood plant, and Joyce Mylon, 32, employed by a Prince George electronics firm, had never ridden horses before beginning their journey. They said they expect to reach Halifax the third week of September and then continue by car down the eastern seaboard to Florida, California and home to B.C.

Relaxing here before continuing their trip today with new gear and mounts, they recounted some of their experiences since leaving Clinton. They said they had been bucked and thrown several times

and have often thought of abandoning their journey.

Near Kamloops, they decided to cut across country with a minimum of supplies and a .22-calibre rifle. They lost their way and ran out of food. They shot a squirrel and lived for two days on squirrel stew until finding their route again.

Sleeping under a bridge near Natal one morning, they awoke to find the bridge moving away from its footing. They lost their supplies and while they were searching for their equipment the two horses ran away.

They were delayed for two days at Lethbridge when a train frightened their horses away.

June 24ᵗʰ - Sept 10ᵗʰ   Sept 12-16ᵗʰ

Map of Ontario

June 25 & 26, 1965
Kenora

We Rode into Kenora this afternoon and headed for the post office. Tied the horses out the back and J. C. watched them while I ran in to grab the mail. While the post woman was handing me the mail, a woman behind me in line introduced herself as Mrs. Weatherall. She said, they heard on the radio we were coming into Kenora and would like to invite us both to stay with them. "We have room for the horses out in the pasture, and you can stay the week with us if you choose, as we also have a spare trailer."

We walked out to where J. C. was and talked about it. We were both very excited and said," thank you very much". She told us how to get there. They would be looking for us. It could not have come at a better time. How blessed can we be!

This was decision time, as the journey has become very trying. The main problem we feel is the bugs... mosquitos, black flies, now caterpillars and new flies. It was very exhausting, and our main concern was for the horses. Believe us. We had our hands full.

We finally arrived at the Weatheralls. We were greeted and taken to the trailer. There was water and a fenced in pasture, we could strip them right down and let them be free for a week. Packed all our tack to the trailer. There was a washer and dryer, running water, cook stove, everything you would need. Even laundry soap, we didn't need anything.

We cleaned up and laid out flat to sleep for a few hours. That evening, they asked us to join them and their company for dinner. They had three missionaries visiting from way up north, and one brother. With all the kids, the Weatheralls and ourselves, we sat around a very large table. She had put out a huge spread for us all.

We were about ready to eat when Mr. Weatherall held up a bible and started to say a prayer. It was an experience for both of us, as we have not sat down to dinner with a missionary family before. It was very educational but thought the meal was going to get cold. They are very nice people, and sure say long prayers. We felt very blessed to share that with them. They have four girls, and one son, Robbie-Joe. They introduced the girls as Ruth, Grace, Eddie, and Axel.

During the meal Joyce had her sleeves rolled up and had quite a rash on her arms. It seemed to bother her quite a bit. She was wiggling in her chair. Mr. Weatherall noticed and said he had some lotion that would stop the itch. Well the response was "Nonono no", and I have never needed to laugh so hard in my life. To see the expression on her face, and hear the noise that came out of me, I've never heard before.

Well, the story about the rash was not to be explained at the table, as coming into Kenora we had stopped in the woods to relieve ourselves. J. C. by mistake used poison ivy leaves. That's all there is to that story.

The meal they put out was wonderful. We asked, if we could help clean up but they insisted no, that it was fine. I asked the Weatheralls if they knew of a vet in town, as we'd like to get our horses checked before we pull out. We thanked them, excused ourselves, and headed out for the trailer. Great folks. We had a wonderful evening.

Checked the horses out. Saw the barrel was full of water, and their heads were all down grazing. The rest of the evening, we just hung out and rested. We decided to wash our clothes tomorrow. Sorted all our gear and laundry out and played a couple hands of 500 rummy. We were sure blessed, to run into this family, for the much- needed rest for the horses and for ourselves. We bedded down around eleven.

We didn't get up too early this morning. We knew, we had to get our laundry done and hung out to dry during the day. We knew tonight their guests from the north were going to stay in the trailer, and we were already prepared to set up out back.

That evening they asked questions, about our trail ride, which I sure had a lot to tell. I realized I was over talking. They took lots of pictures. Said, they want a copy of the book. That will happen.

We have made the decision to sell Scout. We feel it will make the trip easier on both of us, as there will be one less animal to worry about. We put an ad in the paper today. It was a real hard decision as to which horse to leave. I knew I was not parting with my mare, even though she had her uncanny ways about her. J.C. said, she's decided to keep Belva Dear as Scout was: the hardest to handle, and the oldest, and didn't get along with the other two most of the time. We will miss him, but feel it will be the only answer to our solution. Then, we could use the extra money, which was not the reason. I did receive funds from home in the mail, which we were glad to receive, as we arrived in Kenora with eighty- two cents in our jeans, and some groceries.

The next morning a vet came to the Weatheralls to have a look at the horses. He gave us some drops for them, the same as we had been giving them. He was very interested in the ride. He asked us, about how many miles a day do we travel etc. He checked the horses, and told us they looked good to him, but what about us? We had to laugh at that. The rest will do us all good. I told him about Frankie tripping. He said well, she had made it this far and we had nothing to be concerned about. He also said they were in remarkable shape for the miles they had travelled.

We went back to the post office as J. C. money has not arrived, nor our pictures. They were to be sent here (dropped off two films in Creighton, B.C.) I got letters from home, and we both got letters from people we had met along the way.

We slept well last night back at the trailer. We did our laundry, got it all hung up to dry, played cards, slept a while, walked out to see the horses, talked to the Weatheralls a little while, it was just a peaceful quiet afternoon. Most of all we just played cards and slept. We had picked up a newspaper in town and it showed an article of us coming thru Saskatchewan in the Moose Jaw Herald. We kept the clipping to send home.

We camped out back and it was great to look up at the stars, the cool evening, with a slight breeze, so there wasn't many mosquitos. What a blessing that is.

June 27, 1965
Kenora

We got up this morning and there was a van outside. It was a cruiser from the newspaper looking for us. Said they had been there awhile, and we found out it was around noon. They asked us if we would play ball with the missionaries today. We said "TODAY?" Oh, brother. Of course, we said, we would love to. Yippee it was rained out. We were still exhausted, but would have played anyways.

We had lunch, meat paste sandwiches, and just laid around and played Canasta. I think we're more tired from laying around doing nothing. It was a very lazy day today.

Later that afternoon, a man had phoned regarding the ad in the paper about Scout. We set a time for him to come out and see him today. He looked him over and said, he wants a horse for his teenage daughter, and would get back to us. He looked like a nice fellow, so we thought Scout would get a good home there.

We just laid around the rest of the day, played card, made plans, and made a list of what we need when we are in town. We will need a new map soon.

June 28 & 29, 1965

Slept in again. There has been a lot of thunder and lightning off and on, short bursts of it with no rain. The horses are in a safe place and don't seem to mind it. When I checked them, Frankie came up to the fence, probably looking for oats. I scratched her ear for a little while and talked to her. Went back to the trailer and read most of the day, but that's becoming very boring.

Decided to go to town. We can see the horses out in the field just standing there looking at us, not feeding. I went to the fence. Frankie came over right away. I got her saddled up and had to entice Scout with a handful of oats. J.C. saddled him up and got ready to ride out. I looked for ticks but never saw any. I checked her knees and they are almost healed. As we were leaving I looked back, saw Belva Dear standing there alone looking at us. I really felt bad. It must be the thought of leaving one behind.

It was around 2:00 p.m. when we left, and we asked the Weatheralls' if they needed anything from town. We headed out to check the mail again. No luck. We stopped at a grocery store to pick up some soup. When we went to pay, the grocer insisted on giving us a bag of groceries. He had packed up everything to make a stew. He said he had heard our interview on the radio and we had said that our favorite meal was a stew cooked out on an open fire. We got a real kick out of that, and thanked him.

That night we had dinner with the Weatheralls' and also, Jane, Edgar, and the five kids. They said all the kids had passed in school and young fella had passed from grade two to grade four. He was an honor student. That evening the newspaper came out to interview us again. They wanted to see me put a shoe on Scout. When we left, we had a shower and played card until 10:00 p.m. It started to rain and we bedded down for the night.

Shoeing horse

June 30 - July 1, 1965

We rode Frankie and Scout to town today. It looked like people were getting ready for a parade. We went to the back of town and up on a grassy slope. There was good grazing and no one around. There was a long huge wooden beam laying at the top of the hill. It looked good and sturdy, so we tied the horses to it, while we went down to the post office just down the hill. We thought it would only take about twenty minutes or so. Tucked the saddles off back in the corner. We planned to come back, lay out, and read our mail while they were grazing.

We got our mail, and while we were leaving the post office, we heard quite a commotion outside. We ran up the hill to see the horses gone. Yes, and the beam also. Oh Boy! By the trail they left, they were heading for town. Oh Brother is not exactly what we said. Something must have spooked them. It looks like they took off on the run.

They were, tied together with this long beam between them. It looks like they've headed through town. The rope let go from Frankie. They ran down the alley and a man was carrying two trays of bread into the side of a store. He tossed the trays and ran. They say the bread was all the way up the alley.

Terrified they would hurt someone, we were after them right away. Panic set in. We split up looking for them. A woman picked up Joyce and they followed the tracks. A police car drove up beside me and he said to get in! (Yes, I saw the bread!)

We finally found them on the way back towards the farm. The Policeman stopped his patrol car on the road. Scout took off into the bush on the left hand side, and Frankie ran into the back yard of a home. They ran when the Police- man put his flashers on. I took off after her, running through the woman's yard. The police got out of his car to come and help. The woman looked out her window wondering what the lights were, and saw a Policeman heading in behind her house. She wondered what was up. She later said that I was lucky she did not jump me. She thought for a minute that the police were after me until she saw the horse.

Then I manage to walk to the other side of the road to get Scout, while the police held onto Frankie. They both had very short ropes left on their halters. I walked them both a mile and a half to the trailer. What a long walk along the roadway with two uncooperative animals. I nearly lost them again when a passing car tooted their horn. The police cruiser drove by a couple of times to make sure I got them back to the farm safe. I was so great full for their help and thanked him. He said, we'll it was quite exciting, have a great day.

I wondered where J. C. was. After I took care of the horses, I was walking back to town when the cruiser picked me up and gave me a ride. He let me know that J.C. was at the police station, and she knows that the horses are back at the farm. I met up with her and we went back to the hillside for our gear. Packed it all up on our shoulders (saddles and bridals) and started back to the Weatherall's. Boy, are they heavy. Believe it!

A car pulled up and a couple asked if we would like a ride, then join them for a sandwich and a cold drink. They would drop us off at the farm right after. We sure agreed to that and had a great time visiting them. The sandwich and cool drink was a real treat as we were truly exhausted. They drove us back to the trailer and we thanked them for their kindness.

When we got back, and as they were leaving, we noticed our bridals were missing. We figured we dropped them on the roadside when we got a ride. Oh Brother, now what next? Realizing they were missing, we just caught them before they were out of sight. We returned with our ride to back where they had picked us up. No bridals. We drove all the way back to the hillside. No luck at all. The next day the same family came out and asked us to dinner, and if we would like to stay a day or two with them. We told them we would love to and thanked them. We let the Weatherall,s know where we would be.

We were feeling frustrated. No bridals is quite serious, when you have eighty-two cents in your pocket. We really had a good laugh at ourselves over that, but nobody knows we hope. Then we remembered I got twenty dollars from mom. Our mail was still in my saddle-bags.

We repeated the ad in the paper to sell Scout, and advertised on the radio about the lost bridals.

The family we stayed with overnight went out of their way to find bridals for us. They finally found bits to make bridals. They were so excited to have found the parts. They were starting to make them up when their phone rang. It was a highway patrol man. He found the bridals on the road, and knew where they belonged. He said he'd be right over with them, and that he had found them the night before on the side of the road and people were running over them. Then he remembered us. Oh God, we could have both kissed him. He said, do you know you are the talk of the town.? Oh Lordie.

We sat around having a few beers after dinner. Our host was telling us some of the stories he had heard yesterday. He said they ran through a red light, cars screeching, horns blowing and nearly wiped out a boat. He heard a man say that two horses went by so fast, but didn't know what the object was behind them. He also heard about the bread up the alley, saying the man may have crapped himself, as there wasn't much room in that alley. Some of the stories they told.

Before I continue. I have to confess that I had this couples name written on our map, and the map has gone missing. I wish to thank them for all their effort in helping us, as well as their wonderful hospitality. I hope, one day you read this journal.

We found out later on that a couple of kid's crawled up the bank to have a peek at the horses. THAT WOULD DO IT. Frankie would be long gone.

We sold Scout today for fifty dollars. The father bought it for his young daughter, Mr. Heidinga (Sp). We felt bad leaving him behind. We had to make a decision. Less oats and shoes for sure. Hope we are making a wise decision. Also sold my .22 rifle for five dollars, but kept the scabbard to carry the shoeing tools in, etc. With the twenty dollars from mom, we now have seventy dollars in our pocket, and a good supply of oats, extra horse-shoes and nails. We are rested and ready to move out.

We cleaned up the trailer and went to see the Weatheralls to thank them for their hospitality in case we missed them in the morning. Told them we would drop a line, and it was a blessing to have met them. We also got ahold of the family we spent the night with last night, and thanked them for their generosity and thoughtfulness in helping us. They said they would send us a copy of the newspaper to let us know that the town of Kenora may never forget us. I told him to hold back on some of those stories until, we are gone a day.

Scout, we will miss you!

July 2, 1965
Leaving Kenora

We got up early, to make sure the trailer was clean. Then got ready to pull out. We had to stop at the post office in town, prior to heading east, to check on any more mail, and to send the pack saddle home. Also to put in a forwarding address.

It was 2:10 p.m. when we left Kenora and Scout behind, not looking back, heading for Sturgeons Falls. J. C. still has not heard from home. The pictures did not come in from Wardner. We dropped a line to the Kodak Company.

We've talked to several people today. Already find it much easier travelling without the extra horse. We should have thought of it much sooner. I sent the pack- saddle home also. It cost us four dollars and eighty cents. It sure cost a lot.

We passed through some construction work and yes, the mosquitos are very bad. They didn't seem that bad in Kenora. One thing that's good though is that the ticks seem to be gone. J. C. says, it's because we are out of 'pine' country and into 'poplar'. Maybe it is the weather as its been a lot cooler.

Camped approximately eighteen miles east of Kenora at about 8:20 p.m. As much as we miss Scout, we are noticing, how much less work is it with one less horse. We set up camp, and its good to be back on the road again. Bedded down by 9:30.

July 3-6, 1965
Travelling East

We have lost part of our diary since leaving Kenora. We rode along the highway for the past five days. We camped out at nights and had campfires every night except one, as it rained. The country through here reminds us very much like British Columbia. Its very nice to have campfires again. It makes all the difference.

We are seeing moose and deer tracks a lot lately. Being as we are travelling mostly highways, we are now thankful that Scout has a good home. We are travelling well and the weather is a lot warmer.

Stopped for afternoon grazing for a couple of hours and played a few hands of rummy. About 2:30 p.m. we headed back out. Went on another ten or twelve miles and got an early night. We went off the road in behind a clearing of small timber. The grazing looked good. We staked out the horses and made camp. Had a small fire and a meat paste sandwich with soup. Put the fire out and bedded down with no idea of the time.

Woke up near dawn. When I sat up, I looked out at the horses. There were four of them. I nudged J.C. and motioned to her, Shhh. She said,"what s up", and laid back down. I whispered 'there are four horses'. Well she popped up right now.

Back behind the mare, off in the distance a bit, was a cow moose and a calf slowly moving out. Felt quite relieved to see her walking off into the timber, as they are a fair size and really don't know anything about them. I heard they could be quite danger-ous. Damn, wish we had film left.

Up at 8:40. There was a pond out back where we took the horses to drink, and they did. Got on the road by 9:30. As soon as we were on the road a vehicle pulled over and yelled out, that we were only 'days behind the covered wagon'. Heard they had a bit of trouble with one horse. Apparently one was hit and came up lame. Told them we were very sorry to hear that, and they pulled out.

Travelled on and pulled in about 2:30 p.m. We were on the highway and to the left there was a culvert with a creek running through it. From up on the highway the culvert looked straight down, but the creek looked like clear cold running water. Up ahead a hundred yards, we saw where it tapered off and we could get down to the creek.

Took the horses over for a drink down off the highway where the culvert was. We put their halter and ropes on them and led them about one hundred and fifty yards back from the highway, as the grass near the culvert was cut grass. Back in further near the trees they could graze for about an hour while we washed up where we couldn't be seen.

We stripped down to our underwear washing up, when we heard a vehicle pull up. You could hear the people above us, and we hoped they couldn't see us. We sat there quite calm for about fifteen minutes. You could hear them talking. It sounded like they had a southern drawl, and that a movie camera was running. They said "Wait until we get back home and show them how close we got to these moose". They soon pulled out. We got a chuckle out of that.

We had a good wash up. It's always nice to come to a creek to have a better bath, than just a quick stop at the gas stations. We didn't know what time it was and honestly didn't care. Went over and got the horses. A few more people were talking to us from up above on the road, as we saddled them up. We told them about the people who filmed the horses, thinking they were moose. They got a chuckle out of that.

When we got up on the road, we were asked if we would like an orange crush. We gladly accepted, talked awhile, and pulled out. They said they were from Saskatchewan. I asked them if they were coming or going. They said they were in Ottawa for a couple of weeks. I told them if they hadn't been out there for a while, they would be in for a surprise due to the amount of mosquitos. They said "Oh, that's normal". J. C. and I just looked and each other thinking O.K.?

We rode on another twenty-two miles approximately, and pulled in off the road to a beautiful spot. Made a nice campfire and our usual stew with biscuits. A couple of guys pulled over and sat by the fire with us for about half an hour talking about their horses back home in Alberta. Then they left. We bedded down around 10:30 p.m. We've travelled a hundred and sixty miles. Since weve left Kenora, we have gone thru Dryden, Vermillion, and near Ignace tomorrow.

July 7, 1965
Heading for Port Arthur and Fort William

We were up at 7:00 a.m. On the road shortly after. We met a farmer who stopped to chat. He said, he would be passing back this way, would look for us and bring us some oats from Fort William tonight. He also told us that the boys from the covered wagon stayed with them for eight days. He said their names were Cecil Rivers, and Jacques Pelletier, and they are only two days ahead of us.

We have been anxious to meet these wagon burners ever since we heard they were on a journey also. Hearsay, they plan to publish a book. He said their horses names are Rhonda and Spike. We will catch them and get their autograph. If all goes according to our plan, we will be half way in two or three days.

The horses are travelling much better. That week in Kenora, even with all that excitement, seems to have done the trick. One less horse, and a lighter load. Everything is starting to look up. We decided last night that we will, not quit now. It is the east coast FOR SURE!

YES! The black flies still drive us crazy, but there is a good thing. J.C. is almost over her poison ivy she said, and said she would rather have the poison ivy than the flies. I told her NOT ME! They are too bad for us to stop for noon grazing, so we are heading for a watering hole. We got off and sprayed the horse's blankets again. Tried to put more salve on their bellies. Well, forget that. Belva-Dear is not bad, but the mare, I was glad not to be riding her at that moment.

It was about 3:40 in the afternoon when the man returned from Fort William with fifty pounds of oats for us. He said they were, (on the house,) good luck, and to drop a line. His name was in the seven missing days of the diary. It's so easy to remember the incidents that happen, but not that easy to remember the names, as we've spoken to so many people.

We rode thirty miles before stopping for the night. One good thing we've noticed is that the flies have died down. We watered the horses and they are grazing right away. There is more clover than most stops. We checked their shoes, put two on Frankie, and one on Belva Dear. We have lost track of how many shoes I've put on. The best time we found to do this is at dusk. Even then it's a risk. Remember these flies are not horse flies. They are the ones that they felt they had to 'bring in' from Italy. Can you believe that? REALLY? To get rid of mosquitos?

J.C. has a great fire burning and we are having canned stew tonight. Today we saw our first Black Bear, and glad to see him run off. It looked like a young one, and yes, Frankie was a little excited.

Like two kids, we have made a game up as we travel, one point for a Deer, three points for a Moose, five points for a Bear/Duck or Owl. J.C. says she already has five points as she saw the bear. Whoever has the most points when we reach Quebec wins. What? We have not decided on that yet. It's the first time we have been able to travel together. Not having the pack horse has made the difference.

As we sat around the fire, two young women stopped to talk with us. They insisted we have a drink with them. They said a moose ran out in front of them, and they missed it by inches. They turned so sharp, they nearly rolled their car and said to watch out for them as they are very aggressive. Now that we are seeing a lot of moose tracks, it wasn't a good time to hear that. Well, we had a drink of the Southern Comfort that they had poured for us. Then they headed out, saying they are heading for Calgary, looking for work. We did enjoy their company. We let the fire burn down, and it was after 10:30 sometime, when we bedded down .

July 8, 1965
Heading for Atikoken

The mosquitos are extreme this morning. We woke up during the night cursing. Neither one were happy campers, but have not heard much from the horses. The spray must be effective. We are not crazy, but this is extreme, believe us.

We woke up this morning under our tarp, very tired, and it's raining. I yelled YES! (I've never been so happy!) It scared the hell out of J.C. She wondered what's wrong, and I repeated "it's raining!" She whipped the tarp back over her head, mumbled something under her breath, and went back to sleep.

Don't know what time we started this morning but it was later afternoon when we stopped for grazing. Two men came into camp with a sack of oats. The driver introduced himself as George Martin. There was a French speaking Man with him. He handed us three dollars. We just looked at him, but he insisted, saying it was towards the trip. Then they left. Now we are wondering what's up as this is the third time people have come to us and wished us well, gave us a dollar or two, and said it was for the trip.

Apparently, in one of the newspapers it made the statement that 'the girls are travelling on a shoestring'. We never ever made that statement. We did say in Kenora when interviewed, that we were waiting for funds, which arrived when we picked up our mail. Also, we mentioned that we were possibly thinking of selling the pack- horse, and that we needed a well-earned rest before we moved on.

We weren't on the road more than an hour when we met Mr. Martin again. He stopped to tell us that he left two sacks of oats with the police for us at Atikoken, forty-five miles ahead. He said they would be looking for us when we arrived, and really went all out to make us welcome. He also told us to call before we hit the Fort. They will come out and meet us.

We definitely need a new map, as I believe we are not headed for Atikoken. I think we are on a wrong road.

We made camp, when, another man stopped and introduced himself as Zennie Dubinski, saying he was a real estate rep. He said we could have a free motel for a few days, and a place to put the horses.

It was 1:00 a.m. and we were still sitting around the fire. We were asked, if we wanted to go down the road a mile, for a meal, but we chose not to leave the horses. He had just left when a kid went by on a loud motor bike. Another one came behind him. When they spotted us, they stopped roaring their motorcycles. What a racket. Then, they left.

We went to bed and shortly after, they came back with two cans of something. It was quite dark out, but we could tell it was the kid's voice. They asked us if there was anything else they could do. I was sitting up at this time, and asked what are you talking about, would you please go home and let us sleep. They said they would. Well that went easy, and J.C. asked "whats that, soup or corn. "

We just got back to sleep and back they came! They rode right up to us. They had brought us some pop, and insisted we have a bottle. I said, "Please", but they insisted. We took the pop. I told them if they didn't bugger off we would call the cops. They promised if we drank the pop with them, they would leave and not return. We told them to please, go home. They left.

YES, they came back. It was still dark out. They said they forgot to get our autographs. We had nothing to write on. I used my saddlebag as a pillow, reached in and found a card that someone gave us of the covered wagon guys. We put our names down on that and gave it to them. They were really happy with that. They stayed and chatted. I asked if they knew what time it was. The older of the two, who was about fifteen years old, said it was nearly five o'clock in the morning. As they were leaving they yelled to us to stop for breakfast in the morning when we get to the café.

I started to laugh. I laughed so hard and J.C started laughing too. We couldn't get our breath. We both had to get up to pee. Got back to bed and we ached from laughing. We couldn't laugh anymore. J.C. asked why I was laughing and I told her I forgot. She said "Where were you going to call the cops from?" and away we went laughing again. We finally fell asleep.

Two and a half hous later, we were up, around 7:30 a.m. The boys had said they were from Upsula.

Note: The main thing we remember was that we were camped in a farmer's field, and had permission to have a bonfire. We had travelled until eleven p.m. It was the longest day since Kaslo.

July 9, 1965
Heading for Port Arthur

Got started about 8:30 in the morning. It was still raining. We were close to the gas station when the owner asked us if we would like to have some breakfast with them. We were waiting for them to mention the boys. They served us a great meal, told us we could get water for the horses, and they let us wash up before breakfast. We thanked them, and were back on the road again.

The horses are really moving out this morning and we are really tired. We managed to make sixteen miles before we stopped and grazed, and to have a cat nap. There are lots of moose tracks in this area. A woman that had stopped and gave us a dollar a week ago, stopped again to chat. She said the covered wagon is now at the Lake Head, which we assumed she meant Port Arthur and Fort Williams.

As we travelled along, apparently we both had the same thing on our minds. J.C. said it, and I was thinking it. 'Hope those kids don't show up again tonight!' We realize they meant no harm, just overly interested in the trip (probably nothing better to do). Bastards' is what I said, in the middle of the night, but, I TAKE THAT BACK. I know they were just kids, and meant well. Thank you, you little devils.

We got an invitation from the John Street Riding Stables. The owner gave us her name as Helga Aalto. We thanked her. Then, down the road we met a 'totem pole' carver. Him and his wife invited us in for snacks, and gave us some spray for the horses. It's the same as we are using. We were thankful for that, as it works quite well. (They said they were Old Indian herbs). They read about our journey in one of the newspapers and wished us all the best. We made sure we let them know how much we enjoyed the tour and seeing his carvings. They were beautiful. We really enjoyed the visit.

We rode on a little further and took up John Streets' invitation, staying overnight at their stables. A reporter came and took our pictures, and asked about our trip. It was a half hour interview talking on the air.

We were watching television that evening and there we were on the news from a prior interview a few weeks back. Its sure strange watching yourself on TV. J.C. said we looked like two old 'Prospectors'. (That is true). We had a great night's sleep and the horses are doing well at the stables. (Thank you Helga)

July 10, 1965
Hillcrest Park

They had a big breakfast ready for us before we left. We thanked them for their hospitality, and pulled out around 10:00 a.m. Met the news cruiser again. We told them that we had tried to contact the guys from the covered wagon. We heard that they were up with a pilot taking pictures of the area. Then they were supposed to meet the mayor tomorrow at Hillcrest Park. The news team asked us if we could be there to meet them at 10:00 a.m. tomorrow. We agreed as we would be in the area about then.

We spent the day picking up a new tarp, and new Stetsons, as ours are frazzled to nothing. They were used to feed the horses their oats in, and had been stepped on too many times. We hate new hats, as if you abuse them, they do not fit well any more. Most cowboys prefer that. Spent the day grazing the horses on the outskirts of the park, and camped. Called it a night.

July 11, 1965
Lake Head

The next day, we went to the park at 10:30 with the horses. By eleven, we were ready to leave. As we were leaving, the news crew showed up, saying the men from the wagon were supposed to be there but they didn't show up. They stopped and interviewed us, took our pictures, and wished us all the best. We learned a great deal about the area from them. They were great guys. This, picture was taken as we were leaving Fort William, by Lorne Delinski. We purchased them from him at a later date. The area there is beautiful.

The Lake Head, Hillcrest Park

We never did get to meet the men in the covered wagon, nor did we hear anything further. Sorry, we missed them, and wished them all the best. To meet them was supposed to be a surprise. Well it was. We were told to call a Mr. ... ... where they were staying at. He told us we could not see them for three days. We would love to have met them since we have travelled a long time behind them. Not being able to, was a big letdown. Oh well fellows, now, try and catch us and good luck.

We left the Lake Head after talking to the reporter as its nearly 2:00 p.m. and it looks like a storm is coming in. We are heading out towards Nipigon, and will make camp as soon as we can. The storm is coming in fast.

We got to the outskirts of town, and quickly made a shelter off the side of the road. Watered the horses, and gave them their oats. Now the rain is coming, but it sure keeps the flies away. This will be our camp for the night. Got a nice fire going, made dinner, and played rummy under the tarp. We are so glad to be in Ontario, it reminds us of home. We talked about some of the jobs we have had. I asked J.C. about plans she had for after the trip. She said she would like to go ranching, talked about her job at Len Kirk Electric and would probably go back there after the ride. I talked about getting a place for my daughter and I, preferably in the country, as I've always loved the Cariboo.

July 12, 1965
Travelling to Nipigon

We'd been on the road about an hour, and it was near noon when a man pulled up to talk to us. He introduced himself as Jacques Pelletier. He said he was a producer from the covered wagon. He had wanted to come out and meet us. He wondered why we never came to see them in the Fort. We told him what Mr. .... said. You could tell he was not happy about hearing that. He gave us five dollars and said he was in a hurry. Said he was on his way to pick up more film in the Sault, and when we get to Montreal to phone him collect and he would show us the town. Then he said whenever we finish our trip, wherever we are in North America, call him collect and he would fly out to meet us. It was nice, to finally meet one of the wagon crew. It was a quick visit, and we both felt it was a strange request? Oh well. We finally got to meet one of the wagon team.

We did not travel very far when a red Volkswagen pulled up, parked right in the middle of the road, and a woman jumped out. She left her door open and come running over to us. She said to come and visit her in Nipigon. The traffic, was tied up on both sides. I told her she was parked in the middle of the road, but she kept on talking. She was very friendly and actually made us promise we would come to see her. She kept on talking, and again I said, "The traffic is lined up". Then people from two other cars got out and came over to talk. They wanted to know if we would sign autographs, and they took pictures. We kind of got a kick out of that.

We had to laugh at how patient the other people in line were. She continued to talk. Her husband had died, said she was from Craven Hurst, and they were selling his house as they had been separated. She returned to her vehicle and yelled back to not forget to go and see her. She waved, and away she went. Tooting the horn, and yelling again not to forget to stop. The other vehicles just waved and smiled as they pulled out.

We got a late start, so never stopped for noon grazing. Near evening, a woman stopped us to pass on a message. She said a Mr. Trombridge was a school Teacher, and would like to know if we would like to stay in his cabin at Black Bay, on the beach. Well yes, we said. We rode there and he met us. We thanked him for the offer. After we took care of the horses, he showed us to our cabin. He had a big campfire going on the beach. Wow, this is really living! We roasted wieners and had hotdogs with a couple of beer. It was a beautiful full moon. It reminds us of home. He took pictures. A friend dropped down and we sat there another hour and went to bed quite late. Had no idea what time it was. Had a great evening.

July 13, 1965
Leaving Black Bay

We had a great sleep, and this morning we got up, put the coffee on, went out gave the horses their oats and water, and J.C. started breakfast for the school Teacher and his friend. We made hotcakes and bacon, with lots of coffee. Before we left, quite a few pictures of us and the horses (were taken) on the beach. We were supposed to swap pictures after the trip was over, for the kids in his classroom. He also took autographs for them. We had to smile again at that. He obviously is a very caring man (teacher).

We were very fortunate to have met and spent time with him and his friend. Where does the time go?

We left this afternoon heading for Nipigon, and thanked him for the wonderful time there. As we were travelling along a narrow road, a dog barked. Just then a car went by, and Frankie freaked, going down hard. She took me with her. Her head was down under her leg, and my leg was pinned under her and twisted. The mare got up faster than I did. It took me a few minutes before I could walk. We finally managed to get everything under control. It was not a good situation with the traffic. A woman ran out to help (Mrs. Untulic). (Tanya) The mare seemed fine. I told her I was ok, and I would just have to walk it out. We took the horses in back of the Untulic residence.

J.C. bent down to untangle Belva Dear. He kicked her in the head. Oh boy that did not look good at all. She went down like a ton of bricks, and got right back up. Her hand was on her head, and I could see the blood through her fingers. Mrs. Untulic, looked at it, and ran in to get an ice pack. Right away. I wanted her to go in for stitches but she refused. She should have had four stitches in it for sure, as it was quite a gash. Mrs Untulic asked us to stay the night, as there was room for the horses out back. It did not take much convincing, as it was getting on in the evening. J.C. went in and laid down for half an hour, and said she was ok as it just glanced off of her. She turned and said "IM FINE! " We cleansed and taped the gap, and put a patch over it. It didn't look good to me.

Just before dark, about 7 o'clock, I put two shoes on Belva Dear. How I manage to shoe him, I will never know. We were again asked to please stay for the night, because I could barely put my weight on my ankle now, and J.C. was as pale as a ghost. What company we were. What a remarkable woman to take on two injured riders at the same time, its like a nightmare. Bless you gal. J.C. said she is going to be o.k., that she never had a headache, and can't stand the ice on her head.

July 14, 1965
Nipigon

We stayed and mowed her lawn for her the next day. It was really a God send, as I could still barely bare any weight. J.C. was still pale. Tanya asked us to stay another night. Through it all, we remember all the laughs we've had, and would never trade a day of all the experiences we've endured to date. Thank you Tanya.

July 15, 1965
Leaving Nipigon

Thanked this wonderful woman for her hospitality and headed out. As we were leaving the Untulic residence, a Mr. Tom Hebert brought us some oats, and wished us all the best on our journey. As J.C. was getting on Belva Dear, he bit her. Boy did he ever get a slap for that! Actually two! What Next! I laughed till I could hardly breath. This is past being funny. J.C. finally started laughing also. Thank God. We finally got on the road. There was no conversation between us at all. There was no place to ride to see a doctor either. She said she was FINE.

We travelled on until 1:00 p.m., and camped near a beach. We are both pretty stiff and sore. We tethered the horses out, grabbed a blanket each, and walked down to the beach. The lump on J.C's forehead is really something, she looks like a 'space alien' (but swears she doesn't have a headache.)

At the beach we met people from B.C. They had a Pan abode House near, and asked us to join them. Sitting on the beach, we had a couple of beer, hot dogs, and then coffee. We spent a good couple of hours enjoying the day. Great people. J.C. was hurting, and not saying much. (She is very stubborn). We look like we have both been in fights. Hope no one thinks its us going at it. Who would believe the truth.

When it was time to go, we thanked them, packed up, and started east again. Don't know how many miles we travelled today, but everything is going well. Just before we camped for the evening, a man came out and called us from his store. He wanted to know if we wanted to look at his hides. He had Bear, Wolf, Fox, and Moose, mounted heads and horns. He said he had an empty trailer out back and we were welcome to use it.

The grazing was good, and there was water at the trailer. We took him up on his offer and thanked him. The trapper took a whole roll of film and said he would send us some pictures. His wife told us that their daughter had been drug by a horse and been unconscious for fourteen days. We hardly got unpacked and J.C. was out like a light by 9:30 p.m. I kept an eye on her for awhile as she was quite pale. We managed to sleep well.

July 16, 1965
Twenty Four Mile to Schreiber

Packed up and ready to roll by 9:00 a.m. I've noticed J.C. has a bit more color this morning. We thanked the couple for the stay and the tour, and hoped their daughter would be ok. We only travelled two hundred yards, when an older man from a station house asked us in for coffee. We were about to tell him we needed to make up time, but he asked us to 'Please' join him. We did and had the strongest coffee I've ever drank in my life. Chatted awhile, thanked him, and started out again. Very interesting, nice older gentleman.

Finally on the road, we went through to the outskirt of Roseport. J.C. walked into town for potatoes and bacon. She asked at the café where the nearest store was. They said, it was closed, but there was another one a couple blocks up. People at the café had heard her request, and said they would take her back to the horses, as it's the last day of their trip, and they had extra food she would like to give to us. They left us pota-toes, bacon and eggs, and onions. We thanked them very much and they left. I made dinner and we headed for Schreiber. J.C. is still not feeling good, but managed to eat a good meal. I've come to the conclusion that she. is very stubborn. She say it's the bite that bothers her the most and next stop we need to pick up some aspirin.

It was just starting to get dark. It looked like we were about a quarter of a mile this side of town, and looking for a good place to camp. Just as we were about to pull in, there was a bunch of cars stopped on the side of the road looking at moose feeding, and taking pictures. It was just browsing peacefully. As we got closer, we realized there was another one on the other side of the road. We rode toward them not knowing what reaction we would get.

Frankie started to get a little spooky so we stayed back. There was a beach up ahead and we rode off in that direction hoping to get some pictures. It was too dark but I would like to get some of the pictures the people took of us, and the moose, from the other side of the road. We bedded down by the beach for the night. J.C. tucked in right away. I walked to the beach and sat there quite a while watching the reflection in the water.

July 17, 1965
On The Road

We were up around 7:30 and found moose tracks approximately twenty yards from where we were bedded down, between, the horses and us. I would like to think the tracks were there prior to camping. We thought the horses would have spooked or snorted, or something. We found it quite amazing anyways. J.C. says she I feeling better, and looks better too.

We left camp heading east and a man stopped and gave us ice-cream. He introduced himself as Henry Miller. He said he was a mechanical engineer for the paper mill. He invited us to come back some time, if we are ever through here again, to visit him. He said he would take us flying and boating in Lake Superior, as he owns his own plane.

Several people have stopped us today just to get pictures. Don't know what's going on, but they ask if we minded if they get our pictures. We travelled twenty four miles and camped off the road, around the corner, in a gravel pit.

People came, said they followed our tracks, to take our pictures. As we were setting up camp, a couple drove in towards the gravel pit, took us to get water, and bought us each an ice-cream cone before taking us back to camp. Then, they left.

We built a small 'smudge' to keep the flies away. We sprayed the horses. Built a nice fire, had a stew with biscuit and coffee. It was quite a nice night, but started to cloud over again. Decided to stay the night, as we all seem to be a little tired. We saw two moose in the area again, and almost rode up on them. We decided to bed down just outside of White River for the night. All is well.

July 18, 1965
Heading for White River

On the road again. People stopped us shortly after we started, to take our picture. They said they were going to have Christmas cards made out of them. They said they were from Minnesota. Just after that, along came two young fellows from Chatham New Brunswick, who said they were heading home to Ontario from Calgary. They had started out on horseback from Drum Heller to Chatham. As soon as they hit the Trans-Canada Highway, midway thru Alberta, and all the way to Brandon Manitoba, they had heard many stories about us as they travelled.

Their horses went lame in Brandon, so they folded. They had travelled eight hundred miles and were to weeks behind us all the time, hoping to catch us. We told them how we were behind the covered wagon and how we were hoping to catch them. We talked and compared experiences off the highway, for two hours. We had many laughs. They were very glad to have met us, and we thoroughly enjoyed their company. They told us that the producer from the covered wagon had left, and there was a new producer. (Hearsay).

We travelled on for a few more mile, and met them again just before we camped. At a café, we had dinner with them. A fellow from the Marathon Press came in and took our story. He said he would meet us later this weekend, on the highway and give us a copy of the paper. He said the name of the newspaper will be 'The Mercury Marathon'. I told him the two men eating with us rode across the 'prairies' on horseback. He said we would be in the paper this weekend, and left.

Somewhere we have lost a day, but we camped outside the café in the back, for afternoon grazing. It may have been a mistake, as too many people arrived to take pictures, talk with us, and get our story. We met Americans also. Everyone seems to know who we are. They know much more than we do, and what we are going to do. We got quite a chuckle out of that. Apparently some bridge gave way and we lost all our gear. That was a new one for us.

Everyone is so friendly though, and seems genuinely interested in our 'ride'. We haven't made many miles in the past two days because of this. It's hard to keep the horses just standing while we talk. While we were taking our break, we heard, we were in the weekend magazine, sometime in mid-July.

Travelled on again until 6:00 p.m. Watching for water and a good place to camp. We were outside a drive-in café with no intentions on stopping. We noticed the drive-in was closed. The owner spotted us, came out, and said he would open the café and make us hamburgers and fries and gave us each a drink. He told us we could set up camp for the night behind the café, as there was a good spot for the horses.

We talked for a little over an hour and went out and bedded down. Just then, we heard a noise. J.C. said someone was calling us. I told her No, I thought it was Black Birds. We sat up and looked. Off in the distance was an East Indian woman, and four French women, wanting to see the horses. We told them it was ok, and they probably didn't understand us, then they left.

July 19, 1965
Belva- Dear

Up at 7:30 this morning and noticed Belva- Dears limping slightly. We packed up and headed out around 9:00 a.m. to go to town and get groceries. As we were leaving, I noticed Belva- Dear was limping quite noticeably. We were quite worried. J.C. rode Frankie, and I walked Belva Dear down to the cafe. We got them water and then went in for a coffee.

While having coffee we talked to a landscaper working on the O P Property. His name was Dick Mast. He told us he had seen us on TV and was very interested in our trip. After we left the café I walked Belva- Dear several miles instead of riding him. We ran into Dick Mast again. He had come back and told us that he would call a vet for us today and see if we could get medicine for the horses. I stopped and put liniment on Belva- Dear's knee and wrapped it. We are looking for a grazing spot to pull off the road until we can get some help.

He said he believes he can make a deal to swap a horse for us with the Bar X Ranch in Sault Saint Marie if we were unable to carry on. He told us to find camp for the night and soak Belva Dear's hoof. Then he said, he would be back and track us down.

It was about 10:30 at night when he returned. He said he was sorry for being late, that he was held up making long distance calls. He brought us dinner back to camp. Said he didn't know what we like, but brought us fried chicken, mashed potatoes and peas. We had a beautiful bonfire going. He had half a mickey of rum, and three beer. We sat around the bonfire and chatted until 2:00 a.m. He was a great guy. We had lots of laughs, and let him know how thoughtful he was.

He said he was a 'Gorilla' in Holland during the war. It was very interesting to listen to him. He listened to our story regarding the journey and said we were 'about one hundred percent'. He was quite cheerful, and laughed a lot. He said he was a member of parliament, and the head of the Dutch Immigration and has been all over the world. He also says he has five sons and one daughter. We got to meet two of them. Dick Jr. and Jon. He asked if we would please write him. He left at 2:30 a.m. Mr. Mast gave us the number to the Bar x, and said they wanted us to please call collect, about the horses. We checked the horses then went to bed and slept soundly.

July 20, 1965
Hammer Lake

Up early this morning. Put on coffee. We have to make some decisions as Belva Dear looks like he is hurting very bad. We are not going on until we can get some help for him. We love our animals and won't carry on like this. Found it different the other day walking instead of riding. (It actually was good exercise).

The owner let us keep our gear out back of the café. While in town we met an American tourist. He stopped and gave us fish and a can of potatoes. As we walked through town we met a man at a garage. He stopped us to talk, and told us he was dying of cancer and could he take our picture. Then he gave us pop, chocolate bars, gum, and fish hooks. He never gave us his name, but we wished him the best. We gave him a hug, told him not to worry, to try to think positive, and thanked him.

Back at the café we asked if there were any phones we could use, as we needed to call the Sault. He told us there are no phones in this area, but he would drive us to White River and would drop us there to use a phone, as he was going through.

From a pay phone, we called the Bar X. They accepted the call and said they were very glad to hear from us, and thanked us for calling. He said not to go anywhere, stay until Sunday. He said that's only two and a half more days. He introduced himself as Lloyd Avery and would ship a horse out to us on Sunday from the ranch. He said to trust him and to stay there. It's only one hundred and ninety nine miles away. He said he would take Belva Dear back to the Sault to his place and doctor him up for us. He also sent a message out with a construction worker to confirm it. It read:

Dear Girls;

I got a phone call last night from a Port Arthur man saying you're in trouble with one horse. We will bring him back to the Sault and will doctor him up for you. Please phone me collect.

Howard Avery,

Bar X Ranch

It took us nearly two hours to hitch hike back to hammer lake. When we got there, the forestry crew came to the café and bought us dinner. They sure were a bunch of real nice guys. We got to see a twenty two pound Pike, caught by a seventy four year old American. It was interesting as I'd never seen a Pike before.

While we were at the café, we heard a terrible screeching of tires. There was a bad accident about two hundred feet past were the horses were grazing. We hoped they were not looking at the horses. Everybody ran out. There was a man and a woman in the vehicle. Looks like they hit a soft shoulder, crossed the road, and hit guard rail. Nearly rolled into the lake!

There were no phone in the area, and it was quite a panicky situation. A man jumped in his car and headed out for help. He drove twenty miles before he could get ahold of the police. The woman had to be taken to the hospital, looks like her arm was nearly severed. The forestry crew sure did a good job trying to stop the bleeding. She was approximately sixty years old. The husband was ok but badly shaken up. After the wrecker had taken the car away, and the police left, two of the crewman said there was only a big boulder stopping them from going into the lake. They found sunglasses and a twenty-six ounce of brandy (Chaubonnaire). It had been open and a couple of inches were missing. It had been tucked under a bush.

The owner of the Hammer Lake lodge gave us a huge house tent to use for two days while waiting for the Avery's to arrive. Belva Dear is eating well, but still limping. We soaked his leg for half an hour, put liniment on, and wrapped it.

While setting up for the night, we saw a black bear cub run off into the bush. The owners say that he comes there almost every day. Oh goody! We were given a huge bed to sleep on in the tent. We were just thinking of bedding down early, when we got company. Mr. Mast and his sons dropped in for half an hour and visited after a fishing trip.

I had the flashlight on and saw a huge moth on the wall. My God, it's the only fear I have. I HATE moths. I was just about ready to throw the flashlight at it when I realized it was only a small fly walking across the face of the flashlight. So thankful I noticed it before I threw it.

They left, and we went to bed. We laid there talking about what a strange day it has been. Thinking about the man that had cancer and gave all his stuff away, about the car accident, and about how strange it was to have no phones in the area. Finally got a campfire permit in Ontario. And this was our better day.

July 21 -22, 1965
Hammer Lake Lodge

The lodge has boats, motors, fishing equipment and cabins for rent. The gas station owner is Mr ... Just then a man came from the forestry, and introduced himself as Mr. Bernard. Sitting around and no place to go, we checked out the horses. Soaked Belva-Dears leg again today.

Played cards and drank the half bottle of brandy with Mr. Bernard. He gave us five dollars and we gave him a lamb's wool sweater we had found on the road. It fit him perfect. He took the shoes off Belva Dear for us. We kept them.

We had a good meal and a campfire tonight. Did nothing but lay back, just a lazy day, and went to bed around 10:45 pm

Got woken up at three in the morning. A truck and a trailer had pulled in. It was Lloyd Avery from the Sault with a friend Cal Marshal. They loaded up our two horses and left two. We never expected that, but really glad to know Frankie would be with Belva Dear.

Both horses they left were geldings. One named Sailor Boy, the other named Duke. They were our exchange horses for the week. They sent them for us to ride the one hundred and ninety nine miles back to the Sault. We all had a drink and Cal fell asleep on the end of the bed. Lloyd went out to his truck to sleep. So, we just crawled in the other end of the bed and slept fine.

He sure snored loud and the look on his face when he woke up was priceless. He looked around, appeared to be very confused, and left very quickly. We laughed most of the day when we thought about it. They headed out and said they'd see us at the Sault, good luck, and keep in touch.

A man working there was rude and insulting. The woman working there was run ragged. She was yelled at the whole time we were there. She cleans cabins, does the cooking, laundry, cleans, and pumps gas. She looked like she was ready to have a nervous breakdown. We heard the abuse for two days, and nearly stepped in to say something. She was a great woman. Tried to talk to her, and all she would say was, it,s ok, shh. We mentioned it to a few people in the area to watch out for her, they said, they would.

July 23, 1965
Leaving Hammer Lake.

While there, the wagon driver and a woman photographer came to see us. They asked if we knew where Jacques Pelletier was. We told them we had no clue, as we had not seen him in a couple of weeks. We asked who he was. The woman just said 'a photographer'. We were packed up, and ready to head for Wawa.

The horse that I was going to ride was hard to saddle this morning. I had to tie him down to get on him. We managed to make forty one miles today. We only stopped for them to get a drink. We are now on the outskirts of Wawa. Boy do these horses ever move. We both are exhausted trying to hold them in.

We made camp, and a man named Bill Young and his brother brought us out hay and oats for the horses. They wanted us to camp in town, but we had already unpacked. As soon as we took care of the horses, and we set up our bedding and gear, they took us to town and bought us a meal with coffee. They asked us to come for breakfast in the morning.

They dropped us back at camp. We were down and out like a light.

July 24, 1965
Wawa

Went into town and met the Young brothers, Jim and Bill for breakfast. They asked if we would please stay one more day as they have arranged for us to take a tour of the Algona Mines and Magpie Falls. The horses will be taken care of until we got back. We gladly accepted.

They showed us all over the area in Wawa. The Young's own or run the Wawa Bus lines. They went out of their way to show us a great time. We camped the night in Wawa. Jim and Bill came over to where we were camped, sat round the campfire, and talked until nearly midnight. I was telling them how it was quite a challenge to ride Sailor Boy. One of the brothers said, that somebody had to break him. I asked if that was a joke… right. Hmmm.

J.C. realized she was missing her wallet. Then she remembered she had it last at Hammer Lake. Jim called the OPP, and had them pick it up for her. We were down for the night.

July 25, 1965
Magpie Falls Tour

We met with Jim and Bill this morning. They had J.C.'s wallet there. We all had breakfast then headed out on the mine tour, to see Magpie Falls. We spent nearly all day touring, and thoroughly enjoyed ourselves. Two wonderful guys to spend a day with. We had dinner early and retreated to get all our gear ready so we could hit the trail early in the morning.

July 26, 1965
Leaving Wawa

Packed and ready to head out. I went to put the saddle on Sailor Boy. I was just tightening the cinch when he went crazy. He bucked and kicked, and snorted all at the same time. I just backed up. I was not having anything to do with this. He snapped the rope that was tied to a tree, and headed south on the dead gallop, trying to buck the saddle off. I, thought to myself, now what? This is not for me.

The other horse was just calm and being, saddled. I looked over at J.C. She said, "No, no, this one is mine!" Jim went into the bus depot to call the OPP for assistance. Bill had just driven up as J.C. was finished getting Duke ready. Bill and I jumped in his car and went after Sailor Boy. Here comes a man walking up the road with him. He told Bill that there were girls from Vancouver who were riding East, it may be one of theirs.

Bill rode the horse back to the bus depot, and I drove his car back. Then, he had to tie the horse to the tree to get him ready. Was I scared for a moment? I thought there was no way I was going to do this. But, they held onto him and coaxed me up into the saddle. Then they asked if, there was anything, we needed before we got to the Sault. He said to remember to hold him in, and that I was the boss.

Away we rode out of Wawa, and we were making time. The power of this animal is amazing. I never let up on the reins for a second. We were approximately twenty- two miles out. We had oats, and the grazing looked good. I told J.C. that I was afraid to get off my horse, in case he pulls the same thing he did this morning. Cautiously, I managed quite well.

Managed to saddle up. Travelled on until about 6:00 p.m. and a bus pulled up beside us. A man named Bob, from the Sault, said he had a bale of hay and some oats for us. Since it was a good spot, we pulled in off the road right there. I asked him who had sent them, and he replied "The Young's".

We took care of the horses, made a bonfire, started some dinner, and just sat around and talked. I told J.C. I had never ridden a horse with so much energy in my life. It was exhausting holding him back. We washed out one blanket, and hung it to dry. J.C. said her horse rides beautiful, and doesn't seem to want to run as much as the other one. These horses are taller and bigger. It's a long way up to the saddle compared to ours. You almost need something to stand on.

July 27, 1965
One Hundred and Seventy Miles to the Sault

Another day. Sailor is still hard to handle, but I managed to get on him. We were on the road about 9:00 a.m. We decided not to have breakfast until we stopped for grazing. While I was riding along the highway, I decided to put my jacket on. I was not holding my horse in as I was told. He was heading for the white line and there was traffic on the highway. Certainly was a frightening moment. Damn It! That's enough to make you pay more attention.

I still cannot get over the strength of this animal. I will bet he can run like the wind. What a difference in horses. J.C. said she was glad hers wasn't so frisky. Just then another bus stopped to let us know that up ahead about fifteen miles there would be some more hay and oats for the horses.

So, we stepped them up a bit. We made record time and stopped for a couple of hours. They are very thoughtful people. They always drop the hay near water. Laid out for a couple of hours and relaxed. I told J.C. that if we would have had these horses from the start, we would already be in the Maritimes.

A rodeo man stopped and asked when we would be in the Sault, as the radio station and TV want to know when they can pick us up. The same time, a transport driver had stopped and asked why we were back in the bush. I told him, to get way from the radio and TV people, and the rodeo man laughed.

Right after that another couple stopped to take pictures. They had heard on the radio that our horses were lame, and wanted to know which one. We told them they were ok now.

Packed up and headed out. We are glad the bugs aren't as bad. We believe that if the horse flies were like they were two weeks ago, we would not survive to reach the Sault on these horses.

Another bus arrived around 7:45 p.m. When he pulled off the road, he hit a soft spot, and was stuck. Half an hour later a woman and another passenger got off and onto another bus. A freight truck stopped and pulled the coach line out (Bob Young).

We were exhausted. Made a nice campfire, had hamburgers and coffee, and played several hands of rummy. It still amazes us at how well the horses travel, but still have to keep a tight rein on Sailor. He is a rebel. I asked J.C. if she would like to ride him for a day. I cant explain the look she gave me. Oh my!

We could hear the horses during the night but could see nothing. It could be a deer, as we have seen quite a few. Bears are not on our list, even for points. We checked the horses again about 3:00 a.m. and everything looked quiet. We managed to get a good night sleep.

Note: Since we'd been with these horses, we didn't have anyone stop to take pictures unless, we were grazing.

July 28, 1965
Sailor Boy and Duke

Just about ready to start out when the police stopped to see if everything was ok, and if there was anything we needed. We talked to them a few minutes then a lady pulled up and gave us seventy cents. We accepted it politely and rode on. We are now riding on a shoestring, but will not admit it.

Sailor Boy is not getting much easier to ride and it is tiring. I told J.C. if I were an expert and a better rider, I'd run him until he was pooped, and really make time. No comment came from my buddy. It was quite a jaunt.

The Bar X drops hay off for us twice a day, wherever we decide to stop. There is enough hay left between here and Wawa for another four horses. We cannot make the connection between the Avery's and the Young's. They have both gone more than out of their way, to help us, these last two hundred miles.

When we were about ten miles out of the Sault, Lloyd and Howard Avery came out on the highway and met us. They brought us dinner, T-Bone steaks and the works. Then they headed back to the ranch, the Bar X.

We were about six miles out from the Bar X when six riders came out of nowhere, surrounding us. Then, ten more, from the other side of the road. They were yelling, "String them up!" then, they all circled and introduced themselves. We got a real charge out of it. We all rode together into the Bar X. It really was great fun! They were quite amazed at how calm Sailor boy was. I asked if there was something we were supposed to know? Several of them laughed. Here we were eighteen cowboys and cowgirls. Lloyd said they were looking for a hanging tree. Then he said "Oh look how tame the horses are, we sent them out for you to break in." We all laughed. Real wonderful people. Lloyd is such a kidder, and very well liked, by all. It was a wonderful ride.

When we arrived, they took care of the horses and gave us a cabin. They said we could stay as long as we wished. We thanked them for the hay and oats that were dropped off the last couple hundred miles. Lloyd said he is not taking credit for that, as it was Jim Young. (Steel City Coach Lines). From Wawa who sent the oats and hay, they were good friends.

July 29 – Aug 4, 1965
Bar X

The horses looked ready. Belva-Dear is not limping at all. They looked great. First plan we had was to find a job and pick up some spare cash. Right away Jim Young offered us job at the Steel City Coach Lines.

The next day we met Mrs. Marie Young. She purchased us new jeans to wear to get our picture taken with the Toronto Star. Mr. Young is a Policeman, and owns a Palomino Stallion like we've never seen before. He has offered me the chance to ride him. He is breath taking, absolutely a 'perfect' horse. I thanked him and said he was too much horse for me.

If you can believe it or not, after being here three days, and wanting a rest, we went horseback riding. I rode Jim Young's horse 'Goldie'. He tried to buck me off. Yahoo, but he didn't. These animals are a different breed, than our range horses, believe me. I love my mare, and J.C. has decided to carry on with Belva-Dear. We started with them, and will end with them, if possible. They aren't near as high spirited, so we feel it safer near the highways. The other horses are great for very experienced riders. There is a vast difference in the ride. We are grateful during this journey to have had the experience to learn that difference.

That afternoon, we met John Gerahety and Lila Rahn. They run the Bar X trailer court. They asked us to join them for a cold beer. Well, when we got there we met a whole bunch of ranch folks, and had a great evening. We signed autographs. Lila and John then announced that we were 'pride of the bar' we sucked it up, and had lot's of laughs. Yes we stayed until closing time.

We were told that the World Famous Chuck wagon race crew, with Buddy Heaton, the buffalo rider, were going to be at the Sault tomorrow. We were asked to meet them, at the Avery arena and ride in with them on our own horses. We rode in and as we entered the circle, everyone, got introduced. They then announced that they were holding a benefit dance for the 'Long Distance Riders' tomorrow night at the Bar X. And they offered us new horses.

The owner of the World Famous Chuck Wagons, Cliff Clagget, got up and announced that the lead rider Lou Alwood's dad Dewane, used to work for him in B.C. for seven years. Here we had to come all the way to Ontario to meet. He said, These are brave women." Then he said, "Is it o.k. Buddy if she rides your Buffalo tomorrow?" Ride a Buffalo, My response to that request got a laugh.

Turned in around 1:00 am., and could still hear the party go on until the wee hours of the morning. We are staying at an island lake with the Young family. They offered us a job for a couple of weeks, cleaning the stagecoach buses, which we gladly accepted. The busses parked for a few days at a time, in a compound. Our job was to scour the inside of them thoroughly. The weather was good, and we were really enjoying our job.

Our cabin was over a small bridge with a stream running under it. We have, been totally blessed in meeting all the folks we have met on our journey east: The Avery' family, The Young family, and the Mills Family from the Sault area, and the hundreds of great people we have met across the country.

They had a benefit dance for us last night and it was a great turnout. Then asked to tell of our journey, on stage. I was glad people were asking questions. It made it very easy, as I'm not much of a public speaker. We sure had many laughs.

Later on J.C. played the guitar and sang. Everyone just loved her. She is very good, and has a wonderful singing voice. Everyone was dancing to it. I was amazed at her talent, as I'd heard her play only once at the Eddy family's place in Crawford B.C. Even though she has a noticeable stutter, when she sings it is clear as a bell.

Then they announced that Cliff Clagget and I would open the dance. Well, we did and I was very happy everyone joined in right away, as I've been known to have two left feet.

At the dance we met a wee gal about seven years old who had started a scrap book. She has our picture on the front of it, and wants our autograph. It was wonderful for kids to make scrap books regardless of what it's about. We thanked her and her mother for bringing her. Now I miss my five, year old daughter.

Buddy Heaton asked us if we would be interested to ride in an 'All Female' Rodeo. We now have been offered three jobs to ride in rodeos. Later that night he asked us if we would consider driving one of his chuck wagons from Sault Ste Marie, Canada to Hell, MI, USA to make a grand entry in the rodeo there. He said he wasn't kidding. That got us thinking about the covered wagon we followed. We asked if he knew them. "Hell No!" was his answer.

We met a thirteen year old gal named Debbie Kay Carter. She said she had been on TV also, that she was making records in eastern Canada, and has been on TV all over

North America. She is leaving for the P.N.E in Vancouver, B.C. Her father is a disc jockey who we met and spent time talking with at the Bar X last week. She wanted to ride my mare Frankie, so she rode her in the pasture for twenty minutes.

The next day, we heard her sing on the radio while we were cleaning buses. They announced her name as Debbie Laurie Kay. She has a great voice, and is so young. Her dad Dave Carter plays a big bass and Lloyd Avery calls the square dances. Together they are super.

Most people have brought their kids. It's amazing how much fun everyone is having. Had two dances with Cliff just before they pulled out, for Barry Ontario for their show the next day. He said to say hello to my dad, and to please remember when we write this book, to make sure we call his outfit the 'World Famous Chuck' wagons, not a 'rodeo'. Believe me, they are. He gave me a letter to give to my dad when we get back.

Note: Cliff Clagget is very much the gentleman. I actually had met him in 1959. He was seriously injured, in a race last year, rolled his outfit, broke his hip, arm, leg, and several ribs. It today shows in his stride, but he is no quitter. Believe me, the young riders have a hard time keeping up with him. He is top in his field. He says his home is in Nakusp, and has not been home for a year, as that's how long he's been in the hospital. The people who don't know him, have no idea what he has endured. My hat is off to him.

We have had a great time and the horses are like new. It will be strange riding them again after riding these other horses. We love our animals. Spent the next week cleaning buses and odd jobs, as well as visiting with the Avery's.

August 5 - 15, 1965
Steel City Coach Lines.

It is sunny and warm, and just the perfect day to work on buses. What we really like is, regardless of the weather, we both still have jobs, inside huge buses. We love it. After work we were supposed to go riding with Debbie Laurie Kay, and we forgot. Apparently we set the date two nights ago at the dance. She was very good about it, as she got to go riding with another family.

Lloyd's wife was there to pick us up to go to the lake. She made homemade chili, the best we'd ever eaten. We all played scrabble and had a great evening. They returned us back to the cabin about 11:00 p.m. and there was a message left there for us. It said she was from Bruce Mines. She said she came out to the Bar X to see us, sorry she missed us, and she wanted us to phone her. It was signed Denise Fex. She still wants to ride with us to the east coast.

We worked the rest of that week cleaning buses and made three hundred dollars. We both were extremely happy with that. For the past two days we have been at a beach party out at the Avery's. We were asked what our ages were, and I said I had turned twenty nine in Saskatchewan, and J.C. said she thought she had missed her birthday. She said I am now thirty four. We had a huge fire and wiener roast on the beach. We sat around the fire until late in the evening and slept well. Had a great time.

Note: Until this summer of 2013, looking back, August the 15th was her birthday, but no one knew.

Aug 16 – 24, 1965
Winding Down

Mr. Howie James put a hard surface on the new shoes and Frank Hill shod our horses. We let them out Saturday and ran with them a bit. The next day we rode them around a little in the corrals to get a feel being back on them again. They really were in good spirits.

We have had a wonderful time working at the Steel City Coach Lines. We went back the next day too visit all the fellows we had worked with; Paul, Shane, Bob, Jim Young, Lucien, Stan, and Ken Allen. Later that night we went to a movie.

The next morning we met Howard Avery and he claims that the 'Wagon Master' and his partner said they were going to travel with us when we left the city. He's telling everyone that. Then he laughs. His daughter says Lloyd is retiring this year and hopes for a Grand Champion with his horse Danny Boy next year. We wish him the best, 'what a horse'.

The next day we ran into Bill Young from Wawa. He said there was an offer out there for us. He suggests we look into going home on skidoos. We haven't seen what they are yet, but it sounds interesting. We had a roast beef dinner with Bill Young, then went to the Bar X to say goodbye and thank them for everything.

The next morning we went to see Howard Avery and the Rohns. Howard gave us sixty-two dollars proceeds from the dance. We were surprised. We thanked him, He said it was the folks at the dance. Well, we met some genuine folks there and will not soon forget them. We decided to take our own horses. He said if we ever come back, we could have our pick of horses. Went and met other people that we spent time with, thanked them for everything, wished them well, and told them we would be leaving in the morning.

Aug 25, 1965
Leaving the Sault

We are pulling out this morning. Phew is it very hard to say so long. They were such great people we've met here this last month. They have become like family. We have packed up and sent parcels home. J.C. is sending her jeans home as a souvenir of how she arrived in the Sault.

We went to the barn and packed up all our remaining gear. We rode on to Howie James home to say our goodbyes to him and his family. Marie has shown us how to take the back dirt road to the highway. We then went to the coach lines and said our final goodbyes to Jimmy and the boys.

We were going to stop at Lloyd Avery's, but we met him on the highway. He said as long as we aren't passed Montreal, he would send us new horses if we needed them. Then he insisted on giving us fifteen dollars each for a chicken dinner tonight. We stopped at their house to see <u>Mildred</u>. She was washing clothes. She took several pictures of us with the kids, then we pulled out. There were tears in our eyes when we left. We will never forget the past month. They are great people and sure made it possible for us to complete this journey. Marie James came out several times before we hit the highway to make sure we were on the right road. The wonderful people we met at the Sault, we will never forget.

We travelled through the Ojibwa Indian Reservation. Several kids came running out and asked us for a ride. We told them sorry we couldn't do that. They then picked up stones and threw them at us. I turned my mare towards them. Boy did they take off. They dropped their stones and ran.

We rode on a ways and stopped across from the Ojibwa crafts, and went inside to have a look. Real awesome work! The kids were following us everywhere and since they were very calm, we let them pet the horses. Nice kids. Jay said I actually said that with a half smile.

Marie James and a friend drove up to see us, and said they may see us later tonight. Along the highway, a service man asked us in for a coke. Riding along the highway, a young girl ran out and stopped us. She asked us to stay at their place tonight. She said her grandpa has a pack of pigs that he hooks up to wagon and drives people around in. We both thought that we would like to see this. We went up the road to their place and they told us, that if we put the horses in the barn they would feed them. They make you feel at home right away. They asked us to stay over for the night, and we accepted. We chose to sleep in the hay loft, as there were lots of people there. We had a great sleep. Marie and the family would have a good laugh to see us riding pigs. I remember riding a pig when I was a kid, and the outcome was not good, as it ran into the pig house with my legs wrapped around him. There was only room for him. That was not good for either of us. (My mom was not impressed).

Aug 26, 1965
Leaving For Bruce Mines.

Up in the morning and went into the family's' house for breakfast. We had eggs, toast, coffee, and a great visit. They feel they may be related to the Wagon Master. We told them that it was a privilege meeting them, and thanked them for the night stay. There were lots of laughs, and a great time.

We started out again this morning with no idea what time it is, but it looks like rain. We have even lost track of the date. We made about sixteen miles then stopped for afternoon grazing near a farm. The owner said we could put our horses in his field. It was raining and there was a café nearby. We had a bowl of soup each and we split a hamburger.

When we got back to the horses, the rain had stopped. We decided to sit back and relax awhile. We had just sat down when a big voice came over the fence. He sounded angry and wanted to know how many cards we had left of theirs that his ex-partner had given us? We assumed he was the other half of the covered wagon.

He said he came out to warn us about sending any on, as his first partner was 'a crook' and it wouldn't do any good. We told him we were disappointed in him coming so far to relay a message like that. We actually were. I told him we were looking forward to running into the both of them. I asked, "Why do you think we would pass on any of your cards, let alone have any of them?"

Then, as he was leaving I asked him to please wait a minute, I told him that someone, had stopped and talked to us about a month ago, and gave us one of his cards. He had told us he was leaving for Montreal. During that week, some young kids kept coming into camp bugging us in the middle of the night for our autographs. We remembered we had nothing to write on, so just to get rid of them; the only thing we found was that post card that had been given to us by Jacques. We both signed our names on it and gave it to them. That's the only card we ever had. He then laughed. I think he may have just had a bad moment. He then stayed and chatted for about half an hour, turned and walked away from the ranch where we were grazing. He walked to the highway and thumbed a ride back down the road.

We packed up and travelled on this afternoon. We ran into Denise Fex just before Bruce mines and she asked us in for a hamburger. She told us when we get to town, we have permission to leave the horses at the racetrack. We rode on into Bruce Mines, had a milkshake and took the animals to the track. Denise called a man named Al Crockford, and he brought us out some oats. Soon there was dozen of people there.

Al Crockford phoned a Mrs. Cameron, whose family Mary Bosonquet stayed part time with, while riding across Canada in 1939. We had never heard of Mary Bosonquets' ride. We found that quite interesting. We got invited to stay with the Cameron's the next day.

We told a long story to the local reporter. There were far too many people around. Denise asked us to stay with her tonight, so we accepted her invitation. We went down with her to have dinner and a drink.

There were a lot of people who wanted to talk to us when we took the horses to the track, and also at the café. J.C. had stayed at the café to talk to the people, while Denise rode Frankie and I rode Belva-Dear to the track. We stayed overnight and visited.

August 27, 1965
Heading For Dayton

We got up early and headed for Dayton. We met the Crockford kids on ponies at the turn off into Dayton, (where Mary spent her winter). We met Harold Gordon, Mrs. Cameron's brother while he was haying. The two young kids were sent to show us where the Cameron's lived.

When we arrived we met the Cameron family, who told us about Mary Bosonquet. She had ridden a horse from B.C to the Great Lakes, then sent them by rail to Sault Ste Marie. Back then there were no roads through that area. Then she rode onto Montreal and down to New York the following year. Edith and Gordon Cameron showed us Mary's book and said she now lives back in England. They could not believe that twice in twenty six years, that they would have women who rode across the country, stay with them. We got a chuckle out of that.

We put the horses in the barn, unpacked our gear, tended the animals, and they drove us around to show us the sights. We went to meet an elderly doctor in a lodge at a beautiful bay. We all had dinner, talked until about ten, and had a great visit.

It was wonderful meeting these people. Then we slept outside under an oak tree, watched the stars through the branches and reminisced about the past month, and all our experiences. What would we do if we had to do it again? We had some good laughs. Still don't know the answer to why. Why? How can I answer that? J.C. said, "Well, Why?" I said to her, "Same reason you came I guess". I got no response. We then called it a night.

During the night I layed back thinking of when I was a child riding off on horseback, out back of our ten acres on the mountain. I'd sit by a creek for hours, day dreaming of someday when I would make this journey.

August 28 - 29, 1965
Leaving Dayton

We were up early and had breakfast with the family. We thanked them so much for their thoughtfulness, then headed out to meet Mrs. Skerton. Another place Mary had stayed. We had tea with her, talked about our trip to here, and enjoyed the visit. Then we headed out for Spanish.

I noticed Belva-Dear has a small sore on his leg, but he's not limping. We came out on highway number seventeen near Iron Bridge, heading for Spanish. It is quite cold this afternoon, and is starting to rain. We only stopped an hour for the horses today, then took cover at Spanish. We rubbed ointment on Belva-Dear, cared for the horses, set up shelter, and had an early night. Whew its cold.

Next morning we were up early and J.C. is not feeling well. I got that 'look' when I asked her if she wanted the liniment. We spoiled ourselves and had breakfast in a small cabin along the route.

We had only travelled a few miles when a vehicle stopped to talk to us. They asked if we would ride in the parade in their town of Massey tomorrow. They said they would like us to lead the parade.

The next day they held up the parade for us. The horses behaved beautifully, until the pipe band went past. We continued through town and the fellow riding with us introduced himself as Karl Liski. He said they owned the Ponderosa Ranch, and he has invited us to stay over with them tonight.

We headed into the fair grounds and they announced for the two lead riders of the parade to go to the judging area. J.C. won first place on Belva-Dear for the 'Best Western Horse Rider'. She was just beaming, GOOD FOR HER! We really had a great time. They presented us both with a small bottle of perfume. It was very nice of them.

We headed out for the ranch, and there were dozens of people there. We put the horses in the barn, and they insisted on taking care of them. Then we were invited in for a beer with all the people. We stayed for a couple of hours and had a wonderful time getting to know about the area, swapping horse stories, and the journey we have been on.

Karl and Myrtle Liski asked us to go back to the fairgrounds, and then out to the legion, and onto another club. They told us not to worry about the horses as they were cared for.

During that evening, we met a lot of great folks. People thought it was quite neat that 'Massey' the town we were in, was my mother's maiden name. They announced it at the bar. Thank you to the Liski family and their friends. They have an exclusive place; a really old ranch house with three hundred acres on the Spanish River. We had a great stay-over with them.

We were told that some people we met in Espanola heard we were here, and are going to drive out tomorrow to meet us along the way. They also said to let us know, they are going to bring a lunch with them. Called it a night around midnight.

August 30, 1965
Heading for Espanola

We thanked the Liski family for the wonderful time we had, and managed to be on the road by 8:00 a.m.

We arrived at the Espanola turnoff around noon when we are greeted by the family who said they would bring lunch out to us today. They introduced themselves as Mrs.

Viola Spence and company. What a spread: corn on the cob, tomato sandwiches, chicken, carrots, cucumbers, apple pie and tea. All on a table, they even brought a table.

There were a lot of kids around. The horses had their water, and were grazing, and of course, all the kids wanted to pet them (Thank You Lord, school starts next week!).

They put on a spread that was out of this world, and we thanked them so much for their time. We didn't get started back on the road until 5:00 p.m. We had just pulled out when an elderly couple stopped to give us each a cold pop, and we got our picture taken with them. Thanked them and started out again.

We ran into Karl Liski who was on his way back to the ranch. He said he just came back from the dentist, as he had fallen off his barn roof last week. We had a good day travelling, but lost track of the miles.

We've decided to camp for the evening outside of Webbwood in a field, as there is water and excellent grazing. Gave the horses their tonic. What faces they make! Belva-Dear has a slight limp. We checked his front hoofs and they look o.k. We rubbed him with liniment again.

We built a great lean-to tonight, and only had a snack as the lunch this afternoon was good for two days. It started raining pretty hard, but not as cool as it has been. We decided not to have a fire tonight as it's a little too damp, and besides its nearly ten p.m.

Two guys stopped by to see if we would like a drink. We said we had a long day but thank you anyways. They were very polite, left, and said that maybe they would see us another time then. All is well, and we bedded down for the evening.

August 31, 1965
Heading for Sudbury

It got quite chilly during the night. Actually, miserable and cold. It's going to be good to get to the other side of Sudbury. Raining hard, and kind of a miserable way to start the day, but we have to move on.

We were on the radio and TV again, as we'd been told by the first vehicle that stopped us. They asked us how far we had come today. I told them, "From the field behind us". They said, "Oh, do you know you are on TV?" We did not, but guess we will, as there is a Sudbury news cruiser just up ahead of us.

The rain helped as people never got out of their vehicles, they just waved and tooted their horns. That's better than getting wet, as it was really coming down. We both felt like drowned dogs. J.C. said we are drowned rats not dogs.

The Sudbury Star got their pictures and story, then we pulled out heading for Sudbury again. At 4:30 p.m. arriving in the outskirts a Mr. Miller from the Bar M Ranch met us and invited us to his place. He has riding stables.

We were following him in his car when a man hollered out his window so loud he scared us. Then he roared his engine, blew his horn, and took off. Frankie spooked and went down on her knees again quite badly. Both knees were bleeding. She goes down nearly every time she is suddenly frightened, where Belva-Dear would run.

A rancher from the area saw what happened, and stopped. He asked if I was o.k. and took a look at her. He said it wasn't that bad, and believe me she will be just fine. He went to his pick up and got some 'Hydrocortisone Nupercainal B F. Anesthetic Ointment' for the horses. He said that she wasn't limping and that was good. He said some people just do not think sometimes, and they appeared intoxicated.

Another TV man stopped us to take pictures. There must be a lot of TV stations in the area. Another rancher stopped us and invited us to come to their place. We told him we were heading to the Bar M Ranch. He said "And so am I". It sure seems like a long way out there.

Mr. Miller, his son, and two friends came to meet us, which was one of the people who had just asked us. They insisted we get in the car and take a ride to the ranch. They said we were wet enough, and that's the truth. We were drenched. The son and a friend led the horses back.

They have a real nice spread. They said they were just starting up and their house wasn't quite finished yet, but it would be by September for the 'Harvest' dance. The clubhouse has no roof, but will be done by then also. They have the nicest stables that either one of us had ever seen.

They brought out enough vet supplies to stock a hospital, then, took care of Frankie's knees, and went to check Belva-Dears legs. They are so helpful and we are thankful for the help.

We all sat around, ate, and talked until midnight. There we were again, on TV. They kind of had the story a little mixed up. They said we went through ninety six shoes for the horses, and wore out six pair of jeans. I myself am still in my tattered original, and purchased one pair at the Sault. They also said it cost us two thousand dollars, and the truth is we have spent less than eight hundred. We do our own cooking, and live out in the bush a great deal of the time. We did buy new Stetsons.

We are more than half way. We know the horses have been taken care of. Laid in bed and watched the Late Show. Then we watched us again on TV. I do not feel I look like what I see. J.C. said that also. Guess we never see ourselves as we really are. Who are those two old gals? Now we are old gals, last time we looked like old prospectors (It is nice to still be able to laugh).

They have a Westminster Chime clock outside our door. It chimes ever hour and sure sounds nice. It rained and chimed all night. At least it wasn't cold. Guess you could say we had a great night's sleep.

September 1, 1965
Leaving Sudbury

Up at 7:30 and having breakfast. Mr. Miller just got home from the graveyard shift at the mine. They asked us to stay another day, but we explained how we had to make up time. They said they understood. We had a big breakfast and lots of coffee with the family.

We thanked the Miller family for all their help. It was a blessing running into them. We had a wonderful time and managed to get all our gear dry. He gave us a package of anesthetic ointment for the horses to take, and we thanked him again. The horses look great and Belva-Dear is not limping.

Just as we were leaving, we were told, a man called last night, and said he would be dropping off some oats on the side of the highway. Mr. Miller and his oldest son, with a friend rode out eight miles with us to see us off. It was great company.

Travelled another half hour approximately. Met two fellows in a pickup truck. They said they wanted to take a horseback trip to Vancouver, but couldn't get anyone else to go with them.

Right behind us, it looks like a fair size thunderstorm is rolling in. A woman stopped to take pictures as we headed for shelter. She asked us in until after the storm. We tied the horses out back and covered our gear. Headed for shelter at her place.

This one didn't last long. The lady gave us warm water to clean Frankie's knees. We applied ointment and wrapped her leg again. It wasn't as swollen today, but we will still take it easy for another day. We left the horses out to graze and crawled under a tarp for a short nap. Another storm looks like it may come in, but it seems quite a distance away.

We left the area and covered another ten miles. Figured we did well today, considering we never got away until 11:00 a.m. The horses are doing well. We pulled into a park and camped with the owners. It was raining lightly so we set up a small shelter and camped for the night.

The Sudbury Star

7th Year—No. 196   WEDNESDAY, SEPTEMBER 1, 1965   Pages 15 to

Sudbury Star News

September 2, 1965
Sturgeon Falls

We slept in this morning. It was cold and damp. We managed to be on the road by 9:00 a.m. Went straight through to Sturgeon Falls. Travelled thirty miles, stopping only half an hour to let the horses graze, and water them.

We signed several post cards, books, and autographs when we stopped to get mail from home. We got our mail from the Kodak Company. They found our pictures, and will forward them to Grand Falls in New Brunswick , which will be our next mailing address. I also got mail from an old friend Rose Plant. She says its 'fan' mail. Got a good laugh out of that. Phoned home to talk to my little girl. All is well at home.

They took pictures of us from a plane today at Sturgeon Falls and gave us a free motel room at the Lincold Motel. We were the guests of Joe Fortin. Took care of the horses, and called it a night.

Leaving Lincold Motel

September 3, 1965
Leaving Sturgeon Falls

Last night at the laundromat, we managed to get all our gear and horse blankets washed up. Talked to several people while we were there. The man that took our pictures from the plane came and gave us some real nice photos. It was great being able to see our tracks behind us going down the highway.

During our overnight stay we met a few great people and they were good company. We were given a half sack of oats prior to leaving today. We stayed up until 2:00 last night answering letters.

Pulled out around 9:00 a.m. and travelled on to just this side of North Bay at noon. Grabbed a snack, and played a few hands of Canasta. Finally pulled out at 6:00 p.m., just as far as the outskirts, as we were waiting for pictures.

A Watkins man came over to talk to us. He gave us a bottle of liniment, two jars of ointment, some suave, and some cream for our hands.

Other people stopped us and said we were in the New Brunswick newspaper in 'French'. Several French people have stopped us just to take pictures. I cannot figure out one word of what they are saying. Until this day I have not had it translated.

We finally got our pictures and moved on for another six to ten miles east of North Bay to camp for the night. It was clear and cool, which sure helps with the mosquitos. First time we seen the little dipper since we left British Columbia.

September 4, 1965
Leaving For Mattawa

Up at 8:15 a.m. All appears well, and it looks like it's going to be a great day. As we are riding through town, we came across a seven year old boy who was sitting by the road crying. He had a bike accident and his fender was all bent. He said he couldn't ride his bike with tears in his eyes. We fixed it for him and gave him a quarter for him to get a pop. We said to tell his mom that we gave him the quarter for the pop to help him feel better.

Belva-Dears leg seems to be sore again. We pulled in beside a creek and soaked it for twenty minutes. Put liniment on his leg and wrapped it. We let the horses graze for an hour. The mosquitos are starting up again. Damn things!

We are getting near the end of our oats, so we will be picking some up with groceries tomorrow. We are pulling out. Its 4:30 and we are leaving for the Mattawa area.

We made about thirty six miles today, then set up a shelter and hoped to keep half dry. As we were grazing late in the afternoon, and having a bite to eat, a couple from Vancouver came over to talk to us. We all stood under the four by six foot tarp and tried to keep dry. We talked for an hour and really enjoyed their company. It is extremely hard to tolerate these darned mosquitoes.

September 5, 1965
Deux Riviers

Its quite cool this morning. Looks like it might be another good day. Leaving camp just before 8:00 a.m. It rained hard most of the night and everything got soaked. The horses were travelling quite well until a bird flew passed us, and Frankie panicked again and fell on her knees, taking the scabs off, when they were nearly healed. She is so nervous.

So, we pulled in and camped this side of Deux Riviers. We went to look for drinking water. By the time we got settled, it was dark. The water for the horses laid on the ground in pools, and smelled like gas to us, but they drank it. We bedded down wet and cranky. We are not allowed to be cranky, just wet. In the past few days we've had fairly good grazing spots. I wish I understood why the mare is so afraid of so many things. She even jerks if I cough.

NOTE: Had a visitor last night, about half an hour after we were down for the evening. I thought my partner was quite restless. Her arm hit the back of my head, then she bumped into my back. For several moments it didn't dawn on me that she was in front of me and not behind me. I laid there perfectly still. I could feel 'heavy' from my neck to my butt, and for some reason it was quite calming. I was not frightened at all. A thought never came to my mind, but just then J.C. said "Did you hear that?" When I tapped her and said ssshhh, it got up and moved right away. I could feel the push as it moved. We just stayed quite still, put our heads under the covers, and actually slept quite well.

We could see no trail in the grass in the morning, as the horses were grazing all around. They had not made a sound at all. We talked about it, and suspect it may have been a small deer. With all the equipment being carried by horses, and us underneath the tarps and all, there may not have been any human scent they could detect. We will never know.

I told J.C. that I thought it was a wonderful experience, as how often do you ever get to experience something like that? I know it was not a horse, as they are tethered quite a ways back from us always. The only other animal we had seen in the area in the past day, was a wolf. Could not imagine a wolf laying down next to a human. It was quite a heavy weight. We may have heard from the horses had it been a wolf. It will remain a mystery that I will never forget, but feel blessed by the experience.

September 6, 1965
Heading for Pembrook

We pulled out around 9:00 a.m. and Frankie's knee is still a little swollen. She is travelling well despite of it, but we are still going to travel slower and take more time as the traffic is real wicked today.

We travelled about eight miles, came to a motel, and the grazing in the area looked great. There was a place to turn the horses out in. We found out it was a long weekend, and with the traffic being as it is, we made the decision to stop. It would also do Frankie good to rest one more day. She does not limp, and there is no swelling at all.

The horses are staked out back. We noticed railroad tracks. We double checked, as we remembered the last railroad incident too well. Then we noticed there is a fence between the tracks and the field, so we felt much better.

A rancher dropped off oats and a bale of hay for the horses. We settled in for the day as we both could also use the rest. J.C. is not feeling that great, and my knees are still in bad shape. We are very thankful to be where we are for today anyways. We hope to be in Quebec within four or five days.

Frankie would be fine and not stumble, if she would pick up her one leg. She always digs it in when she walks, but has done so since day one. Still, the vet says there is nothing wrong with her. Other than that, she is great to ride, and loves to be combed. Belva-Dear always kicks you when you comb his backside, and now bites. You always have to be cautious around him.

We settled in and did a load of laundry and played cards. J.C. went to bed early. We finally got a chance to dry out some more of our gear.

September 7, 1965
Pembrook

We were up at 7:00 a.m. Horses had just finished their last bale of hay. We were packed up and rolling by 8:00 a.m. heading for Pembrook. We've decided to take it easy over the long weekend, and only travel half days until the traffic dies down.

We only travelled four hours this morning when a vehicle pulled over. The man talked to us for just a few minutes. He told us he had a ranch up the road a few mile, and would love to have us as their guests if we had the time. We thanked him and explained what we had planned for the next few days, and would love to accept their invitation. They told us to look for the Ponderosa sign a few miles up the road.

We arrived by 2:00 p.m. They introduced themselves as the Angus Campbell family, and said they were pleased we stopped in. He is the Mayor of Pembrook, and in the next election he would like to run for MP.

A friend of his took us on tour of the McDonald jewelry store. The Campbell's gave us a town house to stay in and asked if we were looking for jobs. We were offered jobs driving tractor in the cornfield. Also we were offered jobs for the winter if we wished to stay. We thanked them, but we definitely need to reach Halifax before winter, and I have a little girl who is waiting for her mom to return.

I put a shoe on Frankie last night. We had dinner with the family and had a wonderful visit. Everything seems to be falling into place. We talked until around 11:30 p.m. then went to the townhouse for the evening. Wrote down the day's events and planned for tomorrow. We really learned a lot about the area and thanked them so much. They were great people.

I used the rest of the liniment on myself and put ointment on Frankie's knees again. They really look good. Before we left, J.C. phoned her friend Sharon McMullen in regards to her mail. I called home and talked to my mom and my daughter Dana, who starts grade one this week. Sure miss all my family and I'm sure J.C. does as well.

My mother said my father is very glad I have finally decided to take this journey, but still can't believe I actually did it. He said he really believed it was just a childhood dream. I returned a message to my father: "Sometimes when I wake up, I feel it is. Thank you. P.S. I love you".

Heading out from the Ponderosa in the Pembrook area

September 8-9, 1965
Heading for Renfrew area

We pulled out this morning after thanking the Campbell family for a wonderful stay. We truly enjoyed our visit with them, thank-you so much. It was great travelling in the morning, then the rain started about 11:30.

It was really coming down in buckets when a woman drove up and asked if we would like to stay at their farm for the night. She said her husband had passed us on the road earlier and told her how to find us. We had surpassed our half days ride, and accepted.

We rode on to their farm and were introduced to Mable and Herb Smith. They were so friendly. Once we got unpacked, and the horses were taken care of, she said "after you get dried off, we wanted to know if you would like to go to the fair in town with us tonight?"

Herb said he gave the horses a bale of hay and some oats, and there was lots of water. After drying off we headed for the fair and sure enough, we ran into Buddy Heaton and Cliff Clagget with the chuck wagons. Buddy spotted us and yelled across the room "I told you they would make it!" We had a great visit. We introduced the Smiths to the bunch traveling with Claggets World Famous chuck wagons.

They insisted we all have a beer with them, all sitting around in a group on bales of hay. We thanked them, had fun, and caught an hour of the fair. Went for dinner then Mable and Herb took us over to Portage du Fort. We all had a couple more drinks and headed back to the farm. We visited until 12:30 a.m., checked the horses, and then bedded down for the night. We talked about making a day tomorrow, as J.C. is feeling a lot better and the traffic has died down.

The past three days have been really great. We met some wonderful folks, and oh yes... we were told a newspaper reporter was looking for us and had missed us at the Ponderosa

QUEBEC

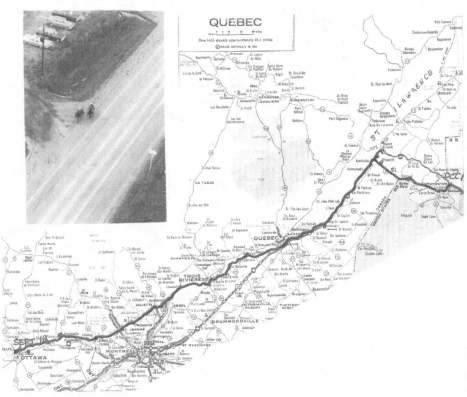

Map of Quebec

September 10, 1965
Quebec

The horses are really feeling their oats this morning. We were packed and ready to start out in a new province at 1:00 p.m. today. We met the mayor (female) of Portage du Fort. She gave us clippings from the Ottawa Citizen Newspaper, and told us of a short cut to Shaw Ville. We really enjoyed talking with her. She introduced herself as Mrs. Elsie Gibbons.

We travelled on and missed the turn. She drove out to show us where to go. We ended up stopping at Stacks Corner for grazing. An editor from Shaw Ville came out to meet us with a retired Minister. He wanted her to take pictures of himself and us riders in front of his church. We got talking about the horses and she noticed Frankie's knees and said she knew a vet who would come out and take a look at them.

She called from the church. He came out within half an hour. He walked them around and checked them out thoroughly. He told us they appeared to be in VERY good shape for all the miles they had travelled. I asked if it was a wise decision to carry on with them. He laughed and said, "Well are you girls up to it?" then gave us some blue ointment for Frankie and wished us all the best. He would not take a dime, stating it was his pleasure. Then he told us to keep doing whatever it was we had been doing. We thanked them and left Stacks Corner at 5:30 p.m. for Shaw Ville.

We camped in the back of a school yard. Had a bite to eat, took care of the horses, set up camp, and crawled in for the night. It's been quite windy, but not too cold. No mosquitos!

September 11, 1965
Heading East

Slept well last night, and we got up at 8:20 a.m. Gave the horses the last of their oats, then packed up and hit the trail. We travelled until noon, and we're just outside of Queyon.

Several people stopped to talk to us from different parts of the country. It has to be holiday season. A man brought some oats out for the horses, then went in and got them water as well. We packed the oats with us, as they had already had their fill this morning. We thanked him, and he left. We never did get his name, as there were two other groups of people asking questions. More often we do not get the chance to thank the people we need to.

We got a nice fire going and cooked a meal. Like we've said before, there's nothing better than a good hot meal cooked over an outdoor campfire when it's cold out. We had hamburger, corn, potatoes and a pot of coffee. A family came by to talk to us while we were making dinner. We asked if they would like to join us. They just wanted to take pictures, and left.

We travelled on a few more miles this afternoon and ran into another family and they asked us to stay overnight with them. They asked if we would mind if a few of their friends came over to join us. We were so exhausted. After visiting a few hours with the family, someone, said, we were fabulous. Well, that, for some unknown reason struck me funny. I had to laugh, I mean LAUGH.

J.C. said," what is the matter with you"? I could not stop laughing, and felt like a damn fool. I said to her to 'Please Shut Up'. Everyone was looking at me. When I got my breath, I said "Fabulous" and laughed even harder. By this time I had everyone laughing. Later I tried to apologize and told them I was sorry and that I just must be tired. Then the laughter started up again.

We visited until nearly eleven then headed out to camp. We had a great time, and yes, lots of laughs. We had to move out as we have a very busy day planned for tomorrow. We thanked them for the invitation. They were all loads of fun.

Another newspaper came out to interview us. I told J.C. to tell them everything, as I was going for a nap. We won't have to rely on the water soaked diary. We'll just keep the newspaper clippings if they send them on home.

The diary had been stomped on, through a flood, left behind one day, and not easy to remember every daily event (But We Did). Camped near Hull.

September 12-15, 1965
Back in Ontario

We went through Hull, I called an old air force buddy (Doc Moore's). She wasn't home but her sister Coleen came out to meet us. We called around and got an offer to put our horses up at the Mountain Road Riding Stables until we were ready to leave. We were told the horses were in excellent hands.

We drove into Ottawa and we were one block from the Parliament building. Spent the evening with the Moore's and found out there was eight more air force buddies from the past, in the area. A get together was planned.

We decided to go check on the horses the next morning, to make sure they had everything they needed. Spent the afternoon touring the Gatineau's. We ended up staying five days touring the city. A couple nights we got together with my old buddies and had a wonderful visit.

Went and saw the Parliament buildings, picked up groceries, and had a great visit. If it were not for the trail ride, I may have never seen them again as they live the opposite side of Canada. We all move on, reminisce over the 'remember when times' that seemed so long ago.

On the 15th, a man called and said he would put our horses out to pasture outside of Hull, to graze until we were ready to go. He trucked them out of town for a couple of days and said to call him when we were ready to leave. He took all our gear as well, and said he would meet us on the highway when we were ready. He introduced himself as Jon.

We spent the next couple of days staying with a couple of other buddies.We stayed our last night with the Moore's, and thanked them all, 'Wasn't That a Party!'

September 16, 1965
Leaving Ottawa

Said goodbye to the Moore's, and left a note for Doc. She had gone to work by the time we were ready to leave. Called Jon and he said he would meet us on the highway at 2:30 p.m. We grabbed a ride to meet him. It was only a couple miles out.

As we were saddling the horses, people were stopping to talk to us. Jon helped us saddle up. We thanked him so much, and he would not take anything for caring for the horses. He gave us his address to send a card along the way.

By 3:30 we headed for the Lachute area back in Quebec. It sure was a long way around the city. It seemed like miles before we stopped for the night. We had lots of advice from well-meaning people, on which route to take, but no water for the horses.

We pulled in off the road and we could see a farm about a quarter of a mile away. Then J.C. walked quite a ways across the field to see if we could get water for the horses. It was a fenced in area. When she arrived, the man asked her where we were located. She pointed out towards the highway. He said, " If you just go a few hundred yards up the highway, there is a gate that you could bring the horses in through to graze for the night."

He drove her down to the gate and opened it up for us. He said we could water the horses now and before we leave in the morning. We were very thankful for the invitation. He told us to ride in and camp for the night.

We visited for half an hour. They said we would find lots of water on the route we were travelling. There were lots of gas stations and restaurants. Seeing we have a large bucket everything is perfect. We thanked them, then said we had to get an early start in the morning. We asked if they minded that we graze just inside their fence out by the highway, as it was getting late.

They told us to come back after we are settled, and they would put the coffee on. We went back to thank them, and went in for coffee and cake. It never entered my mind prior to this trail ride, that we would meet so many wonderful people. We were down by 10:40 p.m. We could hear the traffic off and on all night, but managed to sleep.

September 17, 1965
Heading for Lachute

Up at 8:00 a.m. It was cool and damp last night, but we managed to sleep quite well. We packed up and headed out. The horses are frisky and stepping out well.

We went on to just this side of Lachute, along the Ottawa River, and camped for noon grazing. There was water. We couldn't have a camp fire as we did not have a Quebec fire permit. We had cold bean sandwiches. They were really good. Played a couple hands of rummy, checked out the horses' shoes, gave them a quick comb down, and headed out around 3:30.

Very beautiful country through here. One thing that is great, there isn't as many people stopping to talk. It sure helps in making better time. It could be the language barrier. If all goes well, we plan to arrive in Halifax in thirty one days.

We travelled on to this side of Rte. Au Chime. It's raining, but warm. We made camp and crawled in for the night. We talked about the past week, (the stopover in Ottawa), all the people we had met, and the bugs on the prairies (we may never forget them). We wondered about the name of the place we were in, and that RTE. might mean turn here.

We have not met too many English speaking people. I tried to talk with one gentleman and he just shrugged. We chose to have it mean, 'cannot speak English'. We are having a time finding anyone to tell us where we can obtain a fire permit for the province of Quebec.

September 18, 1965
Highway 41

We slept fairly well last night. The first thing J.C. said when she got up, was that she had had a bad dream last night, and woke up to hatched spider eggs all over her. Only believe me, it wasn't a dream, there WAS a hatch of tiny baby spiders all over her. (What a dance). I instantly grabbed my sleeping bag and checked it. Phew, thank God there was none in mine. Haven't any idea where they came from. She finally stopped swinging her sleeping bag, whew, what a moment. I yelled to her "Get away from me, get away from me!" We had no idea where they came from. But, I am sure, there are none living after that. That was almost as bad as the bee's. I couldn't stop laughing.

Getting a good start today, up and on the road by 8:15. Frankie's leg has no swelling. I will put a new shoe on her this afternoon and take it easy travelling. We are heading for Trios Rivers for tonight.

We travelled twenty five miles then stopped for noon grazing. I checked the mare when we stopped for water, and she hasn't been limping this afternoon. I trimmed and put a new shoe on her, and she always stands so well for it. There is still no swelling in her leg. We let her stand in water above her knees for twenty minutes this morning, hoping the cool water would help.

While we were camped, we wrote a few thank you letters to people we had stayed with on the trail. While we were in Ottawa, we had spent twenty five dollars that we didn't have in our budget. Will have to tighten our belts for a week.

It is a cool light drizzle, and we hope that is all. I have lost my rain slicker along the way, so I won't be able to bug J.C. anymore about losing things. Today we decided to not take such long stops while grazing, as the days are getting shorter, and the nights are really long. We decided that wherever we can, we ARE going to have a campfire. It is too cold in the evenings, and bedding down by 8:00 p.m. makes the nights far too long. It's dark by 7:00 p.m. now.

We both noticed that the horses have not been travelling quite as well as they were prior to Ottawa. They seem to be grazing well and are getting plenty of water and oats. We'll give them another shot of tonic tonight and take one day at a time.

We grazed the horses, and set up camp. Walked down the road, to a nearby hotel and had dinner. We hadn't eaten all day and were starving. We ordered a hot chicken meal each with coffee. Four dollars and thirty cents for two meals. We ate it down right away, it was quite delicious.

We were given oats for the horses from a man who said they were from his brother who owned a riding stable. Both families asked us to stay with them. We thanked them very much, but we already had camp set up.

While at the café we talked to a fellow who owns stables, and got some good heads-up about what was ahead. He said a lady named Mary Bosenquet had stayed with his brother's family for a while in 1940. She went back to Ontario, got her horse, and travelled down to the USA from Montreal. He said she had written a book, but that's all he knew.

Headed back to camp and within half an hour we really had belly aches. We had noticed the sage in the dressing was very strong. We had noticed it at the time, but did not want to complain as we were very hungry. We are both quite sick, and didn't want them to know it.

Just as we arrived at camp, a couple were looking at our western gear, and were chatting. They noticed I was looking, said something in French, and I nodded back to them. The rancher said he didn't speak a lot of French, but thought it was a compliment. That got a smile.

As soon as they left, we were both very sick for the next hour and a half. We must have food poisoning. Oh, My God were we sick. We both were up and down all night (who would take care of who), and had a problem on both ends. It wasn't pleasant at all. It really wasn't! I poured some water over my head and got looks. I've never been so sick. Couldn't even get up for the last trip. I think we both had an accident. I admitted it?

September 19, 1965
Heading for Trios Riviers

Up at 7:30 a.m. Wet and cold. It was quite miserable all night. We're hanging our sleeping bags on the fence by the highway and it looks like a Chinese laundry as they are soaking wet. We both are not feeling that great still but have to ride on.

After a few miles we stopped and laid down an hour. Then I had to put another shoe on Frankie, but I notice she isn't limping at all. A French man came by and could not speak any English. He was quite elderly and we liked him right away, something special about him. He motioned to the pasture and the water and nodded to show we were welcome to be there. He was watching me shoe Frankie, and kept nodding and smiling. We thanked him, then he left.

We grazed the horses until near noon, waiting for some of our gear to dry. We had bread and beans. Packed up and started out again. We were travelling along a narrow road and went across a small bridge, thru a countryside town. On the walkway was a little dog, a Terrier, and he appeared to be dead.

I thought I saw some motion and got off my horse. His eyes were moving, so I gently picked him up, not knowing what to do with him. Joyce led Frankie along and I walked with him gently cradled in my arm. We knocked on a couple of doors, but nobody spoke English, but a woman pointed down to a house further along. Finally a woman came out and said something in French "chapeau". The dog moved his tail when she called him. I carefully handed him over and she thanked us crying.

Sure felt good that we found the owner. What else could you do? We don't believe he will make it, but at least he has a very caring woman taking care of him. They said it was an English speaking village, called New Glasgow, but the first three houses we went to, no one spoke English.

We travelled on for several miles. It was nearing time to find a camp when J.C. noticed that she had lost her left spur. We are just outside of St Alesis. We went off the road, and put the horses out back under cover. The grazing didn't appear to be that good.

We walked up the road a bit, to 'steal' a bale of hay, as there were no farms in the area. We had seen the bales when we rode in after dark. The traffic was terrible. We finally got out to the hay, ducking a hundred times in the wet grass, like two bank robbers trying to escape, only to find out it was straw! Good for nothing straw! Oh we just laid in the grass howling. Never heard J.C. laugh so hard. For not only sneaking out to steal it, but for finding out what it was. We cannot believe we did that. What were we thinking! Now we have to sneak back out to the road.

By the time we got back and made camp we were soaking wet. Gave the horses their oats and they already had their water. Bedded down for the night. Stealing straw! We're not funny, but we are wet and cold. We woke up laughing.

September 20, 1965
Heading for Jolliet

It was damp and foggy this morning, but surprisingly warm. Had a little bit of difficulty getting back into damp clothing. First thing this morning we put a front shoe on Belva-Dear. Managed to get away by 9:00 a.m. heading out for Jolliet.

We travelled nearly eighteen miles and then pulled in to a good area for afternoon grazing, about four miles this side of town. We washed all our clothes and had a bath in a creek. Boy it was cold, but it felt good.

Pulling out around 2:00 p.m. and its a very hot overcast day for a change. We plan on making it to Number 2 road tonight. As we went through Jolliet, we grabbed a sandwich to go As in the distance it looks like a wicked storm is approaching fast.

We just got to the edge of town when a Policeman guiding traffic yelled out to us something in French. I did not understand him. An Englishman walking along the sidewalk said in English to us that the Policeman said to clear the street. We thought we were off to the side of the road.

We were making time and keeping away from the traffic. He yelled again, quite angry. I hollered back "What the Hell do you think we are doing!" The English speaking man hesitated then said something to the Policeman. The Policeman then smiled and waved us on.

It was quite hectic for a few moments. We had not travelled five miles when a storm was on top of us. We headed for shelter and had to tie the horses as they were nervous, mostly the mare. It was quite wicked. We waited for about another half hour to make sure it was gone.

We rode on about a mile and half, and there were downed trees and branches all over the road. We were very happy to have been in a sheltered area. Believe me it's quite an achievement to outrun those sudden storms. We finally got a chance to eat our sandwich. We still were not feeling a hundred percent after that chicken dinner.

We've been extremely fortunate so far, as we have no way of knowing what is coming our way, day by day. We made camp at a racetrack area, on highway Number Two, east of Louis Ville. The grazing looks fair, and we still have oats. Noticed a shelter outback for the horses. We will stash our gear under there, hang a tarp over the fence, and hoped to keep fairly dry, as there is only a few holes in it.

Another storm came up during the evening. We are beside a wire fence, oh pain! Managed to keep reasonably dry. All we ate today was a sandwich, but we are far to tired to think about making a meal. It's about 8:30 and we are just going to bed down.

PS: We have not seen lightening so intense for some time. It was quite a chore calming the horses down. During the night we heard them whinny, and noticed they saw another horse on the other side of a fence. No one came by to say we were trespassing, and we slept well.

September 21, 1965
The Highway

Five months ago, we left Clinton, B.C. Now, we were on highway number two east of Louis Ville, Quebec. We were up at 6:30 a.m. as had to put two shoes on Belva-Dear this morning. I adjusted the blanket, as I noticed a slight rub spot on him..

Made a nice campfire and cooked up bacon, eggs, and coffee. Sitting there with a slight breeze, back in the country, great meal, what could be more rewarding? We have no fire permit, "no comprendez" (we don't understand French).

Started out around 9:00 a.m. Travelled through some real nice countryside for about seventeen miles before we stopped for noon grazing. It rained off and on most of the day, and was far from being warm.

As we were preparing lunch, there was either a child or a midget watching us from out on his tractor in the field. Maybe, we are grazing on his property. He never came over, just kept on going, so we stayed.

The other day we tried to pick up more horseshoes and nails from the race track. No one spoke English. We still have one shoe left. It will be shoe number fifty five. Thirty-one we put on ourselves. We will also have to get some oats soon. What the horses are eating along the road appear to be oats growing there. We wondered if that was a wise decision, but they seemed to be ok and grazing fine.

We washed out a few things and once again, it looks like a 'Chinese' laundry, as we have clothes hanging everywhere. The weather is warm and windy this afternoon. We would much rather travel through open fields and back roads, but there doesn't appear to be any. Quebec seems to be a little different from the other provinces. Never thought to look into these things when planning this ride, but then I was only nine years old Mom said. And most of all, we wouldn't of met so many wonderful people.

We travelled for another few miles heading up the St Lawrence Seaway, and pulled in for the night around 8:20 p.m. It was already dark out but there is running water and the grazing looked good. We asked the owners in the area if he minded we camped there. They spoke no English, so we pointed to the field and horses. They then said "Oui", nodded and smiled, so we thanked him, then set up camp for the evening.

We took care of the horses, gave them a light combing then went across the street for a drink and a sandwich. We met a lot of people, Someone sent us a beer over, next thing we were sitting around with a group of people, and the beer kept coming. We paid for it later on, oh boy, was the meal terrific. All we went in for was a sandwich. People are so friendly. When we ordered a sandwich, it never came.

Instead: They brought us out chicken, mashed potatoes, corn on the cob, salad, dessert (which we turned down), and bottles of beer. It was so nice to meet people, and talk about the area and their families, without having to give a play by play of our trip. How refreshing! We had a great time. They never felt like strangers for a second.

September 22, 1965
St Lawrence Seaway

We started out around 6:30 a.m. Oh boy! We were up a few times in the night, 3:00 a.m. etc. Early in the morning, we walked out in the field in our bare feet in about three inches of water to get a drink from the creek. Oh Lord, it tastes like grass. J.C. said, (while I was filling out the diary) "what you actually said was it tastes like lamb shit". Argh! I did not, did I!

We both went back to bed for the second time. I told her my feet felt ok, but can't say much for the rest of me... that's it no more beer! We only had three, but not being drinkers, we certainly paid for it.

Travelled until about 12:30. Frankie was so full of life. She started out at a trot, which is not like her. Then, she stumbled and went down hard again. I never had time to jump, and smack, hit the ground. Oh Boy! Face first. At first I couldn't get up. She jumped up and I was still on the ground. She stayed right there, and so did I! Oh God, so did I!

A woman from a house across the street saw me go down, and came running over to help. She asked us to her house, where she helped me clean up and put ice on my split lip. It was swollen and blue. Other than that, I told her I was fine. She told us we were very fortunate there was no traffic, and asked us to stay awhile to make sure we were all right. Then she gave me another ice pack and orange juice. That ice sure hurt.

We stayed for three hours, and it sure did help. It turned out to be the hottest day we've had so far. Finally, we pulled out and left, thanking her so much for her thoughtfulness.

Frankie is doing well. She's always so darn clumsy, so no more trotting for her. We arrived at the St Lawrence ferry this morning and took the ferry to the east side. The horses were absolute angels. Once we were on the other side and had cleared the underpass, we stopped for noon grazing for an hour about 3:30 in the afternoon.

We started out again just after 4:00 p.m. A car blew his horn, and Frankie went sideways about three steps and down she went again, then right back up. I wrenched my back. I told J.C. I thought the rider was getting battered. The roads are so narrow people go by tooting their horns meaning well, but not a good idea when you are on the back of a horse. Just about all I can take.

I'm quite concerned, very hot, and a little cranky at this moment. It almost feels like we are not in Canada anymore. Very few people speak English. It can be very frustrating at times, but then we don't speak French either, oh well.

We only travelled twenty eight miles today. Found a nice spot on a slope overlooking the St Lawrence. It's beautiful at St Pierles-Becquets. The mosquitos are in the millions and we are out of bug spray, and not too happy about it, right now. When filling in the diary, I said, I can't remember what I had said, J.C. said," "Oh you remember alright". Yes, the mosquitoes are extreme.

We put blankets on the horses and liniment on their legs seems to help. Frankie's one knee has a scab on it again which is a good sign she is healing. My lip is still quite swollen and weeping. I'm feeling battered, and yes, bitchy.

It's 6:30 p.m. we put purple lotion on Frankie's knee which we got from a vet. J.C. said she didn't know who looked worse, the mare, or the rider. I do know who doesn't complain. I told her that when I talk to people from now on, I was going to tell them that she beat me up. That damn fall really hurt! I must have lost one point for complaining.

Bunked down for the night around 10:00 p.m. It sure was beautiful looking over the St Laurence seaway at night with all the lights, the ships, the stars, and the DAMN mosquitos. Right now, I wish I were home. J.C. said to chalk a point up for her also, as she also feels that way. Really, hard to take. The horses do not seem to be bothered tonight, at all. I should have had two diaries, one for thoughts only. Damnit I hurt everywhere. With a warm blanket pulled up over my swollen lip. I looked out over the seaway. It was so calming. Someone is watching over us.

September 23, 1965
Heading for Lorbinier

Slept quite well in spite of all the mosquitos. Warm and clear. Saw three sputniks last night, and we think they are the same three we saw in B.C. We figured the time difference. Then we decided… Yep… same three. One was much faster than the other two, going in different directions.

Up at 6:00 a.m. this morning. Packed up and were on the road by 7:00. A few hours later, around 10:00 a.m. we had to stop for a funeral procession. There were people walking behind a hearse. A few French men stopped to talk with us and wished us well. We were dismounted at the side of the road, near this lady's yard, and we hadn't noticed, but the horses had helped themselves to most of the plumage on one side of the tree. What could we say? We rode at the tail end of the funeral procession for about two blocks, then rode out of town. (fast)

We travelled until about 12:30, covering nearly twenty one miles, and stopped to graze the other side of Lorbinier, near the St. Lawrence River. Being high on the ridge we have seen all kinds of different ships in the St Lawrence from everywhere. Mom would really like it up here, except for the language barrier.

It's much cooler today, but still quite warm with a beautiful wind. We've heard it's supposed to rain later. We had to move our entire camp again last night, as once again a million baby black spiders appeared from nowhere. Moving higher had one advantage. It kept the mosquitos at bay.

Went down the hillside into the water waist deep with our running shoes on, and had a bath. The water was very cool, but nice. It's always a great treat to be able to jump right in. By time we went back to the horses, it was cooling off considerably. It will be good for travelling.

We loaded up and off we went. Still terribly sore from the fall, but Frankie seems to be traveling well. Sure miss my little girl, and wish she was here to ride the rest of the way with me. We travelled until after dark making it to St Croix.

A French American from Michigan came by and went up to a house on the side of the road to ask the people if we could camp on their property. They came out to see us but never spoke English, just smiled and said "Oui". We figured the American must also ranch around here somewhere, as we are near the border of Maine, U.S.A. He sold us half a sack of oats for seventy five cents. Then he told us that two houses up from where we are camping, seven people were killed yesterday. Then he left, saying that in Quebec the people drive so fast, to please be careful and make sure we stay back off the road.

We took care of the horses. Just as we were bunking down, it started to rain. Who cares, we are too tired and just went to sleep.

September 24, 1965
East of Quebec City

We were up at 6:30 a.m. this morning, cared for the horses, got a real nice fire going and made breakfast. We still do not have a campfire permit, but no one has approached us. We always make sure it's out before we leave. The one thing we miss most is not having our campfires in the evenings. As I've said before, the evenings are so long when you have to bed down so early. It's dark by 6 P.M.

We headed out around 8:20 for north of Quebec City on the east side of the St. Lawrence. As we travelled through this populated area, a beautiful big Collie ran out and barked at the horses. A car hit him, and ran over his hind quarters, but did not kill him. He was in horrible pain. Several people ran out to try to care for him. There was nothing, they could do.

That bothered us all day. My God what a horrible tragedy. He was such a beauty. The people did not appear angry, but we could not understand anything they were saying. I tried to tell them we were sorry. There was nothing, we could do. One man said, "In broken English" that the dog chased cars all the time, and not to feel bad, it was o.k. They would take care of it. Motioned for us to go.

We rode on, I had tears in my eyes, and felt sick about it. Only travelled another three quarters of a mile when another dog ran out after us. Belva-Dear kicked him in the side of the head. He ran and yelped. Frankie went sideways, she never went down this time. Well, we cleared out of there fast and so glad to get away from the populated area. This is a horrible way, to end a day. Those poor dogs.

Travelled twenty three miles this morning. Stopped for noon grazing under a bridge crossing over to Quebec City. The horses are travelling well. We decided since the rain had stopped we would hang our clothes out to dry. Grabbed a snack, and played a couple hands of rummy. The wind is just enough to cool off the warm day and dry our gear. (Perfect). We laid back and caught a nap.

We were woke up by two women, who came down to see the horses. They did not speak English. They said something in French then shrugged. We said, "Hello", but they just shrugged their shoulders again and left. It would be great to be able to understand even a few words. Well, other than the few we do know.

We managed to pick up three more Horse Shoes and nails from the farmer we met, when we camped in his field. Frankie needs two. It cost us three dollars. I will put them on her this afternoon, and keep the other one for an emergency. Belva-Dear should be good for the rest of the ride.

We are leaving for Rivier du Loop. Yahoo! It's going to be good to be out of the skinny roads in Quebec. It may be o.k. in a car, but not for horses. The countryside is beautiful. We are overlooking the St. Lawrence River here at noon, and the view is spectacular. The colors of fall, the churches, and the sound of church bells early in the morning, is something to experience. The scenery is as beautiful as I have seen anywhere. J.C. agrees.

Travelled approximately another eight miles. Frankie stepped on uneven pavement and bang, down she went again. This time she went down with her head under her leg, and my leg caught in between. J.C. sat there stunned. I yelled to her to help us. I twisted around to try and free my leg, grabbed her mane, and tried to free her.

She jumped up suddenly and twisted my leg the other way. She reared back and I managed to catch her. She had a pretty bad cut above her eye. Most of the time when she goes down a car is passing too close to us and blowing their horn. She is so nervous. She struts out so well all day, and doesn't seem to be tired. I am quite concerned about her, and may have to make some decisions.

I've decided to walk her about a mile and see how she does. My leg feels like pins and needles, so the walk will do us both good. Made a decision to stop for a couple of days and have them both looked at. That's if we can make arrangements to put the horses out to graze. Without them, we are going nowhere. J.C. says the mare and I are ready for pasture. She is not funny.

We are still in the Quebec City roundabout, the traffic is heavy and the horses are jumpy. A Policeman was directing traffic and yelled something out in French. We thought we were travelling well, but he hollered out, again. I yelled back at the top of my lungs, "Will you please, shut up!" J.C. said Oh My God. She was right, but no time to be yelling. It is nerve racking, with the traffic, horns, and yelling Policeman. Guess he never spoke English. We were doing the best we could, considering circumstances. Well! we never got a ticket.

There were two lanes and a small shoulder to walk the horses around. I do not mean to be rude, but there seems to be no speed limit, no road space, and yes, we realize it was not a good place for us to be. We had no sense of direction except the road signs and 'yes' in French. It is extremely frustrating.

We managed to get out of town and stop for the night. Only travelled eight miles this afternoon. Checked out the mare, and she doesn't seem to be limping at all. While she was grazing, I combed her down. Every time Frankie lays down, she bounces up good.

The grazing looks real good and there is water. We gave them their oats, made a good camp, had a small fire, and just had soup for dinner tonight. We will find a good stop for tomorrow once we are totally out of town. We all could use a couple of days, and the stress level for both of us, is high .J.C. is not feeling well. I asked if she still had that cactus thorn. Oh, Oh wrong question. What a day.

September 25, 1965
Heading For Rivier du Loop

Up at 6:30 a.m. A French man was looking at us, and I needed to pee. I think he was wondering about the horses. We doctored up Frankie. She's not limping, and her knee isn't swollen. One thing I am glad of is that she seems to heal fast. With that now comes the tonic and the faces. I tried a dab on my split lip. DON'T DO THAT. We will start out slow this morning and see how things go.

On the road at 7:30 heading for Rivier du Loop. We made fifteen miles with no problem and stopped for noon grazing. We hung our gear to dry once again. The temperature has dropped and it's quite cold this afternoon, but sunny. I would not be surprised if it snowed. It's the coldest day we've had this week. Very cold, boy oh boy, oh boy is it a cool one.

We saw a nice creek running near and pulled in for noon grazing. Horses and riders are taking it easy. We wrote home to a few friends this afternoon then had a nap. Looked over and Frankie's laid right out. She woke herself up, went to the creek, drank, and then started grazing. We both got a charge out of it. It looked like she was dreaming.

Decided to take it easy and only travel a few more miles this afternoon to look for a better grazing spot. The slower pace will do us all good. Came to an old barn at the side of the road. The grazing looked fair. The barn did not appear to be occupied. We rode in, took care of the animals, and gave them their oats. Then we tethered them out. Frankie got spooked by a snake in the grass.

We made a lean to up against the wall of the barn using the tarp and two horse shoe nails. It was too cold to do much, and too early to bunk down. There was nothing we could light a fire with. So, we had beans with a bread roll, and shared a chocolate bar that had been in the saddlebags awhile, 'Oh Henry'.

Swept up some rat poop and cleared an area on the barn floor. Played a couple hands of Canasta and bunked down, after dark, around 8:00 p.m. It was a very cold night. You could hear mice running around during the night. Sure hoped they didn't walk on us. There was no sound from the horse.

September 26, 1965
Montmagny

Up at 6:00 a.m. gave the horses the last of their oats. We packed up and were headed out by 7:10 a.m. Frankie is looking good in spite of her wounds. J.C. says she's not feeling a hundred percent, I told her I felt like I was dropped from a plane. (Yes, we can complain but not quit!).I suggested a motel for a night..

It is bitter cold this morning. We are so thankful it didn't rain, as we know it would have been snow. It feels more like November. Frankie has not tripped since her new set of shoes, and steps out quite well. A car went by and yelled out 'Good Luck Girls', and we hollered back 'Yes B.C.'. (B.C. plates).

We only travelled approximately ten miles this morning, before we stopped for grazing and warm up. We started a small bonfire and made some hot coffee and soup. Just as we were getting ready to pull out, a couple pulled in. They introduced themselves as Mr. and Mrs. Claude Cote. They asked if we would join them for lunch, and they just lived up the road a bit at Montmagny. They made us chicken and pork. They offered to do our laundry for us while we had a couple of beers with them. We accepted there offer, and thanked them so much.

Last time I swore I would never touch a beer again. Well, we had a couple, and they called the radio station. A man came out and put us on the French radio. He would ask questions, then repeat what we had said in French live over the air. Then, he wondered why we chose to travel this way, as it's very different. He asked several questions. Half an hour later (approximately) he left.

Mr. Cote said he would pick up a newspaper and send it on to us later, as he was sure the interview was to be in the paper also. We pulled out around 4:30 p.m. and thanked the Cote family for the great visit and meal. They tried their hardest to get us to stay, but the grazing was not sufficient for the horses. They understood.

We have to pick up oats, so made the choice to move out. They offered us leotards, socks, and even a navy jacket. We figured we would be o.k. and thanked them anyways, as we had rain slickers. They were the first French family that we spent time with. Great people! When we told them that we had a deadline to meet, they totally understood.

We headed out in the evening and only got about three mile past their place when the freezing rain came. It came down in torrents. We got absolutely soaking wet. J.C. was quite sick. We found a cabin and shelter for the horses. We were brought a bale of hay for them from a nearby farmer. Someone is looking out for us. We only had to pack them a bucket of water.

We think the Cote family may have had something to do with it, as we were still so close to their place. We were so cold, believe me, we could hardly put our hands in our pockets to pay the owner for the cabin. The cabin was five dollars and we've never been so glad to be inside.

We barely got settled when the owner knocked on the door with two sandwiches each and a huge pot of coffee. We thanked him. It's so hard to believe how many people have been there for us in times like this. Checked on the horses and they were looking good, out of the freezing rain, and eating hay. We washed up, played cards until 10:00 p.m., did the dishes, and then bedded down. We have to make up time tomorrow. Slept well.

September 27, 1965
2nd Night at Cabin

We were up by 6:00 a.m. J.C. is too sick to travel this morning, and the horses sure could use another day. Paid the cabin owner for another night. Decided to put the horses out during the day to graze, and asked if we could buy another bale of hay from him. He said he would just throw in another bale. He also threw in a quarter sack of oats for us to take. It amazes me how people respond to the situation, and never ask for a thing. We let him know how much we appreciate him, and asked if we could help with anything.

We are just above the St Lawrence River. I walked back a mile and a half for groceries. I'm still quite stiff and thought the exercise might help. It did, but I was sure glad when I got back.

There are a few sunny periods today and winter is sure in the air. Only forty five degrees Fahrenheit this afternoon. It drops considerably at night. I was putting the last shoe on Frankie and noticed a very small stick poked up in her hoof (frog?). It looked a little infected and may explain why she has been tripping so much. I pulled it out and pressed around it, pouring a little bit of liniment around the area. She never flinched at all, and noticed she walked on it o.k. She should be good until Nova Scotia.

They have good grazing and we think maybe, their coats are getting a little thicker. They are two horses to be proud of and believe me, we are. Just laying around doing nothing, and J.C. said her symptoms tell her that she has the flu. She has been down most of the time here. We will take one day at a time.

We wrote home and to the families we met at Sault Ste. Marie talking about how we miss everyone, me specially my daughter. I love her with my whole being and miss her. I hear she is having a great time with all the cousins.

We had a bite to eat, then took care of the horses for the evening. J.C. said she is feeling somewhat better, so we hope to get an early start in the morning. We talked about the trail ride and how so many caring people just seem to show up at the most crucial of times. Realized it was the media, radio stations, television, and newspapers. We have to thank them all for it, as through it all we have met some of the most wonderful people across Canada that we would otherwise never have met.

September 28, 1965
Leaving Montmagny Area

Left the cabin at 9:00 a.m. The horses are looking good. Starting out this morning it is very cold and cloudy. Three hours after we got into the cabin last night we heard it snowed a few miles back, where we had stayed. We sure believe it, as the weather has certainly taken a turn.

Stopped midafternoon. There was all kinds of clover, covered all the way out to the road. We sat off to the side of the road, wrapped in blankets, ate apples and played cards while the horses grazed. The wind blew hard and it became quite uncomfortable. Within the hour we decided to head out again. It was around 3:30 p.m.

After a couple hours travelling I told J.C. it may be her fault, as I think I have the flu. Now I've lost two points for complaining. We travelled on until after dark, and it only looked like fair grazing. Staked out the horses near the highway and crawled under a fence to pick three blankets full of grass for the them. Was it ever cold!

It started to rain so we took shelter fast and tucked in right away until about 3:00 a.m. It stopped raining so we crawled back out and picked another blanket of grass. Boy was it ever cold! You could hear us chatter for fifteen minutes. We dove back into the blankets. If anyone had seen us, I'm sure they would think we had lost our minds. No one wants to be here. The tarp (tent) sure is a blessing. It still helps hold the heat in. Even though it is used only to toss on top of us. (What are we thinking).

September 29, 1965
Heading To Edmundston

We got a good start this morning and the animals look good. You really have to keep moving to stop from shivering. We saddled up and hit the trail, riding on until near noon. Stopped to graze twenty miles south of Rivier du Loop. It will be good to be heading inland away from the St. Lawrence and out of the wind. Today is still very cold and windy.

A couple we met yesterday told us, that we have been in all the newspapers and radio stations all over Quebec. It would be very interesting to know what they have to say.

We have been seeing more Nova Scotia and New Brunswick license plates lately. This afternoon we are turning onto highway number fifty one heading into Edmundston, New Brunswick. We do not know how long we are able to take the cold weather, but we will make it. Like we have said before, we are hoping that being inland will make the difference in our choices.

The horses are still travelling well but know they must be tired too. We will not push them. The cold really bothers my lip and jaw so I ride with a bandana padded over my face when it is windy. It sure helps a lot.

J.C. says she doesn't feel well at all, but isn't going to complain about it. I told her that was one point anyways. I watched her ride on, never complaining, and wondered what was keeping her going.

We camped one mile off the number two highway on number fifty- one heading into Edmundston, New Brunswick. A bunch of cows and a cranky bull came up to the fence. We had to make a decision if that was o.k. with us on this side and them so close. We decided to camp. The horses have only two more days of oats. They have water, and the grazing is fair. We need to stop.

It's twenty degrees Fahrenheit tonight. We staked the horses out and put blankets on them. Bedded down around 8:00 p.m., peeking out of our sleeping bags (what is left of them), and thankful for the worn out tarp, there are a million stars out tonight. One could almost loose themselves, in all the natural beauty up there. They are so beautiful. The ground seems normal to us now. We finally tucked our heads inside the covers and drifted off. Why am I here, who is this companion sticking it out with my stubborn decision to go on. She's remarkable.

Woke up 4:30 a.m. it was very cold. We could see the horses looking at us and there was ice on the outside of the tarp. There is no chance we are moving. About daylight a car pulled up and a Frenchman came over to us and said something. I told him I was sorry we couldn't understand. I thought he said 'when'.

We thought he was just checking the fence and making sure the bull did not get out. (Good Idea!) He left. As I was looking down the fence I could see a gate. I bet he wanted to know when we were leaving so he could go through the gate.

We got up and ready to leave, and he came along again…smiled and said something. He was very patient if that's what he wanted us to do. We were on the road by 7:30 a.m. Yes. It is cold! We must keep moving as the gear we have is insufficient for this weather. We have just about reached our limit. We need to make some definate plans for the next few days, tonight..

We have traveled about eighteen miles up highway fifty one and there is snow on the sides of the road.

We hope we can reach Halifax before long. While we were packing up this afternoon, Belva-Dear bit J.C. again, on the inside of her upper arm. She swung at him like a boxer, but her lips did not turn purple this time. Oooohhh I can see how that hurt! OOOH! She said she was sorry she hit him, but it had to be done. She is right. She said a few other things also. It sure looked painful. Oooohhh I have never, been bit by a horse but after the last time, leaving denture marks, I pray I never do. I suggested she put a snow pack on it right away. It was great no one was listening to her comments. Oh My!

We travelled on until dark, took care of camp, and bedded down early. J.C. was not having a good time at all. I just felt sick for her. We got the camp ready first, and, got her to lay down. I took care of the horses and made a small snack for us. We then called it a night.

October 1, 1965
On the Maine Border.

Up and on the trail by 9:00 a.m. We travelled approximately ten miles and it rained the whole way. We were soaking wet and freezing. Pulled into a small café for coffee. We went out back and it was bitter cold and raining with mixed snow. We asked the hotel employee if there was anywhere in the area for us to put the horses up for the night. We had another coffee while he checked it out for us. He came back with a 'yes'. There was a shelter just out back behind the hotel, where the horses could stay. He said the neighbor will bring a bale of hay and water for two dollars. We were very happy to hear that, and thanked him.

A Frenchman from the state of Maine was at the hotel and heard us talking. He brought us sandwiches and tea to the room, and said he had read about us in the Maine, U.S.A. paper. He was very nice, and we invited him in. He said he had to get back, and asked if we got the the hay he sent out the other day. We thanked him as we didn't know where it had come from.

We were offered a barn for the night half a mile up the road. We are far too cold to move on, and the shelter was quite comfortable. The horses would stay dry, out of the wind, and had feed for the night. We will see how they are doing for the next few days and then make some decisions. What will make the difference is if it warms up just a little. It is still wise to complete the ride now that we've come this far. It will depend entirely on the horses. We are warm and drying out our gear.

Television is only in French so we are playing cards until 10:30. Checked on the horses and put some more ointment on Frankie's knee. It's nearly completely healed. J.C.'s arm is purple. She can't even lift a coffee cup. When we went to bed down, J.C. said she had a rash all over her body and has had it for a month. She said it was o.k. So I asked her what kind of a rash, but she was already asleep.

October 2, 1965
Edmundston, New Brunswick

Up at 7:00 a.m. Can't say either one of us is feeling too good this morning. The horses, they look in great shape. We decided to pull ourselves together, and made the decision to ride. It's a cloudy type of day but so far no rain. Now it will be one day at a time.

Starting out and the horses are travelling well. I tried to convince J.C. it was an Indian summer. As we ride on this afternoon the wind is picking up. It's actually cold as hell. We have lost our map, but Edmundston is just ahead. We have heard that hunting season opens in thirteen days. It would be nice to be out of the woods by then. It wouldn't be fun camping in the timber and getting mistaken for moose, (and the thought did cross our minds).

Sure do wish the cold winds would die down. It's getting quite serious, and almost too cold to ride. We are on the outskirts of Edmundston. We are camping in a farmers' field for the night. Taking care of the horses, grabbing a snack, and crawling into bed right away. Before midnight there was ice on the blankets, and a real heavy frost. Beautiful three quarter moon. Those thoughts came to me again, I have to complete this journey, and do not know why.

NEW BRUNSWICK

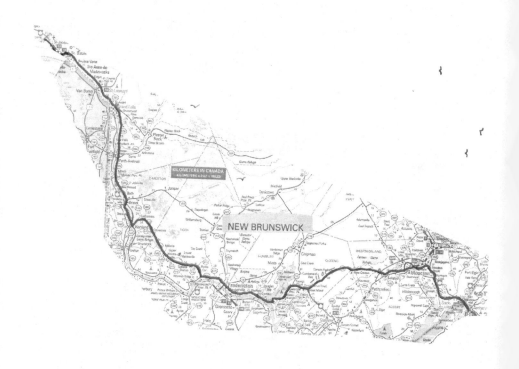

Map of New Brunswick

October 3, 1965
Riding thru Edmundston

Started out at 7:20 a.m., and a man from Cyrs taxi said he would like to buy us breakfast. We had bacon, eggs, hash browns and five cups of coffee, (and a comb for ten cents). We enjoyed his company, and thanked him for such a great meal.

At 9:45 we pulled out and rode through Edmundston. It was cloudy with a very cold wind. It looks like it may rain. We found Edmundston to be a very friendly town. Stopped and talked to several people while going through.

We stopped half an hour for grazing and water for the horses. Then we pulled out as it was too cold to stand around any longer. The animals seem to be holding out quite well.

We travelled for about seventeen miles and with the weather conditions we decided to make camp west of Grand Falls. We took care of the horses and got a small campfire going right away. Put on the coffee, set up camp, and made grilled cheese sandwiches with raw onions (burped them all night). We kept the fire going and just sat around for about an hour playing cards, with the tent wrapped around us.

Put liniment on Frankie's knee, and it's almost healed. She hasn't limped or stumbled at all. We finally made a wind barrier with tree branches, let the fire die down, and crawled under. It was about 8:40 p.m. when we bedded down.

Note: Must have had too much coffee, as we were up and down most of the night. We purchased gloves a few days ago. They are great as long as they are dry. It was mixed rain and snow off and on all day.

Visiteuses peu ordinaires à Edmundston

Helen Alwood, 29 ans, de Port Alberni, C.-B., et Joyce Myhon, 33 ans, de Prince George, C.-B., passaient à Edmundston dimanche au cours d'un voyage à travers le Canada à cheval.

Les deux jeunes femmes sont parties de Port Albernie le 21 avril à dos de cheval dans le but de se rendre à Halifax. Ce voyage est un rêve qu'Hélène caressait depuis son jeune âge mais pour lequel elle n'avait jamais encore trouvé de compagne.

C'est donc campées sur des chevaux âgés respectivement de 7 et 9 ans, que Helen et Joyce ont pris la route.

A un certain endroit, dans les montagnes Rocheuses, il y avait 15 pieds de neige. Parmi les incidents qui se sont produits en cours de route, mentionnons qu'elles ont perdu un de leur chevaux qu'elles ont retrouvé par la suite.

Elles ont dû faire une escale de 8 jours à Montréal parce qu'un des chevaux avait mal à une patte. Ces huit nuits furent les seules passées à l'intérieur. Tout le long du voyage, les jeunes femmes couchent à la belle étoile.

En plus, elles déclarent n'avoir rencontré que très peu de jours sans pluie.

Les chevaux, qui pèsent environ 1000 livres chacun, ont nécessité 59 fers à cheval; c'est Helen qui les pose elle-même.

Afin de nourrir leurs chevaux, elles se procurent de l'avoine pour deux jours à la fois chez les fermiers.

Un fait à remarquer, c'est que ni l'une ni l'autre des voyageuses n'avait monté à cheval avant d'entreprendre ce voyage. Elles n'ont comme équipement que leurs chapeaux et bottes de cowboy avec éperons, des pantalons, coupe-vent, manteaux de pluie et sacs de couchage. Elles préparent elles-mêmes leurs repas ou mangent dans les restaurants.

Leur voyage s'accomplit par étapes de 30 à 35 milles par jour, soit environ 8 heures de marche.

Le photographe du journal "Le Madawaska" les a photographiées dimanche matin alors qu'elles étaient reçues à déjeuner au Coq Royal, propriété de M. et Mme Rodolphe Cyr de Verret. Les deux jeunes femmes comptaient, à ce moment, atteindre Halifax en 13 ou 15 jours.

Une fois rendues à Halifax, elles ont l'intention de chercher des acheteurs pour leurs montures et se procurer une automobile pour retourner en Colombie-Britannique.

Elles disent avoir fait jusqu'à présent un beau voyage et avoir trouvé l'hospitalité tout au long de la route. Elles déclarent n'avoir pas éprouvé de difficulté avec le français dans la province de Québec.

Helen et Joyce prennent des notes au cours du trajet et entendent de publier le récit de leurs aventures à leur retour.

French Edmundston News

October 4, 1965
Grand Falls

Up at 6:30 a.m. and on the road by 7:15. There is rain and snow mixed. With the wind it's very cold. We managed to get slightly wet last night, but not the horses. Their shelter must have been better than ours. We gave them their tonic this morning, then water and oats.

We did not travel very far this morning when Belva-Dear threw a shoe. We need to pick one up. We got a motel and the owner said we could put our horses in with his. Luck is on our side again! Well… they are Shetland Ponies, but there doesn't seem to be a problem so far. We are really glad we made the choice to stop. The wind picked up to forty miles an hour this afternoon, with snow and rain.

Took a taxi to town and picked up our pictures and mail from home. Eighteen dollars and forty cents for the pictures, and the majority of them never turned out. (I think the camera got wet in the flood back in B.C.) We also got mail from Sault Ste. Marie, the Avery's and the Young's. Sure nice to keep in touch with them. They helped us out so much. Mom said all was well at home, and we have two new additions in the family. (A girl Cathy and a boy Wade)

Found a wallet back in the Prairies and mailed it to the owner. Today we got a letter thanking us for the return. He was pick pocketed in a movie theatre. He said he was a Laurentide representative, and was grateful to have it back. We were thankful he received it. (Re: I.D. and personal cards).

We checked on the horses. It's quite comical to see these small Shetlands in with them. But, they don't seem to mind it at all. The motel operator said we will be able to find shoes in the morning. Headed back to the room for the evening. We both made a mad dash for the tub. Rats! Guess I have to go for the sandwiches.

We brought the horse blankets in to dry. Had a good evening. Sure good to be out of the cold, and won't complain about being indoors anymore.

October 5, 1965
Eastward Bound.

Up at 7:30 a.m. Snow flurries. We've heard there is six inches three miles away. The motel owner drove J.C. to town to pick up horse shoes and nails, while I organized the gear and got the horses ready. They returned with the wrong size, but he knew a man that could fix that.

Off they went to his shop to have them sized. It cost two dollars and fifteen cents for both shoes. When they got back, I put one on Belva-Dear. We managed to get on the road by 10:00 a.m. We dropped off our letters to home and friends.

It's snowing with mixed rain. This is not pleasant at all, as I'm missing my rain slicker (and J.C. says I'm not allowed to share hers). The horses are starting out great and we are thankful to have a spare shoe now.

We had only travelled about ten miles when a woman pulled over to talk to us. She asked us if we would like to 'pick potatoes', and even offered to put our horses up if we could help for the day. We thanked her but had to move on.

We managed to make thirty-six miles today with only brief stops for the horses. Wanted to get camped before dark. We saw what appeared to be a barn up ahead, and went in to ask if we could put the horse in for the night. It did not appear to be occupied. They were very concerned about whether or not we smoked. Then the woman asked if I stuttered too. She then asked what J.C. was trying to say.

Standing there we were about frozen and really needed an answer. She then asked if we had eaten yet. We told her we had and thanked her, as we did not want to intrude. (How foolish!). She asked us if we would like to come in for tea after we are settled.

We put the horses in the barn and they gave them hay. It was a real nice barn. We also got a good ration of oats for tomorrow, and then joined the family. We were kept up until almost midnight talking about the 'ride', and really enjoyed their company. We ate nearly all her cookies.

They were the Potato Farmers who had stopped us earlier. We never recognized the woman as the wind was blowing so hard at the time, and her jacket was pulled over her head. They said they had to get their potatoes in before they froze. They were quite concerned, and told us they had two hundred acres to harvest… and that was the small field. We told them that we would love to help, but must carry on, as we are running out of time also. It was a shame winter hit so early.

We brought most of our gear in to dry and they gave us a place to bunk down. Thank you the 'Ball Family' for your hospitality.

October 6, 1965
Heading For Hartville.

We were up at 6:30 to find out there was another time change, so it's 7:30. They called us in and made us a big breakfast. They decided last night to send all their pickers home, as the ground was already frozen. So sorry to hear that. We gave the horses their oats, and started out before noon.

The horses are travelling quite well today but we feel they are looking a little thin. I will put another shoe on Frankie this afternoon. Thought she would be good to Halifax, but better now than have to do it in a storm up ahead. There is still no sign of limping at all, but she still digs her hooves in when she walks.

Boy is it ever cold out this morning. I feel I have a cold coming on with a slight runny nose. No hanky so I blew my nose 'farmer style' (dad called it that). I looked up and there was a farmer off to the side mending his fence. He laughed. God! I could have died. J.C. howled for quite a while. How embarrassing! We made quick tracks.

The R.C.M.P stopped us to chat. They said they had heard we were in the area. (Hope it was not the farmer). We talked a while about the town and how the weather has been. We were told there had been no change in the weather for a while, and wondered how we did it. Then, 'WHY?' It has been the number one question from the start. We just laughed. What can you say, as we really don't know that answer? Actually the question being asked is "what made you do it?" It is explained later in the journal.

Just as the police left a man and a woman stopped to chat. They introduced themselves as Mr. and Mrs. Nevers'. She told us her daughter from Shaw Ville, Quebec sent them a letter to make sure they got our autograph. He said he was the Mayor of Hartville, and asked us to stop in for coffee. We told him we would be glad to and thanked them.

Rode into their place and while we were there I put the other shoe on Frankie. The radio station and newspaper came out to talk to us. They stayed quite a while. The Nevers' asked us to stay and we knew we had to make time. One look at the weather and we agreed and thanked them.

Time seems to be running out for us, but, agreed if the horses do not stop, we will not either. Got the animals settled. We were taken to see their new town hall and the new Baptiste church. They asked us to sign the guest book. We stopped for tea at the church and there was a wedding about to happen.

There we met many people who asked about our 'ride'. We then returned to the Nevers' home. We had a wonderful meal and visit with them, staying up until nearly ten o'clock. Bedded down around 10:30. The cold weather sure can remind you of all the spills, sore joints, swollen knees, horse bites, rashes and floods. It's been cold to the marrow, but have to think positive to make it to Halifax.

October 7, 1965
Leaving For Marysville

Up at 7:30 and the Mayor had fed the horses already. He said he gave them hay and oats at 4:30 a.m. That's the time he gets up each morning. He takes care of fourteen cows and a dozen pigs. They made us a big breakfast before we started out.

They told us the ground had a very heavy frost so to please take it easy. After breakfast, and thanking them for a great time, we started out for Marysville. Hoped to be there by tomorrow morning.

We have sure seen a lot of hunters. A car just went by with one 'buck' and two 'does' on top. It reminded us to be cautious while travelling country roads. We made thirty five miles and camped an hour before going on.

We were going to pull out about 4:00 p.m., but it looks like a heavy rain is coming in. We decided to make some sort of a shelter, take care of the animals, and prepare for the night. We are approximately twenty six miles west of Marysville.

I remember an older woman I had met there in 1954 with her daughter, and always wondered how she was. Her name was Mrs. Lyons. She's the kind of a person you do not forget easily. I would love to stop and say hi if she is still in the area.

We made a huge bonfire. Oh boy, does that put the spark of life back into you. OH! The warmth from it was so rewarding. We made a nice stew with corn, buns and coffee.

Went to bed around 10:00 p.m. and watched the fire until it burned down. We talked about how far we have come, and wondered where I lost my Stetson.

October 8, 1965
Hay Loft

Woke up at 5:00 a.m. It was raining. We pulled all our gear under a tree and went back to bed. The horses are watching us. Frankie came over towards us and snorted, but it's not time for the oats yet.

Oh God, cannot think of riding in the rain again today, without my rain slicker and now, no hat. Finally got up at 8:00 a.m., Got water for the animals and they are grazing. We are going to stay right here until the rain lets up some. We have only approximately ten days to go, if it all works to our plan.

All we had in our saddlebags were a few jelly rolls, which we devoured. We notice a barn full of hay up ahead, so I moved all our gear up to the barn area. J.C. said she would go up ahead to a store for a few items. I got firewood and managed to get a nice fire going, then got water for the horses.

J.C. returned from the store. She met a man from the state of Maine. He bought her potatoes, bacon, juice, cookies, a coat and a 'Readers Digest' book. I told her "Well where is mine?" She just laughed, and me pretending to be cold did not work. We had a lot of laughs about the 'free' coat.

The rain came down hard so we put the horses in the barn and gave them a bit of somebody's hay. It later on turned into snow. We are not going anywhere. I put on a big pot of coffee, cooked potatoes and bacon, and we really enjoyed it.

The whole day was spent in this field. We managed to accomplish what we set out to do, stay dry and dry our gear. We decided to go up to the hay loft and have a sleep. Took our tent, laid it out in the hay, then our sleeping bags on top. We lay there writing letters home, and tried to keep warm. Once you get hay on you, it really, really itched, and that was not good.

We were just about done writing. It was starting to get dark fast. The people who were taking care of this place came by. They told us the people at the store told them we were here. He wanted to know if we would like to come and stay with them. We explained that we did not mean to intrude at all, and sorry we never inquired prior to taking up residence. Honestly, for the first time today we are warm, and cannot bear to move out to the cold right now. We said we hoped no one would mind if we stayed here for the night. He laughed and said "It is absolutely fine. It will be no problem at all." We thanked him so much for the offer and our stay.

October 9, 1965
Marysville

Up at 7:00 a.m. full of straw, and scratchy. Looks like the weather is going to clear up, but right now it's still raining. Took care of the horses, cleaned up the barn, and kicked the fire pit together. Heading out for Marysville. We left a note on the barn wall thanking them.

The country around here sure is beautiful. It's grown some since 1954, but I still remember the area. Went right to Mrs. Lyons' home. She was there. I knocked on the door, she opened it, looked at me, and I felt she didn't recognize me until she started to cry. That got me crying too. Being as tanned and weather-beaten as we were, I'm amazed she remembered me. What a wonderful woman she is. She's seventy eight years old.

I introduced her to J.C, and she introduced us to her son Conway and his wife Shirley. They were staying there taking care of her. They asked us to stay and visit as there was a field out back for the horses. How could we not accept?

We gathered wood and got a bonfire going out in the yard. They brought out a comfy chair and warm blanket for Mrs. Lyons. We all sat around roasting wieners and talking until the wee hours of the night. An older gentleman from next door also joined us. I would not have changed this stop over for anything.

Cleaned up the area, helped put the fire out, and stayed overnight with them at the residence.

October 10, 1965
Sheffield

We left 8:15 a.m. left a note for mom Lyons as she was sleeping soundly and had not been feeling that well. We stopped to say goodbye to the gentleman next door as well. He would tell mom, that we will drop a line when we get to Halifax, we figure in ten days.

We made Sheffield this morning. Two men came out from the Maugerville Newspaper and took our story. We sat out with them and shared a bottle of 'Jewish' wine. Then they said we had to finish the bottle of wine because when we were done, they are going to roll up a copy of our story, a penny, and one cigarette, cap it, and send it down the St. Lawrence River. (Message in a bottle!)

When they left, they wished us all the best. We started out again and went only another four miles before we stopped for a club sandwich and a coffee. Got some water for the horses. Starting out hoping to make it to Youngs' Corner.

We only got a couple of miles from the cafe and we both were sick, vomiting and diarrhea. We managed to travel about another mile, saw a building back off the road, and pulled up. The grazing looked good. It just started to rain and the wind came up. We had no choice but to stay in behind this building for a while. It sheltered us from the rain, the wind, and 'the public view'. Believe both ends were working. At the same time no less. Now this is our second time with food poisoning. Oh, we do know, that travelling now is not good.

We managed to get set up for the night and got into our sleeping bags. We were up and down several times during the night. We emptied both our canteens and prayed for more water, as believe me we were both burning up. I kept my head out of my sleeping bag, tucked the tent around my face, and let the rain cool me off. J.C. is not talking. I asked her if she was still alive. She moaned, (Barley).

October 11, 1965
Heading Towards Moncton

We survived the night and managed to see daylight come morning. It was still raining and hard to get up. We still aren't well by any means. (Afraid to check the sleeping bags, we were really sick). Looked over, and the horses are still grazing at 5:00 a.m.

Up around 8:00 a.m. packed up and pulled out. Both of us are still not feeling well but have to make choices, but leaving was first on our list. Believe me it was close. Both of us started to get up twice and went back down, and stayed down for some time. J.C. is sicker than me. My fever broke, and she is still vomiting. I packed all our gear, and saddled the horses.

We HAD to have water for us, and the horses. We rode two miles this side of Youngs Corner and pulled in. Truly we were not able to carry on. There was water there so we watered the horses and filled our canteens. Tied the horses out without unsaddling them, and laid down for an hour. We know we have to hit the road soon and some of our gear needs to be dried out.

Soon, on the road, we realized the water and the lay down did help a bit. Well... after we started out again we made a few more stops, but nothing! We started out and met the son and his family of people we had stayed with in Upper Kent. We could not chat long, as it was real cold, and I was shivering and didn't want them to know we were not well.

I said to J.C. "Look at you in your damn warm coat". (Sure glad she has it.) It was getting near 5:30 p.m. and starting to get dark. We are heading for highway number thirty to Moncton. We are still wet, and now travelling after dark.

Some people stopped to talk. We asked if they knew were there would be good grazing," or" where we could buy a bale of hay. He said he would give us some oats for twenty- five cents and a bale of hay for thirty cents. We let him know where we would be in about twenty minutes and in which direction. He was a nice young man and said he would drop them off for us.

We pulled off the road about a quarter of a mile further and there was not much feed. It was a blessing getting the hay and the oats. There was water. We made a quick night of it. Flopped the (tarp) tent down with no lean-to. We are both starting to feel about sixty percent better. We wondered in the back of our minds if we had gone far enough. Just before we crashed for the night I told J.C. there was only eight days to go, and she said, that sounded scary.

October 12, 1965
Canaan Forks

We were just about to get up, and the man who we had purchased the hay from (delivered by the young man) came over and invited us to breakfast. Please, he said to us. His wife died three years ago and him, a ninety three year old, and another elderly gentleman all batched together, and would like it if we joined them.

We had not eaten for thirty hours and it probably would be the best thing we could do. He looked like a real nice guy, and was so pleasant. We went to their place and they made us bacon, eggs, toast, and coffee. It was as good as we had ever eaten. (Whew it sure was warm in the tiny house.)

We thoroughly enjoyed their company. They got a kick out of our story of the journey and that question came up again, 'what made you do it, and why?" I think it was so great to see three elderly gentleman batching together, all getting along so well, and such a well-kept place! We thanked them for the great breakfast, their company, and the hay. He asked if the young fellow had dropped it off, just checking. Then he said it was the only hay for miles as it was a real hot summer.

Back on the road we ran into Conway Lyons again. He stopped to talk with us for a while and said he would be in Moncton until Friday. His mom was feeling a lot better. (Family we stayed with from Marysville). We went past Canaan Forks and camped again. The grazing is not that good, but the horses still have oats, and there is water. They are travelling well.

The rain is starting again, but at least there is no snow with it this time. Sure are glad of that as we are still getting over the club sandwich ordeal. We spotted an old barn up ahead and are going to head for it to see what it's like.

It is old but empty and the floor is full of rat poop. We got some branches and kind of swept up an area. The horses will be okay outside tonight as it's not that cold. We are still slightly damp but not suffering from it. We will bed down here tonight.

Earlier today we saw two dead deer along the highway. One was a 'buck' and someone had cut the horns off. A man in a government vehicle stopped and asked us if we saw anyone take the horns. We told him we hadn't but we had just passed and seen the deer. He didn't believe us! As he stated rudely "Well you were here, you must have seen something". By the look we gave him, I'm sure he got the message.

We bedded down early and with the cold weather it's getting a lot harder to spend the long hours out. We talked about the elderly gentleman and how nice it was to have met them. So sorry we neglected to write down their names.

October 13, 1965
Heading for Nova Scotia

We started out at 8:30 a.m. It's very cold and damp, but it looks like it's clearing up some. We have no idea of how far we have travelled this morning, but we are camped for noon and grazing about forty eight miles from Amherst, on highway number two.

This afternoon we took the bypass and hoped to get a good day in, and hoping to pick up more oats. We have no idea where we are, or how far we have travelled, but we are not in Nova Scotia yet. We've not managed to pick up oats yet, but heard we will be able to in Amherst. Two women who stopped to talk to us, for a few minutes, said that they would look for us when we get there.

Earlier we met a woman and her husband from Port Alberni. (My home town.) They said to say hello to Dr. Weaver when we get back. They live on Redford Street (their name may have been Savage).

We stopped at noon and ate in a café while the horses grazed out back. We are camped off the highway and the grazing was not that good. Gave the horses their oats and water and will make up for it tomorrow.

We have less than one hundred and eighty miles left to complete our ride. Now we are feeling we have conquered it! A work horse followed us a few miles yesterday and we could not seem to get rid of him. We chased him into someone's fenced yard and rode on. He jumped the fence and was still coming with us.

We decided to stop at a store along the route and asked if someone could tie him up until we were out of site. We had lots of laughs with him. Someone at the store said "yes we would love to tie him up, then what?" We still howl about that. While there, we got oats for two days from a local man (Jake).

We travelled on to the other side of Moncton and figured we made forty miles today. We bedded down in a lumpy spot,, it did not matter where we tried. We accepted it as being an overgrown plowed field. We made the best of it. All is well. It's a full moon and very cold, a little cooler than usual.

Off in the distance a dog followed us this evening for a while. We were told it may have been a wolf. We figured as he kept way back off the road, that he just may have been. We named him Yeller. He was beautiful.

I told J.C. I had terrible dreams last night, and she said that she did too. How strange is that? We both had a good laugh. I told her I wish I had gone to the store that day as I guessed there was no chance of borrowing her coat. (We can still laugh.) We have grocery money, and for horse needs. And we only have a week to go.

It's far too cold to play cards tonight. We tucked in for the evening and hoped to be in Halifax within the next four days. Cannot complain.

October 14, 1965
Highway Two

We woke up at 5:20 a.m. and saw two men coming into the field to see what we were doing. They left right away after they saw us camped there. We heard them talking. They left. We finally got up at 7:20 a.m. It was quite cool. We were packed up and on the road by 8:30.

We went to Memramcook and Belva-Dear threw a shoe. We only had one used shoe left, but will make it do. We stopped on the side of the road and put it on him. It fits quite well. We rode on into town. We are hoping the shoe will make it there, as we are getting down in funds. All is well.

It's sunny and quite warm this afternoon, which is a real treat. We have only had a few full days of sunshine all summer. A highway crew stopped to talk to us and wished us all the best. They said they wanted to buy us dinner when we came thru the next town.

We travelled towards the Nova Scotia border and asked a farmer if we could purchase a bale of hay. He wanted five dollars for it. We would have paid it, but didn't have the funds. I felt embarrassed turning it down. We thanked him and rode on. The grazing wasn't quite that bad and we still had oats for one more day.

We're just this side of the Nova Scotia border and camping for the night. J.C. went to a nearby farm and got a bale of hay delivered to the site. He wouldn't take anything for it. He said we did not have to thank him, as he knew we would return the favor. What a wonderful young man.

October 15-16, 1965
Going into Nova Scotia

A woman stopped and took a lot of pictures for the Atlantic Winter fair. Then we headed out again, and stopped at a race track to see if we could bargain for a couple of horse shoes, just in case we need them. Two men stopped us and took J.C. to town saying they would find some. The holes were not punched out, and they broke their punch trying. So, they went to a friends to get it done.

They knew we had no cash, and they could not do it. We thanked them. They went to another place and got it done. The men had two trotters and gave us oats for the horses. We thanked them so much for all their troubles.

J.C. arrived back and we have enough spare shoes and enough nails for one. We headed out again and it started to rain. The clouds were coming in. Frankie stumbled again, but did not go down that hard. I caught my foot under her and sprained it again. Phew! That was nasty. She skinned her knee a little again.

We checked her out and she wasn't limping at all. We pulled into a driveway of a farm just to check things out. A family came out and introduced themselves as Murray and Mildred Bickford from Amherst, Nova Scotia. They asked if we would spend the night with them. Oh, it could not have come at a better time. We are now in Nova Scotia.

NOVA SCOTIA

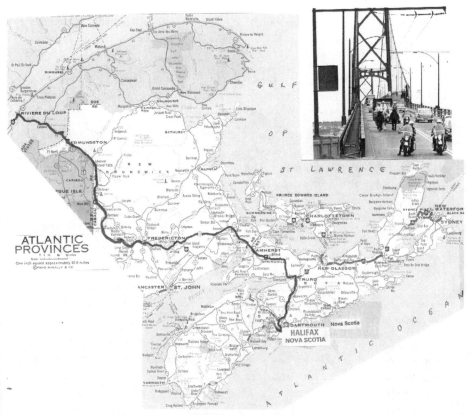

Map of Nova Scotia

October 15-16, 1965
Continued

At the Bickfords' home, the grazing for the horses turned out to be great. After the horses we taken care of, they asked us if we would like to do our laundry. We spent a wonderful evening with them, and really enjoyed our visit.

When I took my boot off, I could not get it back on. It was swollen badly, but it wasn't bruised. I kept ice on it for most of the evening. They made us a great meal and made us feel at home.

The next morning there was no way I could put my boot on. I said, I would just wear two pair of socks and take care of it as we went on. My ankle was swollen so bad you could barely see it was a foot. We all got a good laugh out of that.

Murray and Mildred would not hear of us riding on and insisted we stay another night. We just sat back with ice, visited, ate, slept, ate, and had wonderful visit. We are so fortunate to have met this family. They really saved the day. Hope one day to meet them both again. Thank you so much! Slept well.

October 17, 1965
Sunday Heading for Oxford

Up at 7:20 and the Bickford's had made us a beautiful big breakfast. I managed to get my boot on (barely). We headed out by 10:00 a.m. It was hard to say 'so long' to them. They certainly saved the day. We are all ready for the challenge.

The horses stepped out well this morning. We arrived in Oxford just after noon. People came out and asked if we would join them for lunch. We gladly accepted. They invited us to their home and gave us enough oats to reach Halifax. They were great people.

Back on the road and travelled another eighteen miles. A man stopped us along the highway and said to please go into the P & K Diner when we get there, and ask his wife Pearl for a meal. We thanked him and he left. When we arrived I said to J.C. "You ask" but she said "Nnno you ask". Even though we thanked him, we cannot do that. He also said he was going to arrange a 'Welcome Party' for us in Halifax.

We did stop at the diner for coffee and Pearl introduced herself and said she knew we were coming. She served us a wonderful meal. We visited for nearly an hour, then we got water for the horses, thanked them again, and pulled out.

We did not travel far when a deer walked out right in front of us and calmly walked down the road like we were not even there. I have not seen that since B.C... Hunting season is closed out here on Sundays (GOOD, as we saw five this last hour).

We travelled on until almost dark. Pulled in and camped in an old abandoned school yard. We listened to a rat on the porch all night. The last rat was in B.C. in the cabin outside of Lumby. That was a pack rat though. This is just a small one, or maybe even a mouse.

It's quite cool and frosty this evening. My foot is still swollen and the cold bothers it some, but I cannot complain. Took care of the horses and bedded down.

October 18, 1965
Going Ahead

Slept with my boot on last night just in case I wasn't able to put it on in the morning. That was not a wise choice. It was extremely hard to sleep, so I whipped it off about 4:00 in the morning.

Up at 7:00 a.m. It's getting a little harder to move out in the morning. The horses look great. I put ointment on the mare's knees. I'm going to walk her a while this morning and see if I can get circulation in my foot. I didn't walk far when I realized the mare was not limping, and was full of spirit. So, I mounted and rode on. We took our time, and will take a slow pace today.

We rode about ten miles, then stopped for grazing for a couple of hours. A family that introduced themselves as 'The Millers' had pulled up and brought us coffee. They said they were from the state of Maine, and had heard of our ride back at the restaurant. They took pictures and said they would send them home to our families. We thanked them and rode on.

J.C. and I talked about the horses, as we have had several offers to buy them. Cannot think of letting them go... Phew what a horrible thought... but, we have to be realistic and cannot take them back to the city. I do not know what J.C.'s plans are after the ride. Wishful thinking and hoping someone will buy them and put them to pasture for life, (as pets). A riding school has made us an offer (all the way from British Columbia, to come and see the horses). They said they would use them for advertising. We got a chuckle out of that.

They will do well once they are to pasture for a few months. We know and its winter, so by spring they should be good to go, as the Avery's took them for three weeks in Sault Ste. Marie and they were in beautiful shape when we got them back, and they have made it to Nova Scotia. I can tear up just thinking of letting them go. I cannot think of it right now. Last week we were thinking we cannot wait until the trip is over, but now we feel sick about arriving and dismounting (why?). J.C. thinks I'm too emotional.

Rode on a couple more miles looking for a spot to camp. A strange thing happened. A man came out and asked us in for a cup of tea, eggs and toast. We thanked him for the meal. He sat down with his coffee, and just as we were about to eat he said "You will have to hurry up and eat, my wife won't like it if she knew you were here, and the kids will be home soon". We wolfed down our meal. Glad we never took the saddles off the horses. We took off right away and thanked him.

We hardly got out of sight and it struck me funny. We wolfed our meal down so fast, like we were a couple of gangsters who had just robbed a bank and were on the run. J.C. said I'm not funny, and I do not have a good sense of humor. So, I rode behind her quite a ways and howled. When I thought about it later on, J.C. was right. If the woman had returned, the outcome could have been a lot different and not so funny.

We made sure we travelled on for a few more miles and took a short cut through Debert. It was quite dark by this time. We made camp behind an old army hall. It is quite warm and has cleared up. Took care of the horses, gave them water and oats. Frankie is looking good. I took care of her knee again.

We talked more about the horses and tried to figure how far we've come now. We haven't had a campfire for a few weeks. That is what we miss most of all, those beautiful campfires and evening meals.

After we bedded down, we heard strange noises. It sounded like crickets, but we felt it was too cold for them. Went to sleep.

October 19, 1965
Two More Days

Up at 8:00 a.m. and took a look at the horses. The mare has a slight bit of swelling in her knee, and I had quite a bit of swelling in my ankle. Today is going to be a much slower one. Quite a pair we are. Started out this morning walking Frankie and noticed she is not limping at all. I am, so I mounted her and rode.

We only went about seven miles and camped near a creek for the afternoon. I soaked my ankle and J.C. is not feeling well. She's quite pale and where she was bitten, is still quite painful.

We have six cents in our jeans, but we have one potato, four slices of bread and a can of carrots, then we are there.

Could not notice any swelling in the mares' knee by 1:00 p.m. I walked her about a mile. My ankle is feeling a little better. Then we decided to pull in by another creek, gave them their oats, tended Frankie's knee and soaked my foot again. Boy is that water cold.

We managed to get a fair size fire going and tried to bake the one potato. We ended up eating it half raw, with the can of carrots, and it wasn't that bad at all. It struck us funny and we both got to laughing, and could not stop. (Pain)

There was a hint of snow in back of us. We planned for tomorrow, and tucked in for the night. I have only eight more pages left in the daily log.

October 20, 1965
Heading for Dartmouth

Up at 8:10 a.m. We gave the horses their oats and slowly hit the trail. We only travelled about seven miles, then we were stopped by a filming crew from Channel 3, C.B.C. and the radio station. They asked us to, please dismount 'English' style. We had to spend a little time practicing that, believe me. FINALLY we assumed that we were approved of the method of dismounting and the interview carried on.

We were held up for nearly three hours, so this was afternoon grazing. We could never understand why it was so important to dismount "English' style, as they were western range horses. The mare seems to be in good spirits. So glad she is not limping. We never got started again until 5:00 p.m. and decided to take our time and finish the journey in exactly six months to the day. We were told that the city limit sign for Dartmouth was just ahead of us.

Our journey will end in Halifax. We did not know there was a long bridge separating Dartmouth from Halifax. We rode on and there was the city limits. We arrived. We have arrived at last.

We rode on for another half hour and a truck came along. The man introduced himself as Mark Facey. He said he has riding stables and teaches English riding. He asked us if we would like the horses trucked to his place for the night. We thanked him but said no thank-you. He then promised to bring us right back to where he picked us up from first thing in the morning. J.C. and I talked for a moment and said "To the exact spot?" He agreed. We told him we have never accepted a ride before, but seeing we have passed the city limits, it would be o.k. with us.

We weighed the situation and thought of another cold night on the ground, the concern with the horses, then accepted his invitation. The horses were given the very best of care. Mark even treated Frankie's knee and said she was fine. They're a little thin, but then so are we.

We felt sick when we realized the trip was over. I found it really hard to take for a few minutes. J.C. never shows any emotions so I am not sure how she feels. We had dinner with the Facey's, hot shower, and a great visit.

Later on, we had a tour of the stables and checked on the horses. What luxury. We were up during the night a few times just not knowing what tomorrow will bring. We were just a few miles from crossing the bridge, wondered how we would manage that, and if there was sidewalks. Slept well.

Dartmouth was a bonus!

SURROUNDED — The two lady horseback riders from B.C., Helen Alwood, in western hat, left and Joyce Mybon, back to camera, were literally mobbed by youngsters leaving classes at Notting Park School when they visited the Dartmouth Free Press last week. The kids lined up to get autographs from the first two women ever to cross Canada on horseback and Free Press publisher, Ralph Morton, left, waiting his turn, decided to get an autograph for himself. At this point the crowd was thinning out a bit, leaving room for the photographer. (Jamieson)

Notting Park School

October 21-22, 1965
We Have Arrived (Halifax N.S.)

We were up with the sun. Had a wonderful breakfast, then Mark took us back to the exact place he had picked us up. We thanked him so much, and headed into town. We rode ahead a few more miles, and near the entrance to the bridge was a lot of people and four motorcycle police.

We have arrived

They told us they were going to escort us across the Angus L McDonald Bridge into Halifax. Two in front of us, and two behind us. We could not believe the welcome we received. They introduced themselves and asked us to please follow behind. Over the Bridge we went into the city of Halifax Nova Scotia. Our final destination! Wow! Long bridge, but the horses just stepped it up and were absolutely perfect all the way. We looked at each other and I could not hold back the tears. Wow! It was overwhelming. We crossed the bridge then rode to the tourist bureau at city hall. We met the Press, and the deputy mayor of Halifax.

Oct 22nd   Tourist Bureau

We rode to the tourist Bureau, and met the Deputy Mayor of Halifax.

Signing the register at the tourist bureau
Manager of the Maritime winter fair   Deputy Mayors presentation and
Welcome to Halifax N.S.

Not Ready to Leave our Horses.

No matter how much we wanted the Journey to be completed, the last moments were extremely emotional!

October 23, 1965
Horses Sold to 'O Bar M Ranch'

The offers came in. The horses were going to the same place. Oscar L. Murphy purchased them both, which made us feel great as they came from the same field in B.C. At the same time, we got an offer to appear in the Atlantic Winter Fair, and we signed a contract from 25 October thru to November 6. We were still allowed to ride our horses for the daily appearances at the Atlantic Winter Fair. We were also loaned a jeep to use during our contract.

Jeep

At that time, we received a telegram from the radio station in Port Alberni B.C, 'CJAV' who offered to ship the horse back to Vancouver Island if they were not sold. We returned their call and thanked them.

We needed jobs, how perfect can things get. The horses going to a great home, and jobs, which was our plan as we rode into Halifax with four slices of bread, some oats, and six cents in our jeans. We always knew we could find jobs. So, it never bothered us at all.

I had a cousin in town, Jo and husband Paul Boutin, and they have asked us to stay with them. The next day there was a two inch headline in the newspaper that said, we were stranded and broke. We were totally embarrassed as we both had jobs, and a day after we got there we had a sale for the horses. We stayed with my cousin and her husband.

Friday, November 19, 1965   THE CHRONICLE-HERALD   ç

"THE END OF THE TRAIL" — Shown above, left to right are "Frankie" and "Belva-deare" with two of their newly-found friends at the O Bar M Ranch, Upper La Have. Beverley Burke, daughter of Mr. and Mrs. Archibald Burke and Dale Keddy, daughter of Dr. and Mrs. Bruce Keddy, both of Lunenburg. The two western horses arrived at the O Bar M Ranch from Dartmouth after a record breaking trip from British Columbia to the Nova Scotia coast, and are enjoying a well earned rest at their new home. (Rafuse, Halifax Photo Service, Lunenburg)

Two girls on sold horses

April 20, 1965

Clinton, B.C.

Sold to Helen Alwood one cream gelding, brand F left hip. Horse is five years old. Paid in full.

(Sgd) Kenneth Greff

Witness MAPP Alming

CERTIFIED a true copy of the Bill of Sale whereby I acquired ownership of the cream gelding mentioned therein.

DATED at Clinton, B.C. this 10th day of November, 1965.

Helen Alwood

Clinton, B.C. Canada

10 November 1965

Received from Helen Alwood $125.00 for the cream gelding as payment in full for same.

Helen Alwood

The sale of Belva-Dear

BILL OF SALE

April 18, 1965
Clinton, B.C.

Received from Helen Alwood $150.00 on one Brown Mare.

Paid in full.

7 years in June 65

Brand 4-H

(Sgd) Moira Diola

CERTIFIED a true copy of the Bill of Sale whereby
I acquired ownership of the brown mare mentioned
therein.

DATED at Halifax, N.S. this 10th day of November,
1965.

Joyce Doughton
Clare Le Marc

Helen Alwood

BILL OF SALE

Halifax, Nova Scotia

10 November 1965

Received from Oscar L. Murphy $125.00 for above mentioned
brown mare as payment in full for same.

Joyce Doughton
Clare Le Marc
Witness

Helen Alwood
Helen Alwood

The sale of Frankie

For the sum of $150 each we, the undersigned, agree to provide our

services to the 1965 Atlantic Winter Fair, Halifax, Nova Scotia, for

the purpose of publicizing the Fair both on the Halifax Forum grounds

and elsewhere during the period October 25, 1965 to November 6, 1965,

Inclusive. We also agree to release all personal photography, video-tape

recordings and written material effected or produced by and for

Bruce Cochran Associates Limited on behalf of the Atlantic Winter Fair

for both commercial and editorial use. And we the undersigned reserve

the right to accept any other engagements that do not conflict with

the prescribed regular appearances and such official functions as we

may be requested to attend from time to time by Bruce Cochran

Associates Limited.

Signed: Bruce Cochran
Associates Limited for
The 1965 Atlantic Winter
Fair
Signature

Signature ....

Signature ....

This date .October 25, 1965......

Fair contract

HELEN ALWOOD - JOYCE MYHON

AWF TIMETABLE

Wed. - 27 October

— interview   Press interview
Jeep tour

Thurs. - 28 October

Press Chronical
Wes harrison

Fri. - 29 Oct.

Arena 1pm..1;30

5-7 p.m. PRESS RECEPTION - FORUM
Sat. - 30 October

Arena 1.30..2pm
Arena 8.45..9.30

4-5 p.m. - FORUM (JEEP)
8-9 p.m. - FORUM (JEEP)
Sun. -31 October

With Wes Harison

4-5 p.m. - FORUM (JEEP)
11:30-1:30- EXHIBITORS RECEPTION - FORUM
8-9 p.m. -FORUM (JEEP)
Mon. - 1 Nov.

Press Meeting
In Arena riding club

Chronical..Star

8-9 p.m. - FORUM (JEEP)
Tues. -2 November

Wes Harrison Alwood..Myhon

8-9 p.m. - FORUM (JEEP)
Wed. - 3 November

5-7 p.m. - LORD NELSON HOTEL
8-9 p.m. - FORUM (JEEP)
Thurs. - 4 November

Dinner..Press Conference
Long John Baldry? NED landry

8-9 p.m. - FORUM (JEEP)

n.t.p. Trip on Blue Nose 11

Fri. - 5 November

Arena noon to three

8-9 p.m. - FORUM (JEEP)

Lunch, interview public

Atlantic Winter Fair

B.C. COW GIRLS *Show After Each Event*

Tuesday – November 2

After 9:00 Event

Atlantic Pacing Stake

Wednesday – November 3

5:00 Lord Nelson "Bull in the Ballroom" Reception.

After 9:20 Event

Tug of War

Thursday – November 4

After 8:30 Event

Six-Horse Belgian Team

(10:00 Hunt Ball)

Friday – November 5

After 8:45 Event

Champion Four-Horse Draft Team

Saturday – November 6

After 3:15 Event

Pony Jumper

8:45 Event

Championship Six-Horse Draft Team

Cowgirls

Well, our first appearance with the contract? We signed to appear at the Atlantic Winter fair on the 27th.of October, but our manger called on the 25th and said we were invited to attend at a school in the auditorium. We were to meet some people from a riding class and talk about our journey. Well we have told it to so many people along the way, that meeting new people may be fun.

We went to the school and were taken to a stage with two chairs and a speaker. There was a lot of people in the audience, no sitting around with a coffee for small talk. I was simply handed a microphone and they left. I sat there looking at all the people waiting for someone to ask some questions. None came, so I introduced my companion and myself.

Well, I said," there is something different standing on a stage looking out at all you nice folks, than speaking from atop of a horse". Believe me. People laughed, and that broke the ice. Finally all the questions started to come, and we realized it wasn't that uncomfortable. Spent about an hour talking to the people, and hoped all the questions were answered. Then, there was nightly appearances at the Atlantic Winter Fair.

The first night it was good to see our horses again as they had been out at Mark Facey's stables. The rest of the time we were told, they were brought in each night to us at the horse show from the stables at the arena. That way we got to see them during the day.

Of course during our ride in the afternoon at the arena, Wes Harrison was there and as we rode around he made it sound like the horses were galloping over a bridge and of course other sounds. It made it a lot more fun as we were not used to being entertainers. We looked forward to him being there every event, and he was. It got loads of laughs.

The 'Bull in the Ballroom' banquet was with Long John Baldry and Canada's top fiddler Ned Landry, and all the dignitaries. We were required to wear the apparel we had on when we rode into town. All the other women were in gowns, and an actual huge bull was in the center of the ballroom in a tiny cage.

Wes Harrison

The very best part of the banquet for me was listening to Baldrys singing. He has such a beautiful deep voice and is a giant of a man. What a singer!

Picture of us

Right after the banquet, We got a call from a Don Olland and he asked if we would like to go for a cruise on the 'Bluenose'. I hesitated for a moment and asked what was, the Bluenose, He replied "The ship on the back of the dime." I was so embarrassed. Oh my God, I wish I had not asked that question. He laughed. I told him we would love to, and thanked him for the wonderful opportunity.

The next day we were picked up and taken on one of the most memorable trips, that we will ever have in our life time probably. The ship is absolutely magnificent, and you can't believe how big it is, until they set sail.

Bluenose name on ship

Blue Nose with crew

Man climbing mast

Don Olland

Captain Cogins and news crew

We completed our contract and bought a Nash Metropolitan for two hundred dollars. Said our goodbyes to the wonderful people we had met, my cousin and her husband, and Don Olland for the wonderful sailing trip.

Headed out by noon for Florida, then west to Texas, and up the west coast to home, (pushing the car most of the way). That's another story.

There are not enough words to thank all the people we were fortunate to have the privilege of meeting. Proud to be a Canadian. Thank you all for being a part of this journey.

We do know we are the first two women to cross Canada on Horseback. This Journey was never to beat any record. It simply was something I needed to do. And fortunate to have met a companion to take on the challenge with me. I would not have done it alone.

PROLOGUE

Prior to publishing this journal, my daughter and I decided to retrace my steps from Clinton B.C. to Kenora ON, to add any information that may have been missing, and to look up Joyce. I had found a Joyce Myhon in Westlock, AB. I enquired with a long ago friend, and was told she thought she had moved to the Okanagan area, wasn't really sure, but did know she had many health issues.

We started out in Clinton, B.C. and found out quite a bit of information from a couple girls Dina Connon from the Village of Clinton, and Jocelyn Cahill from the Clinton Lariat Newspaper. On we went retracing our journey, except this time on four wheels.

We crossed the Kootney Lake into Crawford Bay and stopped at Gray's Store speaking with a gentleman named Tom . Tom had a bit of information on the Eddy family and the area, a place where we had stayed the night.

We ended up in Monarch AB, and asked at the Post Office regarding the Millwards who had showed us their hospitality during a stop-over there. She directed us to a Barb Beaty, whose mother had once owned the Monarch Hotel where we had stayed back in 1965. Barb was kind enough to fill me in on quite a bit of history of the area.

After a coffee and a nice chat, my daughter and I left for the Monarch Hotel.

A gentleman was renovating it into apartment buildings and it had been closed for the last 12 years approximately. After talking about the Journey, he told me he had two original bar chairs from about 50 years ago that we 'probably sat our butts in'. He said I could have them both, placed them in my trailer, and wished us the best on our travels. I was excited and planned to drop one off for Joyce. So far, three people we had stayed with we found out had passed on. The others like time, had moved on.

Eventually, we ended up in Westlock AB. I enquired with the Government Office in regards to Joyce's whereabouts. They couldn't give me the information, but did place a call to her niece who promptly called me back. I was deflated to hear that Joyce had passed away a few years back from Progressive Super Nuclear Palsy, an illness I had only heard of once before, as it had also claimed my sisters life.

Her niece went on to tell me Joyce was well liked and had lived in the Okanagan for several years before becoming ill. No one in Joyces family had known about her journey in 1965 until after her passing when they had gone through her belongings. Apparently she was quite a private person, yet very close with her mother (who lived to 102 years of age I've been told). While Joyce was in the hospital, according to her niece, Joyce preferred her own company to that of others and chose to be with herself. She was determined to beat her illness. Joyce's niece also stated that Joyce had not married stating "If I ever found a man smarter than myself I may have married." She did have a good long time friend Martha, who preceded her. That was all I learned about my former riding companion, not much more than I had learned on the trip.

Well, things change and life moves on. Most of the pathways and places we travelled through have moved or are no longer in existence. Such a shame such beauty was replaced with larger cities and highways. I will always have my journal and the memories of such an awesome journey and all the beauty that surrounded us in riding across Canada on horseback.